T0247362

THICKER THAN BLOOD

Maitreyabandhu

THICKER THAN BLOOD

Friendship on the Buddhist Path

Published by
Windhorse Publications
169 Mill Road
Cambridge
CB1 3AN,
UK
info@windhorsepublications.com
www.windhorsepublications.com

© Maitreyabandhu 2001
Reprinted 2017

The right of Maitreyabandhu to be identified as the author of this
work has been asserted by him in accordance with the Copyright,
Designs and Patents Act 1988.

Cover design and photographs by Alban Leigh
Printed by Bell & Bain Ltd, Glasgow

British Library Cataloguing in Publication Data
A catalogue record for this book is available from the British Library

ISBN 978 1 899579 39 6

(*W*)indhorse Publications

CONTENTS

To my friends

Acknowledgements

One thing that becomes clear, having written my first book, is that doing so is as much a collective project as an individual endeavour. I have had a great deal of help, encouragement, and advice in the long process of writing this, for which I am very grateful.

It was Nagabodhi who first suggested I write a book on friendship – albeit a considerably slimmer volume than this – and, without his confidence in me, I probably would never have done so. The book recounts my attempt to practise spiritual friendship, as outlined in Subhuti's eight talks on the subject, without which this book could not have been written.

I owe especial thanks to Jnanasiddhi, my unswervingly patient, wise, and helpful editor. Without her invaluable feedback, the book would have been a shambles. I am also grateful to my friends for allowing me to write about them and checking the draft manuscripts, and to Gary for his helpful encouragement.

I would like to thank all those who had the unfortunate task of reading the earlier drafts, especially Sarvananda, my brother John (who had to get up at 5 am to finish reading it), and my old college friend Martin De Sey. Thank you also to Michael Hoey and Heather Priest who volunteered to type up my hand-written first draft.

Being something of a frustrated painter, I had lots of ideas about how the book should look, so thank you to Alban for his lovely design and his willingness to listen to my various suggestions about it. Also thanks to David Waterston and Jnanavaca for feedback, encouragement, and criticism (not to mention spelling corrections) and to all those who helped me in every way from the Windhorse editorial team, and to Gary Dixon who, in a flash of inspiration, came up with the title. Most of all I would like to thank Urgyen Sangharakshita, without whose guidance and inspiration none of the above would have happened.

A VISION OF FRIENDSHIP

All I, myself, can do is to urge you to place friendship above
every other human concern that can be imagined!
   Cicero, *On the Good Life*

'What am I doing here?' That was the question that came to my
mind as we walked towards the snow-covered dormitories of
the retreat centre. A few of us had just made the journey in a
draughty old van, through the inevitable traffic on the Holloway
Road, up to Amaravati, a Buddhist monastery nestling on a
distant snowy plateau just outside Hemel Hempstead. It was
dark by the time we arrived, the headlights of the van lighting up
the cold December night and making the new snow dazzle back
at us as we swung round into the car park. The monastery was
a converted army barracks, its long, low, jerry-built roofs thick
with snow, its toilets – as we were soon to discover – frozen solid.

'What am I doing here?' I said as I turned to the complete
stranger who happened to be walking next to me, as we gingerly
made our way across the snow to our rather bleak barrack room
with its threadbare bit of rug and not very comfortable beds. It was
the December of 1985. The miners' strike was grinding on to its

painful conclusion, and Mrs Thatcher, now in her second term, was becoming the person everyone – at least everyone I knew – loved to hate. I'd done a bit of marching through the streets of London myself shouting 'Maggie, Maggie, Maggie – Out! Out! Out!' I'd donated tins of tomatoes and bars of soap from my student grant, and I'd stood outside Kwik Save shaking a bucket and wearing my 'Coal not Dole' badge. I was twenty-four and deadly serious, though about what exactly, I wasn't sure.

'What am I doing here?' I said, though I didn't expect the man in the leather biker's jacket to answer. He was about my age and looked like he'd just stepped out of Status Quo with his shoulder-length black hair and blue jeans. Anyway, I knew perfectly well why I was there, or thought I did. I had come on retreat to meditate – to gain, I hoped, some fabulous insight into the nature of reality. I'd only been going along to the London Buddhist Centre for a few weeks when I'd heard that a weekend retreat was in the offing, and I'd been quick to sign up for it. They'd hired the place from the monks who lived there.

I was keen to get going. I thought I knew already, in essence, what the spiritual life was all about, and the frozen plumbing and almost frozen dormitories were very much in keeping with my stripped-down no-nonsense view of Buddhism. I expected to rise at five in the morning and to meditate for hours in snow-bound silence. I hoped to build up an incredible intensity and to make a breakthrough slap-bang into the nature of things. I had a lot to learn.

I didn't experience insight on that weekend, huddled in a prickly blanket meditating and trying my best to stay awake, though I do remember finding some of the simplest things – tying my shoelaces after a meditation session, folding a blanket – deeply satisfying, as if they were suddenly invested with a new significance, but on the whole my meditations were a dead loss. That weekend was, however, a decisive and life-changing experience. In a sense I've never looked back. It was the start of Buddhism for me and, though I didn't realize it at the time, the start of a whole new concept of friendship. Not that friendship was something I had gone looking for in Buddhism, or anywhere else for that matter. And I never for one moment thought, as I walked across the snow to our dorm, that the leather-jacketed Mancunian would become one of my best friends.

I'd always had friends, of course – the family of brothers that lived nearby, Toby, and big Helen – but I hadn't realized the significance of friendship or seen the potential in it. Even when I became a Buddhist and developed the strongest friendships of my life – stronger still than those boyhood friendships in the playground – it wasn't until I was away in Spain being ordained – being made a member of the Western Buddhist Order – that I really came to see friendship as a spiritual path in itself.

At the time, Spain was still associated in my mind with over-baked suntans and those fluffy toy donkeys that everyone seemed to have on the plane home. I'd been to Torremolinos in the early days of my nurse training in Coventry. A whole bunch of us had flown out from Birmingham International Airport only to spend the days drinking cheap booze on the hotel balcony – we didn't even make it to the beach, as far as I remember. This time couldn't have been more different. I was to be ordained, and the jeep that took us up to the retreat centre wound its precarious way around hairpin bends and precipitous ravines, among some of the most beautiful landscape I'd ever seen. We were to be there for four months. We settled into our little huts and the retreat began. We meditated in the mornings, studied Buddhist texts before lunch, and at night – beneath a sky scintillating with more stars than I'd ever seen back home – we chanted mantras and performed Buddhist rituals. As we came out of the shrine room on our way to bed, we could just make out the twinkling lights of faraway Benidorm – it had never seemed further away.

Early in the retreat we listened to a series of eight talks. These were given outside, on an outcrop overlooking our beautiful mountain valley. When we'd finished clearing up after supper we would all gather together, try to find a half-comfortable spot, and prepare to listen to that evening's talk. Alan was there, the same leather-jacketed man I'd met on that first frozen retreat in Hemel Hempstead – though by now he'd lost his mop of hair. We sat together wrapped in blankets listening, as the sun went down, to talk after talk on friendship.

It was one of those rare times when everything clicks. There I was, four or so years after that first weekend retreat, about to dedicate my life to Buddhism. As a symbol of that, we would lose our old names – broken toys we no longer had a use for – and take up new Buddhist names. Alan would become Karmabandhu, Ian would become Paramabandhu, David would become Lokabandhu. The four of us were friends; we had worked out in part what friendship between us meant in the years leading up to our ordination, and in those talks I came to see, more clearly than ever before, the deepest meaning of friendship. It was as if a jewel were held up before us – the jewel of friendship. In the fading light we seemed to see that jewel glow first red, then green, pure white, then deepest ultramarine. As each talk unfolded it was as if, by turning that jewel of friendship first one way and then another, we saw facet after beautiful facet of it. I am not given to mystic moments or flights of fancy, but it was as though the valley itself listened, the gently swaying pine trees, the gorse bushes, the towering rocks, and the chorusing cicadas.

This book is a response to those talks and to my own attempts to put those talks into practice. This book is about friendship. It tells a double story. It tells the story of spiritual friendship in Buddhism, and it tells the story of my own experience of it.

It has been my intention to answer four questions. What is real friendship? How can friendship be part of a spiritual path? How can it best be developed? And who can it best be developed with? Of course, to say what something is, you often have to say what it isn't, so that's in here too. I have largely used my own deepening experience of friendship, especially as I have experienced it within the context of the Friends of the Western Buddhist Order. After all, friendship is not an abstraction. It always takes place between two human beings, and to understand friendship you must understand it and get a feel for it in that living context.

Of course, I write from a particular point of view, that of a man (and a white English man at that) and as a member of the Western Buddhist Order. The Western Buddhist Order (WBO) is at the heart of an international Buddhist movement called the Friends of the Western Buddhist Order (FWBO). Founded by an English Buddhist monk – Urgyen Sangharakshita – in 1967, it aims to communicate the message of the Buddha in terms that are both faithful to the Buddhist tradition and at the same time accessible to men and women living in the West. Ordination within the Western Buddhist Order is primarily an expression of commitment to the Buddhist path. At ordination one dedicates one's life to the practice of Buddhism – to the path of positive self-transcendence. Members of the Western Buddhist Order are neither monks nor lay people: they are first and foremost men and women who have committed themselves to the spiritual life. How they choose to express that commitment in terms of particular lifestyles, whilst important, is nevertheless secondary.

At the same time, it has been my intention to write for anyone who has a feeling for friendship and who wants to develop that feeling irrespective of interest in Buddhism as such or of involvement with the FWBO. Every group has its own shorthand – which at worst becomes a kind of jargon – and I have tried to leave that out wherever possible. However, the reader will have to contend with Buddhist names (like my own) which may seem a bit strange and alien at first. In addition to this, many of the friends I talk about in this book changed their name from a 'Christian' name to a Buddhist name – so, to avoid unnecessary confusion, I have mostly stuck to using either one name or the other.

I hope every word of this book is influenced by Sangharakshita, the founder of the Western Buddhist Order, and by his senior disciples (especially Subhuti), to all of whom I owe immense gratitude. What I have tried to do here is show how I have attempted to put those eight talks on friendship – given so memorably in that Spanish valley ten years ago – into practice. I hope that by so doing I can inspire my reader to tread the path of friendship for himself or herself. The best outcome of reading this book would be to make friends, and to take deeper the friendships you already have. I also hope that in my own way I have managed to communicate something of the great ideal of spiritual friendship in Buddhism, an ideal I have learned from my teachers and from my friends.

Potash Farm
Suffolk
1 February 2001

1

GROWING UP FRIENDS

Another thing about John is that he is sensible and nise [sic].
Whenever we are playing rocket ships he never starts laughing
when we get to an awkward point.

I have two friends called Carol and Brenda. I like Brenda
because she is very funny and very small. I like Carol because
when she has any sweets she always gives me some, and she has
lovely curly hair, and she is very nice.

Nine-year-olds quoted in Iona and Peter Opie,
The Lore and Language of Schoolchildren

As a child I spent most of my time in the garden – although
'garden' isn't quite the right word to describe the acre or so of
land behind our house: 'rubbish dump' would probably be better.
My parents ran a small family business – coach and taxi hire,
furniture removals, that sort of thing – so I grew up in a kitchen
full of tea-drinking coach drivers and a garden full of old lorry
bodies, clapped-out cars, and piles of rusting metal. The inevitable debris created by a not very successful coach company was
exacerbated by my father's instinctive tendency to hoard things.
He was a scavenger by nature, and as a consequence large areas

of the garden had become something of a battleground. On the one hand there was my mother's need for a lawn and a few flower beds, on the other my father's tendency to buy rubbish and dump it everywhere. My father tended to win, as my mother, despite her valiant efforts, could never keep up with his ability to buy all manner of 'tat' (as she called it): old baths, rusting motorbike engines, car bodies, and cookers. What this meant for us children (I have three brothers and a sister) was that we grew up in a veritable adventure playground. There was always enough wood and rope and rusty six-inch nails to build tree houses in the silver birches, dens in the backs of old lorry bodies, and secret hideouts among the scrap heaps. It was one afternoon, while I was playing in this junkyard-cum-Disneyland, that a little boy about my age called to me from over the hedge. He and his family of brothers had just moved in nearby and could they come over and play? Well, that was it – we spent the next millennium (or so it seemed) playing in the garden – we were friends.

That family of brothers became my constant companions in adventure, from the moment I was released from the breakfast table to the time my mother called me in for tea. We built dens together, made water pistols out of Fairy Liquid bottles, tried to hatch frog spawn in an old sink, and kept a lookout for UFOs. In between the tedious adult world of brushing your teeth after breakfast and having to wash your face before bedtime was *our* world, a world of rusting lorries, friendship, and imagination – a world in which friendship and play were the very nature of things.

Making friends was easy back then. I remember, for instance, our family beach holidays in Cornwall. After a rigorous search for a suitable spot (far enough away from others and with our backs to a suitably protective sand dune), we would unpack our buckets, books, and frisbees. Deckchairs and windbreaks would go up or be pegged down; my mother would prepare a great leaning tower of sandwiches and my father would wander off in search of scrap metal. Meanwhile I would attach myself to someone else's children, making friends on the spot, chatting happily, and charming their parents. While not all children are as gregarious as I was, a happy, healthy child will naturally make friends. In fact parents tend to take this for granted and become actively concerned if their children do *not* make friends, taking it (quite rightly) as a sign that something is wrong. For most children friendship comes naturally. They don't have to read books about it or to concern themselves with whys and wherefores; they just get on and do it. Friendship is a basic human instinct, as much a sign of health as a healthy appetite and as natural and spontaneous as crossing your arms or the tendency children have to run everywhere.

Then came school. Skulking around the playground in our new oversized school uniforms, it wasn't long before a little band of us gradually crystallized out of invisible affinities and a shared dislike of sport. Like the rest of my contemporaries forming gangs and gaggles on the school playing field, our alliance of friends had its own peculiar banter, running jokes, and nicknames. There was Mark, thin and frizzy; big John, knockabout clown and raconteur; shy Sharon; and of course big Helen.

I can't remember when I started to call Helen 'big Helen'; I can't even remember when I first met her – she had always been there, it seemed, from the very beginning. As a child we'd played mummies and daddies on the little strip of pavement outside her family's maisonette in Rose Avenue. We sang in the church choir together and, dressed in the usual towels and sheets, played Mary and Joseph in the church nativity play. Though we lost touch when I moved to a new junior school – I had failed to learn anything at our local one – we became affectionate, if rather teasing, friends at high school. Every day we would walk to and from school together, Helen complaining, as often as not, that she couldn't walk any faster as she only had 'little legs'. Years later, when I was thinking of becoming an artist, Helen was my first model. I created a little folio of pencil drawings of her sitting in our kitchen among the coach drivers, looking bored, fending off the Alsatian, and drinking tea. In a way those drawings were a testament of friendship.

Then there was Toby. We were about thirteen when Mr Gelthorpe, the new music teacher, initiated his own one-man musical renaissance at our school. Soon we were both playing in the new orchestra, rehearsing in room N, and managing to murder the most innocent of melodies. In our young hands, everything we played turned into Stockhausen. Without my knowing quite how or why, Toby became my best friend. He would regularly come on holidays with my family and, apart from spending all our time together at school, we would often stay over at each other's houses. At night, after we had turned off the lights and were lying in our beds gazing out into the velvet blackness of the room, we would talk. He would usually tell me the latest about how he was in love with my sister and did I think she felt the same about him, and if she didn't how might she come to feel the same. I would chatter about this and that. Toby would make jokes. I would laugh into the darkness. We would talk about schoolteachers, my horrible brothers, and, as often as not, the meaning of life.

Those late-night whisperings were the simple pleasures of friendship: the relish of letting the known world disappear into darkness while our twin voices explored the universe. Of course we were half making it up, it was half ghost story and adolescent fantasy. But it was also something else, a faltering attempt to question life and ask the meaning of it, as if, in the darkness of the bedroom, we were trying to grasp tiny threads of gold that hung tantalizingly down to us from the stars. But it seemed we had to grow up and put such 'childish' things behind us. There came a point in our friendship when Toby seemed to say, 'We must stop talking about these things now. We need to be sensible and grown up. I want to have a career and a family, there are *serious* matters to consider now…' It was as, if in order to 'grow up', we needed to close the door on something.

Many people must feel, at some point or other, that in the process of growing up – of getting your first pay packet, going out on dates, and learning to drive – something has been lost. Without wanting to sentimentalize childhood, it seems to me that children, as well as having a natural capacity for friendship, also have an innate sense of wonder. Recently I saw a small boy looking at a tractor. For its somewhat put-upon driver the tractor was merely a means to an end, a tool, something that needed servicing. For the boy – holding his mother's hand, wide-eyed and slightly fearful – it was a monster, a living toy crammed with miracles. For a child the world is still a place of mysteries. Even at high school the playground buzzes with tales of the supernatural, telepathy, and astral travel. My late-night talks with Toby were an attempt, naïve perhaps, to get to the mystery of things – my question always an incoherent 'Why am I here?' But then the world, with its insistent demands – its mortgage repayments, tax returns, and trips to Tesco – still seemed a long way off. Actually it was just around the corner.

As we grow up, the clock, with its ever more insistent hours and minutes, seems to cut time up into little breathless pieces: an hour for lunch, forty minutes to get to work and twenty for tea breaks. As we live in the modern city, like millions of others, the sheer pace of life, the mind-boggling complexity of it all, can mean that we feel we're always on the move, in a rush, with so many things to do. Our time, once so open and carefree, is taken up more and more with the business of living. Friendship, once our all-day adventure, is squeezed into the occasional lunch date; talking late into the night is replaced by trying to make ourselves heard above the music videos in a trendy pub, after a late meeting in the office.

As we get taller, friendship gets smaller, and the wonder we once felt – the sense of life being full of possibility and magic – gets buried in the humdrum, common-sense, no-time-to-think-about-that-now realities of adulthood. The tractor we once marvelled at becomes an irritation, something we get stuck behind on a country road on our way to *somewhere*.

In our headlong rush, we can fail to notice the simple pleasures of life. Increasingly preoccupied with getting and spending, life becomes ever more dominated by usefulness and convenience. But friendship is neither useful nor convenient. Helen and Toby, and the brothers from over the hedge, didn't improve my career prospects or teach me how better to save money. We were friends for no *reason*; we just liked being with each other, and that was enough. Of course there *are* good reasons to make friends and to stay friends, but we don't really do either because of them. What we get from friendship is what we give to it; the more we are friends just for the sake of it, with no return in mind, the better the friendship will be. By the time we become adults we tend to want to know what's in it for me and how it will help me make my way in the world. But friendship is valuable in itself; it isn't really *for* anything.

So often our childhood friends are the best friends we ever have. For me it was to be many years before I would make another friend as close and important to me as Toby. Indeed it was many years before I again experienced companionship in the way I had with that family of brothers from over the hedge. As we grow older, and our lives become more complicated, friendship increasingly takes a back seat, replaced for the most part by the demands of career and the business of earning a living, or by romance and family responsibilities. We want our 'significant other' to be everything to us: lover, best friend, counsellor, and partner. Weighed down by expectation and burdened by inappropriate needs, the loving couple breaks down only too easily. We put all our eggs into the basket of romantic love and then wonder why it's so painful when it gets dropped.

The end of a love affair can be the beginning of loneliness. I remember at school, after being given the heave-ho by Angela Jeffreys, how distraught and lonely I felt. The agonies of thwarted love are painful enough at high school but the isolation of divorce or separation can be devastating. Our friends came in couples and were met in couples, and now, in our single state, we feel the odd one out. Meanwhile the friends we had before the relationship have got themselves hooked up, or we have disappeared so much from their lives that they are no longer really friends at all. Perhaps, as the psychologist Erich Fromm has suggested, the intensity with which we fall in love in the first place is an indicator of just how isolated we are.

Love or no love, most people experience the pain of loneliness at some point in their life, be it the agony of shyness, the dread of being ostracized at school, or the acute sense of being an outsider or a misfit. There are many different kinds of loneliness, from the acute loneliness of the friendless and marginalized (street kids sleeping in doorways, old ladies in isolated high-rise hells) to the low-lying chronic numbness of having no one to *really* talk to. There is the isolation of bed-sit land, the loneliness of the city, and the gnawing pain of having no friends. But loneliness goes beyond the mere lack of other people. You can be lonely within yourself. You can be lonely even when surrounded by your 'nearest and dearest,' in the midst of married life, or on your holiday of a lifetime.

You can even be lonely among friends. By the time I left school I had become aware of an undertow of loneliness and isolation running alongside the warmth I felt for my little gang of friends. I nursed guilty secrets and, though I didn't realize it at the time, secrets breed loneliness. My jokes and banter were in part a defence, a kind of whistling in the dark. For me, and probably for all of us, there was another story beneath the happy tomfoolery in which we indulged. Behind our wacky stories were all kinds of troubled feelings, unspoken fears and desires, a whole private inner world that for all our mutual affection we dared not reveal. Judging from the number of people who see some kind of therapist, most people experience this kind of loneliness to some degree or other – unless they manage to smother it with drink, drugs, and breakfast television.

Helen was lonely, I suppose. She was an only child, her ageing parents seemingly uninterested in their chubby and rather timid daughter. Her only reliable source of affection was the dog: a small wire-haired creature of boundless energy that Helen doted upon. Unencouraged and miserable, she would tell me how she would sometimes cry into her tea while her parents watched the *Nine O'Clock News*, and her father would send her upstairs to her bedroom so that she didn't disturb them. She was lonely, her overweight a symptom of comfort eating, her shyness a barrier to new and possibly threatening experience. Our friendship helped assuage that. When she came to drink tea in our kitchen I always walked her home and I somehow managed to persuade her to join the local amateur dramatic society with me; it helped her come out of herself, she said.

We have within us a deep need for sharing and companionship. Pain and distress are multiplied and aggravated by loneliness and, as Cicero the Roman philosopher and orator puts it, 'If you are lonely, every pleasure loses its savour.' Real friendship – rather than casual mateship – is the antidote to loneliness. It is an antidote that the world is badly in need of.

But then it depends what we mean by friendship. Your average man or woman in the street will probably say that friendship is still an important part of their life. Despite having the children to dress and get to school, despite the housework, despite the hours at the office, friendship still feels important. But a friend is more than a mate, more than someone we pass the time with or see on the occasional girls' night out. Friendship is, or can be, much more than we usually expect from it.

By the time I moved to London, friendship was no longer something I gave much thought or time to. I still saw Toby; he was living with his girlfriend in rented accommodation near Tufnell Park tube station. I would go over and stay with them sometimes, but Toby and I had stopped talking as we used to. No more late-night talks about how crazy life seemed and what the point of it all was; he was busy with work and decorating the flat. When I went back to Henley-in-Arden to visit my parents I would always go and see Helen. We would go for a drink in the Black Swan and she would tell me the latest gossip about the amateur dramatic society. But the friendships were thinner, lacking the substance they once had. I didn't expect any more from them. In a way I thought that that was what friendship was: congenial, somewhat superficial, nothing compared to *love*, nothing strongly felt or deeply committed. But sometimes, making small talk with Helen over a Guinness or having supper before a concert with Toby and his partner, I would think 'Is this it?' Without really noticing it, my experience of friendship had dwindled. Like just about everyone I knew, I gave friendship less time, less energy, and less thought. Friends I would once have spent all my time with were now mates I met for the occasional pint or another couple invited over for a meal.

There is something about our capacity for friendship, for brotherly or sisterly love, which if not expressed and nurtured withers within us. Friendship may come naturally to most children, but it seems to *go* just as naturally for most adults. As children, nature takes us out into the playground, attracts friends to us, helps us form little gangs and cliques, sets us off on our adventures; but nature can take us only so far. For most people, if friendship is to grow and thrive beyond the sixth form and university, it needs to be deliberately and consciously cultivated.

I keep remembering a night at the local Chinese restaurant one New Year's Eve. I still have the photos. I am in my early twenties, smiling broadly, my hair dyed a slightly punky red, my arm around Helen. Most of us had gone our separate ways by then. Big John was working in Birmingham, Toby was at music college, and only Helen was still living at home, doing secretarial work in a local solicitor's office. But there we were, the old gang ordering bean sprouts and drinking Chinese lager. We probably reminisced, rehearsed once again the old stories and the running jokes, talked about our new lives and our new friends, ate a bit too much. After the meal we went to my place and put some music on Dad's hi-fi. John, playing the fool as usual, started 'pogoing' – jumping up and down and pretending to be a member of a punk band. He hit his head on a brass light fitting and had to be driven to Accident and Emergency; he was not badly injured.

That New Year's Eve sticks in my mind now. For all our fun and our somewhat forced bonhomie, we were drifting apart. We had less to say to each other and more was either not being said or being said behind our backs. The old ways of relating to each other were getting stale and none of us knew how to bring the friendships back to life again. So we stuck to the same stories, the same characters we had built for ourselves. There we were on New Year's Eve, sitting around a table eating our sweet and sour chicken, and none of us knew how to take this thing called friendship further – we didn't even know it could be taken further. It was as though we were all just waiting for marriage, kids, and a career, hanging out with each other out of habit until then. So the friendships began to drift and gradually fade away. What we needed (had we but known it) was a clearer sense of what friendship was and what it could be. What we needed was a *vision* of friendship and a *practice* of it.

This is when friendship becomes real friendship. When you have a vision of what, ideally, friendship could be, and when you start to consciously develop your friendships in that direction – that is when friendship really begins. The rest is a necessary warm-up to the main event. Surely many must feel as I did, sitting around that table – that friendship could add up to much more than this convivial mateyness and yet, like me, not know how to make it more, not know where to start or what to do.

For me, this was where Buddhism came into the picture. It was not long after I moved to London that I started to become interested in Buddhism. I was unhappy. The sense of wonder I had once felt was largely lost, and though I kept the fires of imagination smouldering, I increasingly saw life as something painful and at worst futile. The friendships I was making were on the whole superficial, fair-weather ones. And the friendships I had made back at school were either drifting apart (like my friendship with Helen) or had gone badly wrong (like my friendship with Toby). Love, which by now had become an almost obsessive preoccupation, was proving not to be the universal panacea I had somehow hoped it would be. Of course, people often turn to religion when things get tough. Religion is often sought as a comforter, a kind of metaphysical duvet under which we hope to feel warm, safe, and secure. We look to religion to give us answers, to make everything all right. Buddhism doesn't so much give you answers as exhort you to ask better questions.

In a way, Buddhism doesn't give you anything. It doesn't give you friendship. We already have the potential for friendship. Our capacity to make friends is already there, part of our nature, part of how we naturally function in the world. But, as I have said, nature takes us only so far, and what nature bringeth, nature (very often) taketh away. What Buddhism *does* give you is an ideal of friendship and a way towards that ideal. Instead of losing friendship on the way, we can develop friendship, strengthen it, discover new heights and depths within it. Buddhism doesn't give you friendship; it helps you take it further.

As for wonder, well, unhappiness can prompt you to go comfort-seeking or truth-seeking. My unhappiness prompted me to ask those questions again – the questions I asked late into the night with Toby – but this time with a new urgency. Often it is when we are unhappy, perhaps especially when our life is riven by trauma at the end of a love affair, or at the death of a loved one, that we start to ask big questions. Unhappiness, at best, makes you think. As soon as we start asking the big questions – 'Why am I here?' 'What is the point of it all?' – we start (often without knowing it) to practise the spiritual life.

Remember those friendships of your childhood, how you wondered about the meaning of it all, how you explored the stars together lying out on the school playing field late that summer night? The Buddhist message is that there was real value in that, that you were half-knowingly onto something: friendship and wonder. You don't need to lose that; in fact you can develop it beyond your wildest imaginings.

Of course, childhood isn't one long summer holiday chock-full of simple pleasures, innocent wonder, and noble friendship. Children can be cruel, and childhood for many is a painful and miserable time; a time of harshness and teasing; a time of playground taunts, vendettas, and bullying. Many children grow up largely unloved by their parents, many are lonely and unconfident, and, increasingly, very many come from broken homes or one-parent families. This is without the horror stories we have become so familiar with – the children used, abused, or neglected; the children who do such terrible things that our mind recoils in horror at the very thought of it. Even for me, running wild in the garden among the apple trees and the rusting lorries, life was often painful, unhappy, and confused. My three elder brothers and I waged a constant war in which their relentless teasing was matched by my morbid sensitivity. My sister and I invariably argued, usually over vital matters of principle such as who was going to turn off the light and whose side of the bedroom the light switch was actually on. For many of us, being a happy healthy human being is something yet to be attained. Our natural instinct for friendship and a sense of wonder may never have had much opportunity to manifest itself, even as children.

When we each look back at our life, be it our childhood or our days at school, we can rarely say it was happy or unhappy, good or bad; we usually say it was a mixture of both. Somewhere in that mixture, more or less expressed, is an instinct for friendship and a capacity for wonder. Friendship is a potential within all of us everywhere. It can grow and thrive where you least expect it, and we can become friends with people we would never have dreamt of becoming friends with. In the slums of Dublin, the shanty-towns of India, the suburbs of Paris; in London, New York, Bangkok, and Dubai; from Tokyo to a garden-cum-rubbish dump in Henley-in-Arden – friendship recurs universally, a thread of gold running through the chaos of a battlefield.

But a thread of gold is easily lost. One day, the family of brothers that called to me from over the hedge were suddenly gone. The house was emptied and sold. The removal van came and went, taking furniture, pot plants, and battered chopper bikes to far-off Reading. I never saw them again. As for my friendship with Toby and how that went wrong, that is a longer story and one I will come back to later. And Helen? We gradually lost touch. The last I heard of her, she had moved out of her little maisonette in Henley and was living somewhere in nearby Warwick, working in a solicitor's office. She'd joined a better amateur dramatic society, one that gave her more interesting parts and didn't take her so much for granted.

She visited me in London only once. I was a Buddhist at the time and a painter. She stayed the night, and on seeing my little shrine (an old curtain thrown over a box, a couple of candles, and a miniature Buddha figure) she asked jokingly if she would be expected to get up in the middle of the night and chant something. But between then and now we gradually lost contact: an unexpected phone call, a school reunion that I never went to because I was away from England being ordained – admitted to the Buddhist order – and then nothing. I remember, though, our friendship having one last moment. It was during her visit to London and, like at least one of my other vivid experiences of friendship, it took place on a bus. I can't remember what we talked about now, or where we had been or where we were going; I just remember an exquisite feeling of friendship. It was as if all the years we had known each other – from playing together on the pavement in front of her house to acting in some dreadful comedy at the local parish hall – had been rolled together into one condensed experience of friendship. We had grown up friends, and for the time that bus took to get from where we had been to where we were going, our friendship grew and, for that little time, became more than it had ever been.

2

THREE KINDS OF FRIENDSHIP

Only the friendship of those who are good, and similar in their goodness, is perfect. … And it is those who desire the good of their friends for their friends' sake that are most truly friends, because each loves the other for what he is, and not for any incidental quality.

The Ethics of Aristotle, trans. J.A.K. Thomson

The first time I took LSD I was twenty-one. My mother had brought us up to believe that any drug-taking would inevitably lead to our becoming heroin addicts and overdosing in a squat in Coventry, so, unlike many of my contemporaries, I kept well away from drugs. I was raised in a small provincial town and the issue of recreational drugs simply didn't come up. Henley-in-Arden was (indeed still is) a pretty little town of half-timbered houses fronting onto a high street lined with lime trees. A respectable and rather conservative town, it took years of wrangling for the parish council to agree to a chip shop, and when the Chinese restaurant opened it seemed a risqué break with tradition and a little triumph for multicultural diversity. To me, in those innocent days, drug-taking seemed as far off and as dangerous as the Bronx. Unlike the playgrounds of many provincial schools nowadays, I can't remember anyone sniffing glue, doing E, or getting drunk on alcopops behind the Nissen huts. Experimenting with hallucinogens was a far cry from the Church of England coffee mornings I attended after singing hymns and psalms in the parish church, dressed in my red cassock and crisp white surplice. So it was with some trepidation that, on a sunny afternoon on holiday in Cornwall, I finally decided to 'drop some acid'. Even then it was not entirely my idea – it arose out of friendship.

Sam and I had become friends. We were doing our nurse training in Coventry at the time and a friendship had gradually developed between us. On a hot afternoon in a deserted car park, we were each given what looked like a small square of blotting paper with a picture of Donald Duck on it. I remember holding it in the palm of my hand half thinking that this was the beginning of the end for me, that in a year or so's time I would end up looking like one of those cadaverous young men you see on anti-drug posters with 'Just Say No' written on them. The reason I hadn't 'just said no' was because Sam had done such a good job of reassuring me. He told me it wasn't addictive, that it simply acted as a chemical trigger for aspects of the brain's natural functioning, that he had taken it before and he would look after me. Despite my trepidation I decided to give it a go; I suppose, when it came down to it, I trusted him. We took the tab and, gazing out at the ocean, waited for the world to change.

Drug experiences, like strong dreams, are vivid in the experience and boring in the retelling, so I won't tax the reader's patience with the details. Suffice it to say that the world did seem to change. It became something vibrantly mysterious and wonderful; from a tiny flower to the setting sun, everything seemed transfigured into utmost beauty. Marvelling at all this

I asked Sam if the beauty around me was how things actually were or if it was just in my mind. My insistent question was 'What is real?'

Here again (though admittedly under the influence of illicit substances) was that experience of friendship and wonder that I had felt in touch with as a child. Here again I experienced myself as being in a world of meaning, value, and mystery. Friendship was a large part of it but it was friendship of a particular quality, a quality I was only to begin really understanding years later. As for meaning, in a sense that had to wait too. I never took LSD again. I don't know why; perhaps I intuitively realized that it was a dead end. Perhaps I was lucky. My childhood conditioning had driven a wedge of fear between my desire for new experience and recreational drugs. Nowadays, having met so many people for whom drug-taking has spiralled dangerously out of control, I feel fortunate that I never went far down that particular path in my search for meaning. However, that afternoon with Sam planted a seed of something – a seed encoded with the words, 'There is much more to consciousness than you think.' It was a seed that first flowered years later when, on a Wednesday evening in Bethnal Green, someone with a funny name taught me to meditate.

I have said that Sam and I were friends. But what exactly is friendship? What does it mean to have a friend or to be a friend? By paying a subscription you can become a 'Friend' of the Royal Academy (the friendship consisting of receiving a glossy magazine every quarter, getting an invitation to private views, and – best of all – being able to jump the ticket queues). President Clinton talked of all the people who voted him into Congress as his personal friends. Many think of Jesus or their mother or their spouse or their dog as their friend, even their best friend. I remember having a long talk with a very serious young man about how exactly it was that he thought you could become friends with a dolphin. 'Can you become friends with the dead?' someone asked me at a meditation class. Friendship is as much spoken of as it is misunderstood and undervalued.

Thinking back to my friendship with Sam, it seems to me that there were different elements to it. First, we were of use to each other. We were both in the same year of nurse training and had got to know each other in that context. Working on the wards together, we needed to cooperate with each other and, as we were both new to nursing and in the minority (male nurses were still quite an unusual phenomenon in those days) we found ourselves forming a natural alliance. We helped each other out and that, in part, was what the friendship was based on. Secondly, we were friends for the simple reason that we enjoyed each other's company. In many ways, Sam, born and raised in Northern Ireland and the son of a Protestant minister, was unlike anyone I'd ever met before. He smoked dope, dressed like a tramp, lived in a squat with what seemed to be an open sewer running through the backyard, and, come opening time, drank copious amounts of Guinness. One just didn't come upon this sort of person in provincial Henley-in-Arden. I was fascinated by him, attracted to his extrovert and rebellious nature.

He would laugh at this, but there is a very real sense in which Sam was one of the first genuinely intelligent and cultured men I'd ever met. He was the first person I met as a young man who still asked questions of life, the sort of questions I had asked myself and Toby years before but which I had already almost forgotten. In an incoherent way LSD was part of that questioning: it was his attempt to see beyond the surface of things, to open up his mind. There was something positively dissatisfied about Sam, something about him that just could not fit in, as if he couldn't bring himself to believe in the kind of life that everyone else seemed to assume was the life to live. He had an intense and passionate political conscience and, during our tea breaks from the ward, he would provoke arguments with the other nurses about left-wing politics and the IRA. When you consider that those tea break conversations tended to revolve around ward gossip, boyfriends, and the new range of knitwear at Marks and Spencer's, Sam's argumentative and deeply serious nature tended to rather stick out. But he was so alive! I remember him slumped on one of the grey plastic chairs in the nurses' canteen arguing vehemently about the hunger strikes that were going on at the time, gesticulating with his bacon butty and causing a great stir of indignation. But for all the scandal of his views, we liked him, and as I got to know him better his passionate temperament and positive dissatisfaction rubbed off on me. At the time, though, I was a painfully insecure young man, trying my utmost to fit in and be popular. The movement from my teens to my twenties had been a painful and confusing business, largely preoccupied with one thing: I was gay.

Over the years I had gradually come to what was, for me, at the time, the awful realization that I was gay. It all seemed to start when I was still a little boy. One day, on my way home from school, I happened to stop off at the house of a friend of mine. There was wrestling on television when I arrived and, as I watched those muscular men grappling with each other on the screen in front of me, I experienced a strong feeling of attraction – a feeling I instinctively knew I was not supposed to feel. Growing up, I had no positive role models for being gay, so I vaguely assumed I would end up like one of those effeminate comedians the English television-viewing public seem so keen on. By the time I got to know Sam, the fact that I was gay had become a painful secret. At one point he suggested the two of us go to Amsterdam for a long weekend. I was keen but felt that, if he and I were to spend a weekend together in a cheap hotel, it was only fair that I tell him the truth about myself – just in case he had second thoughts. He was, of course, absolutely fascinated:

what was this dark secret? When, after much mumbling and hesitation, I finally got the 'awful' truth out he laughed for about five minutes flat.

Sam was genuinely open-minded, so he wasn't the slightest bit fazed by my homosexuality. He was, I suppose, much more worldly wise than I was. He was a thinker and a voracious reader, and he'd seen more of life in his home town of Belfast than I'd ever seen in ever-so-nice Henley-in-Arden. I invariably enjoyed being with him. We spent many an evening talking in the local pub, Sam racing ahead on the drinks front, I trying to follow his thought as it twisted and turned from politics to sex to religion.

I've lost contact with him now. He moved back to Belfast and, though he turned up out of the blue one night and we sat down and tried to thrash out just what it was that I saw in this Buddhism lark, I never really managed to get it across to him. I couldn't have explained then how I saw Buddhism as naturally following on from where we had been as friends back in Coventry. I wonder what he'd make of this book. Could I convince him now that friendship could be developed into something more – even into something spiritual? I could of course point him to Aristotle; he would at least know of Aristotle and may have actually read him. I could start with that great figure from the Western tradition and show him how close he was – in some ways at least – to an even greater figure of the East. Among Aristotle's writings (probably lecture notes written by him or taken by his pupils) is an essay on friendship, in which he talks about three kinds of friendship: friendship based on attraction to the usefulness of your friend, to the pleasure they afford you, or to the good they embody. I don't know if Sam would have felt our friendship had an aspect of the good in it, but looking back on it now I do. Yes, we were helpful to each other and we had a lot of fun together on the wards and in the pub, but as I have already said there was something *more* between us, more than use and more than fun.

Looking back on my friendship with Sam it seems there were aspects of it that I now see as having spiritual value. Not that either of us would have thought in those terms, even if we had sat down and talked about our friendship, which of course we never did. In those days we were both fiercely anti-religious, so I am sure we would have poured scorn on any idea that there was a spiritual aspect to our friendship. Yet there was something *good* about my friendship with Sam. I grew as a person through my contact with him. First, he had, despite his apparently anarchic temperament, an educating and refining influence on me. It must be admitted that at the time I was a rather shallow and pretentious young man, and Sam opened my eyes to a larger world of experience and thought. I remember him reading me one of T.S. Eliot's poems, his thick Northern Irish accent ringing out passionately: 'This is the way the world ends / This is the way the world ends / Not with a bang but a whimper.' He'd talk about Camus's novels, Mozart's horn concertos, and the virtues of anarchy over state communism. All this was new to me. I had been brought up on the *Daily Mail* for politics, Agatha Christie for literature, and Barbra Streisand for music.

I could really *talk* to Sam. He was positively unshockable, and the relief I felt in starting to unburden myself to him, especially about my secret sex life, was inestimable. He probably never thought of himself as a virtuous or ethical man, yet there was something very positive, even ethical, about his dissatisfaction with things: a sort of feeling for the truth coupled with a natural hatred of humbug. His politics were in large part an expression of genuine concern for his fellow man. He was highly sensitive to the terrible reality of suffering in many people's lives; it bothered him and he wanted to do something about it. Sam was also – old-fashioned as it might sound – an honourable man. For instance, after I told him I was gay he told me he'd always assumed I was, but felt it was none of his business, and when, in search of a juicy titbit of gossip, some of the other nurses asked him if the rumours about me were true, he simply said he didn't know and they should ask me themselves.

With the benefit of hindsight and with the help of an ancient Greek philosopher, it is clear to me now that my attraction to Sam was, at least in part, an attraction to the *good* in Sam. Clearly, much of what appears to be virtue or goodness isn't really that at all. Often enough, what we take to be goodness is really a matter of *looking* good rather than *being* good. Perhaps we make a bit too much of a show of our generosity, or we are generous only in a way that suits us and doesn't inconvenience us too much. Perhaps we want to be seen as kind and sympathetic, but when it comes to actual practical helpfulness we are nowhere to be seen. Perhaps we think that being good is a matter of always being nice and having no fun. Sam wasn't nice; he didn't speak nicely, eat at sensible times, go to church on Sundays, or wait till he was married before having sex. He certainly didn't *look* good; even in his nurse's uniform he always looked a bit grungy – and he drank far too much Guinness. Yet it was his goodness, his feeling for others, his unwillingness to fit in, and his simple frank truthfulness and idealism that I responded to. I was attracted to those qualities and something of those qualities was stirred within me. Those years as a nurse in Coventry were fallow years in my life, a time when nothing of any real substance seemed to happen, a time when I didn't really grow as a person – apart from my friendship with Sam, that is (and perhaps the painful business of 'coming out'). In Sam's company something in me started to wake up.

If my friendship with Sam was meaningful, most of my friendships at the time were more to do with usefulness or pleasure. Aristotle was right – friendship based on an attraction to the good is rare. If we look honestly at our friendships we will probably find that many of them, if not most, are about wanting something, wanting the perks or the pleasures they give us.

Many friendships are work-based; given the hours and days people spend working together in an average job, this is hardly surprising. While I was a nurse I spent most of my time with other nurses. We lived together in nurses' accommodation, had our own social club in the grounds of the hospital, and took our lunch and tea breaks in the staff canteen. What we all had in common was, above all, nursing, and much of our conversation revolved around that. So most of the friendships I made, while they were warm and convivial, were largely a matter of convenience. If my friendship with Sam was partly an attraction to something *essential* about him – his character, who he really was – then what I had in common with most of my other friends at the time was *incidental*. We simply happened to be in the same year of training or happened to work on the same ward. When I left nursing we told each other we would keep in touch, and we did for a while, but gradually we drifted apart. With less and less in common, the phone calls to arrange times to meet up became more infrequent and, as our fund of ward stories and reminiscences began to die out, we increasingly found ourselves with nothing to say. I remember finding this process confusing; I had felt very warmly for these people, yet with the best will in the world I felt my positive feelings for them gradually seeping away. Most people have this experience. Once the common basis of working together is lost, the friendship peters out. Moving on from job to job, first in this place, then in that, we leave behind us a string of half-forgotten names.

Then there are the friendships that are more overtly useful, the 'how to win friends and influence people' end of friendship. There are the friendships we seek out for the reflective glamour or kudos we hope to get from them. (Remember at school how there were always certain groups of friends hanging out in the playground that were the 'in crowd', the people to be seen with?) Then there are the hangers-on and acolytes of the rich and famous; those with the desire to move in influential circles, to get invited to the right parties, and to associate with the up-and-coming; or the ambitious young bucks at art school who hang out at the bar with the tutors, their eye on the main chance and the posh galleries; the networking, and the golf we play to meet the right people and make the right connections. Perhaps the usefulness we find in our friends is their willingness to be moaned to or talked at or a shoulder to cry on. Perhaps what we want from our friends is support.

What tends to happen is that, when the convenience of working together, and the use you are to each other, wear off, the friendship finishes or fades away. Much the same could be said of friendships based on pleasure. While there is mutual pleasure to be had, the friendship thrives, but when the pleasure fades so does the friendship. Aristotle thought friendships based on pleasure were more common between the young, whose lives, he felt, were governed by their feelings and pleasure-seeking.

I've always liked a laugh myself. When he was on form, talking to Toby could be pure joy. I remember going to a truly awful school concert with Toby and his mother. Toby kept whispering little jokes to me, and what with his mother's comically pained expression as the school orchestra groaned and scraped along, missing two notes out of three, I spent the whole performance curled in a ball, trying desperately to stop myself from roaring with laughter. A sense of humour has always attracted me to someone. With Sam it was his devil-may-care sense of adventure and fun. There was the time he pushed me into the hospital swimming pool while I was on duty – supposedly looking after a young diabetic girl (who of course enjoyed the sight of me dripping wet in my uniform and having to take her back to the ward). Of an evening Sam and I would drink Bushmills Black Bush whiskey and have a laugh, and on the afternoon we took LSD we pretended to be limpets sticking to a rock, letting the huge waves crash over us.

Friendship can bring so much pleasure, but pleasure can wear off or be too forced or start to become an expectation, a kind of pressure. Pleasure is most pleasurable when we are not trying to enjoy ourselves, when it arises spontaneously. That is why I have never liked fancy-dress parties. Once you have dressed up as a vicar or a tart you are obliged to enjoy yourself. You have to show everyone that you are really having fun and know how to have a good time, otherwise you just look stupid and feel daft. Eventually, friendships based on pleasure are a strain; you either hide away when you feel miserable or you put on a show to cover it up. Pleasure-seeking can, strange to say, become boring. It is our sense of meaning that makes us feel that our life is really going somewhere; it is our sense of value that gives us something to do. Pleasure-seeking, at worst, is time-filling, a restless and uncomfortable search for a good time which, we vaguely feel, is always just beyond our grasp.

Of course we tend to assume that anyone remotely spiritual or religious has a downer on pleasure. Pleasure, after all, is often associated with the body, and religion, especially in the West, has historically been very ambivalent about the body. Our image of the spiritual life is often an unsmiling one. Laughing in church was always out of the question, and there is still the worry over whether Christ smiled or not. Perhaps we even associate Buddhism with an unsmiling, spiritually austere discipline; all silent meditation in snow-bound caves and not a decent joke in sight. In my experience, my most developed friendships – friendships based on my instinctive attraction to the good in my friend – are a source of great pleasure and satisfaction. But the pleasure is, as it were, a by-product, something that arises as a result of a deeper and more sustaining resonance.

Kaz and Alison, Debbie, Lorraine, and I would go out to clubs at the weekend. (Nurses could often get in free or cheaply.) We always went in big groups, a dozen or so of us, dressed up to the nines, intent on having a good time. In some ways it was fun, but I was still lonely. We went out in such large groups partly so as not to run the risk of getting to know each other better, of finding out if we *really* liked each other or not and partly because we didn't really know what else to do. No one's life is all pleasure. Sometimes we can't enjoy ourselves however hard we try – and the harder we try the less likely we are to enjoy ourselves anyway. I find that trying to 'get' pleasure is like trying to squeeze 'fun' into a busy day. Every necessary little job becomes an irritating chore to be got through, and when you've finally (and a bit resentfully) got through them, you're too wound up to enjoy the pleasure you'd been promising yourself anyway. But friendship based on the good can, as it develops and matures, include all of us: highs and lows, strengths and shortcomings. We can stop trying to be the life and soul of the party, the comedian, the good-time girl, or the clown, and – in the company of a rare friend – be ourselves. Friendships based on the good are the most reliable friendships we can ever form, the ones most likely to last. Friendships based on pleasure can suddenly disappear. Perhaps you are no longer the flavour of the month, or perhaps you are having a difficult time and no longer much fun to spend time with, or perhaps you decide to give up drinking and everyone thinks you've become a killjoy.

If we are honest with ourselves we will probably find that most of our friendships are based on one or both of these two motives for friendship: use and pleasure. Not that these motives are especially bad. Naked ambition disguised as cordial friendship is probably relatively uncommon, and most pleasure-based friendships don't evaporate the moment we have an off day. Use and pleasure are just the way the world works. In traditional societies, with no welfare state to fall back on, friendships based on mutual usefulness are an indispensable necessity, and for us Westerners most of our pleasure-based and use-based friendships are harmless enough. However, at root both are essentially self-interested. When you think about it, self-interest is the most common and, so to speak, natural motive for action. We are naturally most concerned with our own welfare, just as animals are. This natural self-interest is something we take for granted both in ourselves and in our dealings with others. So, for instance, if we want to get someone to do something, whether to attend a political rally or to read a book on Buddhism, we endeavour to persuade them that it is in their interest to do so. But friendship can go further than self-interest; in fact it can, by gradual degrees and by diligent effort, take us beyond self altogether. This is what I mean by friendship based on the good. This is friendship with a capital F, friendship par excellence.

Many friendships, of course, will have a mixture of all three motives: use, pleasure, *and* goodness. There were certainly elements of all of them in my friendship with Sam. But amongst the use and the pleasure there was a strongly felt attraction to the good in each other; both of us had vague yearnings to go beyond ourselves, to see beyond our own self-concern. Yes, that desire to go beyond ourselves was often misdirected or naïve or expressed incoherently, but nevertheless it was there, buried within us and half-dormant. The LSD we took that day in Cornwall was an attempt at a kind of smash and grab raid on the reality of things outside self-interest. I remember in the midst of our trip Sam saying, 'Buddhists meditate for years to have this kind of experience, why make all that effort when all you have to do is take a tab?' I don't know whether it's with the benefit of hindsight that I now seem to remember thinking he was wrong.

3

THE BUDDHIST TRADITION OF FRIENDSHIP

The friend who is a helper and
The friend in times both good and bad,
The friend who shows the way that's right,
The friend who's full of sympathy:
These four kinds of friends the wise
Should know at their true worth, and he
Should cherish them with care, just like
A mother with her dearest child.
  Sigālaka Sutta, trans. Maurice Walshe

I remember setting off on my bike one cold November evening feeling a strange kind of apprehension. A friend had for some time been trying to get me to visit the London Buddhist Centre, but I had been putting it off because, in the back of my mind, I had a vague presentiment that once I went there my life would never be the same again. I was twenty-four and midway through a fine art degree course at Goldsmiths' College. I had given up nursing a couple of years earlier, as it happens, under the influence of Sam and dope, or more precisely Sam, dope, and Van Gogh. During our long weekend together in Amsterdam, apart from smoking a lot of dope together, we went to the Van Gogh Museum to see an exhibition of his work. By the time we reached the end of the exhibition I knew I had to give up nursing and become an artist: it was as if every canvas was telling me, 'Look what miracles are possible with paint. Now you try!' So it was that I went to London, not in the hope that its streets would be paved with gold but at least with the expectation that, apart from anything else, it was the best place to study art and become famous. After living in digs for a bit, I moved into a run-down house near the college with a bunch of art students and a new friend, Maria. It was from there that I made my first journey to the London Buddhist Centre. I don't remember ringing the doorbell of 51 Roman Road, nor do I remember going into the courtyard with its single willow tree growing beneath the peeling and faded mural of a horse carrying three large jewels on its back. I don't remember going in the reception room or my reaction to the painted scene of an idealized and peaceful landscape. What I do remember is the strange mixture of jubilation and amusement I felt as I entered the shrine room and saw, dominating the room, a large golden statue of the Buddha. I remember deciding halfway through being taught the mindfulness of breathing meditation practice that I was a Buddhist, that in some way I had always been one, and that this was what life was really about. I also remember being disappointed.

An important book that helped to make me more susceptible to living any kind of spiritual life was Christopher Isherwood's *My Guru and his Disciple*. Before then I had been of a predominantly political bent, and had long since rejected any form of religion as repressive and retrograde. In my ignorance I had assumed that religion inevitably meant Christianity, or at least the belief in some all-knowing, all-powerful God, and I had long since ditched both. Isherwood's book opened me up to a new notion of what religion could be. It was a far cry from the monotonous mumbling that stood for prayer in the draughty and half-empty church of my childhood, a far cry from Sunday best and parish fêtes. It was something meditative, mystical, and mysterious, perfumed with the strange intoxicating incense of the East. After reading Isherwood's account of his relationship with his mystical guru-figure – his swami, as he called him, an old saffron-robed Indian mystic – I was rather disappointed not to find one at the London Buddhist Centre. Not really grasping the difference between Isherwood's Hindu Vedanta and my aspiring Buddhism, I had expected to sit at the feet of an ancient, yellow-robed, probably Eastern gentleman, who was completely aloof from the world and whose hushed and mysterious words I could treasure in my heart. I was a bit disappointed to meet these vaguely middle-class English men and women who comprised the Western Buddhist Order. Not a single one of them looked anything like a spiritual being. For all I knew they could have been a bunch of enthusiastic care workers or the sort of people with goatee beards and ponytails you get running youth projects. They were certainly Western, but were they Buddhists? The only visible sign of anything even vaguely Eastern was the strip of white cloth around their necks and the fact that they each had a funny-sounding name which I thought I'd never be able to remember. Where was my guru? Where was all that Eastern promise I'd picked up from Isherwood's book? I asked the man who taught the meditation where the swami was. He looked puzzled and said they didn't have a swami, nor did they wear robes. I was disappointed.

Despite not finding my guru, I kept going to the Buddhist Centre. Meeting Buddhism for the first time was, in some strange way, a coming home to myself, as if in my heart of hearts I had always been a Buddhist and all I needed was to wake up to that fact. Ever since I can remember, before those late-night talks with Toby, long before my trip with Sam, I had always felt that life must be *for* something. It couldn't just be this muddling through until you died, it couldn't be just career and kids and mortgages, there had to be *more*. Going along to the Buddhist Centre that first night I got a provisional answer to the question of my life. It was as if the serene golden Buddha statue – which, I was disappointed to find out later, was made of plaster of Paris – said to me, 'Yes, there is more, and this is where you learn to become more.' The first step was meditation.

Lots of people have all sorts of wonderful experiences when they first start to meditate, feelings of bliss and joy, a deep and powerful sense of contentment, even, occasionally, a mystic inner light show, but I just kept falling asleep and getting frustrated. I had a lot to work with. I came to meditation in a bit of a mess. I was an unhappy and confused young man, and meditation confronted me with myself, with my lack of calm, my lack of psychological integration, and my shortage of positive emotion. But I stuck at it; I meditated every day, went regularly to classes at the Centre, and began to learn about Buddhism.

I soon made friends. After the meditation session there were always tea and biscuits and time to hang around and chat, but I didn't think that was anything to do with Buddhism as such. I thought Buddhism was meditation and lots of it; the rest, as far as I was concerned, was mere decoration, at worst distraction. Although I was immediately struck by how friendly the Buddhists were, it was not till some time later that I started to learn about the Buddhist tradition of friendship and its central importance in the spiritual life. I had thought that Buddhism was a wholly personal and private affair, something you did on your own with your eyes closed.

My ignorance was in many ways justifiable. At first glance Buddhism doesn't seem to have a lot to offer when it comes to teaching on friendship. While the theme of friendship does come up again and again in the many different Buddhist traditions and schools, there is no systematic exploration of it, nor are there any canonical sutras devoted to it. The early disciples of the Buddha probably just took friendship for granted. In those days you couldn't get by without it, especially if, like many of the Buddha's disciples, you'd left your village and family to wander around northern India begging for food and practising the Buddha's teaching. If you got sick on the road you needed friends to look after you. There were no social services to fall back on, no health-care plans or counselling; once you'd left hearth and home all you had to rely on was your friends. So friendship was how those early disciples lived; they didn't need to *teach* it. However, looking more closely at the Buddhist tradition, we *do* find some important teachings on friendship. Probably the most famous of these concerns Ānanda, the Buddha's close friend and attendant for the last twenty-five years of his life.

It seems that one day Ānanda was thinking about friendship and its place in the spiritual life. Perhaps he had been thinking about how important his friendship with the Buddha was to him, or perhaps he had been reflecting on his friendships with his fellow monks (among whom he was universally respected). Whichever it was, we can imagine him mulling it over, much as we might today, and deciding that friendship was of profound spiritual significance. Perhaps rather pleased with his discovery, he went to the Buddha and told him that he had realized that friendship was so important that it constituted half the spiritual life. The Buddha replied by saying, 'Say not so, Ānanda! Say not so, Ānanda! Friendship is the whole, not the half, of the spiritual life.'

One can't help thinking that had Ānanda been a bit more on the ball he would have asked in what way friendship was 'the whole and not the half of the spiritual life' – in modern parlance, a simple 'Could you say more?' would have sufficed. But it was not to be, and the two seemingly wandered off into the Indian jungle without saying much more about it. However, this is an incredible remark: that friendship is the spiritual life and the spiritual life is friendship. The term used in these earliest of Buddhist texts is *kalyāṇa mitratā*. *Mitratā* means, simply, friendship. *Kalyāṇa* is a very rich word, with all sorts of connotations and resonances, meaning lovely, auspicious, morally good, helpful, spiritual, even beautiful. So the Buddha is saying that friendship, friendship which is morally good, perhaps even based on goodness, is the spiritual life *in its entirety*. The profound implications of this remark reverberate down the whole history of Buddhism – they fundamentally challenge our conception of the spiritual life, sweeping aside our exotic and fanciful notions of what Buddhism is and placing us squarely in the essentially human context of deep friendship and love of virtue. For any exploration of the Buddhist Path, be it meditation, ethics, or work, *kalyāṇa mitratā* is a key term that we'll come upon again and again.

But to really understand the Buddhist tradition of friendship, we need to look as closely at what the Buddha and his disciples *did* as much as what the Buddhist tradition tells us they *said*. If the proof of the pudding is in the eating, the proof of any teaching about friendship is in the quality of actual friendships between actual people. It's easy to forget that the Buddha was an actual person. The Buddha I encountered in the shrine room of the London Buddhist Centre was big, golden, and somewhat beefy. He had a funny-looking bump on his head, long ear lobes, and a mystically radiant face. Perhaps I'm stating the obvious, but this is not what the Buddha would have looked like. He wasn't a golden giant with a funny hair-do; he was a man, wore mud-stained robes, probably had a five o'clock shadow, and sometimes got sick. He probably wouldn't have spoken in the rather dry and formal way in which the ancient Pāli suttas speak; he wouldn't have sat on a throne and lectured, and meeting him was probably like meeting a wise friend, an ideal *kalyāṇa mitra*. Nor was he born a Buddha; he was born much like the rest of us except that he was born into a wealthy family in northern India. While he was still a handsome young man he left home, walked out into the night, and after years of searching and struggle he finally attained Enlightenment and became a Buddha – one who is awake.

Earlier I called Ānanda the Buddha's attendant, which is how he is usually described, but we shouldn't think of him as a kind of ancient Indian 'gentleman's gentleman' or personal assistant; he was, first and foremost, a friend. If we read between the lines of the rather formal and at times formulaic Buddhist texts, Ānanda comes across as something of an ideal friend, warm-hearted and kindly, intelligent, patient, and unswervingly loyal. He was the Buddha's constant companion for the last twenty-five years of the Buddha's life and, 'like a shadow that does not depart', was always ready to be of some kind service to his friend, sleeping near at hand in case the Buddha needed him, and organizing the many meetings for those who desired to see the Buddha. He would wash the Buddha's feet, mend his robes, and sweep out his hut. When the Buddha was sick he would look after him and fetch him medicine, and if the Buddha was in discomfort he would massage his back. This is not to say that the friendship was a one-way friendship – which would in any case be a contradiction in terms. Ānanda, it is true, was devoted to the Buddha from the depths of his heart, but the Buddha was in turn deeply appreciative of Ānanda. This is very much in evidence at the time of the Buddha's final passing away.

In the accounts that have come down to us it is clear that Ānanda was deeply saddened by the impending death of the Buddha.

Disconsolate with grief, he took himself away for a while and, leaning on the doorpost of his hut, gave himself over to tears and weeping. The Buddha, enquiring as to Ānanda's whereabouts and being told that he had gone to grieve alone, asked someone to go and fetch him. Ānanda – perhaps a little red-eyed and awkward – returned to where the Buddha lay surrounded by his disciples. The Buddha gently told him not to weep any more. He reminded Ānanda that he had told him many times that all things must change and end – 'how could that not be the case now?' Then, in front of all those assembled, the Buddha rejoiced in Ānanda's qualities: he praised his sensitivity and sincerity, his great kindness, and the positive influence he had on all those who came into contact with him.

The Buddha and Ānanda were friends but, it has to be admitted, the friendship was a profoundly unequal one. Whilst the Buddha clearly appreciated Ānanda, Ānanda clearly looked up to the Buddha with great respect and love. There was what we could call a *vertical* dimension to their friendship: in fact, their friendship embodies this vertical dimension of friendship in a particularly striking and archetypal way.

At the same time, there are very moving accounts of peer friendships amongst the disciples of the Buddha. These friendships we could call *horizontal* friendships inasmuch as they take place between people on much the same level of spiritual evolution. Such a friendship can be seen between the Buddha's two leading disciples, Sāriputta and Moggallāna. Since childhood the two boys had been inseparable, playing, studying, and working together. The sons of wealthy families and popular in the village, they each became the leader of their own little gang of friends. As they grew up, the two sets of friends would engage each other in various sports and games; sometimes Sāriputta and his mates would win and sometimes Moggallāna with his. Every year, the town in which they lived hosted a grand public festival with all kinds of amusements and shows, and every year the two friends reserved seats together so that they could get the best view and really enjoy it. On one occasion it seems that, despite their laughing heartily at all the fooling and clowning about, both were left with a feeling of unease and dissatisfaction. As the festival went on, this aftertaste of discontent grew until one night both friends spent a sleepless night thinking over and over: 'What's the point of all this? Where does it get anybody? In a few years these actors, now so glamorous and exciting, will all be old and feeble. What's the point of a life devoted to pleasure if it only ends up in old age and death? Surely there is more to life than this?' When the two friends met up the next morning they decided that they must go off and search for the truth together. So, discarding their expensive clothes and cutting off their hair, they donned the mud-stained robe of the wandering holy man and set off. Their respective bands of companions were so impressed with their decision that they decided to go with them. Despite meeting many teachers in their wanderings, the two friends didn't find anyone whom they felt really held the key to the riddle of life. After many disappointments they hit on a new plan. They realized they were more likely to find such a person if each went his separate way, thereby doubling their chances of success. This they did, but not before promising each other that whoever found a teacher who could communicate the essential meaning of life would straightaway seek out the other and bring him to that teacher.

It so happened that Sāriputta came across a disciple of the Buddha called Assaji. He was begging for almsfood in one of the tiny villages, the like of which you can still see in parts of India today. Sāriputta was immediately deeply impressed by Assaji's composure and dignified beauty; he intuitively sensed that this man had what he and Moggallāna had been searching for. Sāriputta waited for a convenient time to talk to Assaji, and after only a short conversation Sāriputta realized the Truth. Keen to share it with his friend, he immediately set off to find him. Moggallāna saw Sāriputta coming from a distance and was instantly struck by how his childhood friend had changed: never before had he seen him so beautiful, so serene and composed. He ran up to him and said, 'Dear friend, have you found the way to the deathless?' His friend answered, 'Yes, the deathless has been found.' Then they both set off with their bands of companions to meet the Buddha, and soon afterwards took ordination from him.

The friendship between the two men was to last the rest of their lives. Even when they had both become Enlightened and were the leading disciples of the Buddha they remained inseparable, often sharing the same little room and holding inspired dialogues for the benefit of the other monks. Devoid of the usual competitiveness between peers, they would often praise each other for their very different qualities. Sāriputta, for instance, was known as a meditator and scholar, whereas Moggallāna was known for his psychic powers.

We might think that when people become Enlightened they become just the same as each other. I remember non-Buddhist friends warning me that if I practised Buddhism I'd end up a spiritual clone, a bland Mr Nice Person devoid of all individuality. Sāriputta and Moggallāna were different as boys playing in the village together, and they were different as Enlightened teachers – probably *more* different. On some *thangkas* (traditional Buddhist paintings) they are the tiny figures on each side of the Buddha. They always look the same – saffron robes just so, nicely shaved head, and smile – nothing that really speaks of their unique characters, their still more unique friendship. I prefer to think of them sharing a room (much as I have done these last ten years), talking and meditating together, always appreciating each other, always friends. It's a shame we don't have statues of them on the shrine in the Buddhist Centre: a double statue of two friends who grew up together and became Enlightened friends. It could be an image of perfect friendship – except that to our modern eyes it would probably be mistaken for a gay couple.

Despite the example of Sāriputta and Moggallāna, as well as other examples of friendships between the Buddha's disciples, friendship between peers is not an aspect of the Buddha's teaching that has been brought out very strongly in the 2,500-year history of Buddhism. The teacher–disciple relationship is often the relationship that is most stressed in Buddhism, often at the expense of other types of relationships, especially the more horizontal friendships I have talked about. Many people's conception of Buddhism will be similar to the one I had when I first went to the London Buddhist Centre. Whether they are looking for a swami, a Zen master, or a Tibetan lama, they will expect to sit at the feet of a spiritual teacher and listen to his or her words of wisdom. Unfortunately, even that vertical friendship, like the one exemplified by Ānanda and the Buddha, has tended to degenerate. It has tended to become either more formalized and to have less of the nature of friendship, or the guru or teacher has simply not had the depth of spiritual insight necessary for such a relationship to work.

Most of us, when we look back on our life, find that, yes, we do learn from books and films and so on, but mostly we learn from *people*. Many of us have memories of a particular teacher who took a personal interest in us: perhaps the drama teacher we had at university or the history teacher at school. We learn something when the teacher cares about the subject they are teaching, when they have a deep and vigorous understanding of that subject and when they *want* to communicate it to us. No amount of dry-as-dust lecturing teaches us anything really, be it maths, home economics, or meditation. This is especially true of spiritual life. In spiritual life we don't really have teachers, at least in the modern sense of information dispensers; we have *kalyāṇa mitras*, wise friends. The Buddhist conception of friendship goes well beyond what we usually think of as friendship. It includes within it those 'teachers' who, we feel, are really aware of us and want to help us.

Over the years I have come to see that we don't need gurus after all. What we need is friends, friends we can look up to and learn from, not necessarily in some formal classroom way, but from whom we can catch what spiritual life is because they are already trying to live it. One of the great tragedies of the modern West is that so few people have friends they can reliably look up to and learn from. If this is true, then millions of people are starved of the inspiration, encouragement, guidance, and support that such friendship can bring. Many people don't even realize that *vertical* friendship is possible. Perhaps that is why it sometimes feels as though there is a vacuum in our lives.

Gurus have come to the West but often with pretty disastrous consequences. Like so much that is natural in us, our desire to look up to people needs to be educated. Genuine openness and receptivity to the wise – which has always been emphasized in Buddhism as vital to spiritual growth – needs to be distinguished from other more infantile responses. If we are not careful, our need for a father- or mother-figure gets projected onto idealized spiritual teachers. Instead of friendship based on real communication and mutual goodwill, the guru becomes a kind of living icon, complete with the icon's alluring mystique and rumours of miracles. Sadly, many people, even highly educated and critically minded men and women, are surprisingly gullible and credulous when it comes to charismatic teachers. In such cases the guru (usually, but not always, conveniently Eastern and enigmatic) can do no wrong. This is all the more disastrous because real friendship, and receptivity towards those who are more spiritually developed than us, is essential to spiritual life. Yet for many this seems an almost impossible task – either because of a kind of compulsive tendency to see authoritarianism everywhere or because of naïve trust and a willingness to hand over personal responsibility to the first Tom, Dick, or Harriet who makes spiritual claims for themselves. If someone is spiritually mature it will show in how they live their day-to-day life. We don't need to meet the Buddha, or a saint, or an angel come down to earth promising us magic powers (if we pay the subscription). We need friendship with an ordinary human being who is living the spiritual life a bit more intensively and wholeheartedly than we are. If we want to learn to become spiritually mature the best place to learn it is within friendship.

I had been looking for my swami to learn mystic truths from. I'd wanted secret teachings, mystic soundbites, and saffron robes. I hadn't expected friendship, vertical or horizontal. I suppose I'd been looking for someone special. What I got was a man from Glasgow who had a liking for Zen stories and decent coffee. He was what people called an 'Order member', someone who had been admitted to the Western Buddhist Order. It took me some time to really get a sense of what that was. At first I assumed these men and women with their strange Buddhist names were only a hair's breadth away from Enlightenment. I didn't know how to relate to them. I remember meeting one for tea before a meditation class and feeling painfully self-conscious and tongue-tied; after all, what *does* one say to the Buddhist equivalent of a saint? Later on, when I had got to know some of them better, I swung to the other extreme; they seemed just ordinary – and, sad to say, imperfect – human beings. Gradually, though, I came to see what being an 'Order member' was really about. I began to see that entry into the Western Buddhist Order meant effectively dedicating one's life to Buddhism, to pursuing the ideal of Buddhahood. Order members weren't monks hidden away in incense-filled monasteries. They weren't lay people supporting the monks but not really practising Buddhism themselves. They weren't armchair Buddhists, scholars, Buddhist priests, or mystic lamas. Ordination wasn't spiritual promotion; it marked a decisive, effective orientation towards what that golden figure on the shrine, surrounded by candles and flowers, was attempting to symbolize. And these Order member people, these men and women I met at the classes I attended, were friends. That – I was to come to understand – was what the Order was, a network of friendships, some more vertical and some more horizontal, some more immediately personal and some less so. What the afore-mentioned Glaswegian offered me wasn't answers and certainty but friendship, coffee, and a listening ear. It wasn't long before I decided that I wanted to be an Order member too.

Soon enough I no longer needed my bike. As it turned out, it was probably just as well, as it got nicked from the bike shed outside the Centre. I'd been on a meditation day led by someone who ran retreats in North Wales. The day marked something of a turning point in my meditation practice, and I was in such a good state when it finished that I hadn't minded my bike being stolen at all – I just took the Tube back to Brixton where I was living with Maria. It was no great loss, because not long afterwards I moved in 'upstairs'. Above the Centre was what was commonly referred to as a community; in this case a group of men living together trying to live out the spiritual life. They meditated together, ate together, and every week spent one evening together discussing how they were getting on with their practice of Buddhism. If that meditation day was the beginning of a deeper understanding of meditation, then the day I moved in upstairs was the beginning of a deeper understanding of friendship, of both the vertical and the horizontal variety. Alan, that long-haired leather-jacketed Mancunian, was already there, as was Ian and the afore-mentioned Glaswegian Order member. Moving upstairs was a move towards a deeper involvement with the Friends of the Western Buddhist Order. It was a move towards the heart of Buddhism, a move towards the heart of friendship. In a way it was another beginning.

4

A RARE KIND OF LOVE

*The great secret of morals is love; or a going out of our own
nature, and an identification of ourselves with the beautiful
which exists in thought, action, or person, not our own. A man,
to be greatly good, must imagine intensely and comprehensively;
he must put himself in the place of another and of many others;
the pains and pleasures of his species must become his own.*
  Percy Bysshe Shelley, 'A Defence of Poetry'

A friend of mine had a profound experience of the interconnectedness of all life on the All Hallows-on-Sea to Chatham bus (via Strood). Another experienced bliss while travelling from Baker Street to Hatton Cross. I don't know whether spiritual experiences are especially common on public transport, but I had, if not quite a spiritual experience, at least one of overwhelming love on the top deck of a number 8 bus.

I was on my way back from an art gallery in West London at the time. Buddhism had turned my life upside down – or rather the right way up. The first perceptible change had been in my artwork. I'd been painting pictures of naked figures in claustrophobic interiors, angst-filled nightmares among sinister-seeming wallpaper. Not long after I started meditating, all that changed. For a start, I went outside. The college was next to a small park, and one morning, armed with a little sketchbook of brightly coloured paper and clutching a few oil pastels, I decided to go out and draw trees. I don't know if it was the meditation I had been doing, the recording of *Tristan und Isolde* I was listening to on my Walkman, or the warm sunny beauty of the park, but as I drew I began to feel ecstatic. Each drawing seemed to come about effortlessly, as if it drew itself and I just watched it unfold before me. It was pure spontaneity, each drawing a little riot of colour, a packed starburst of ticks and dashes, spots and smudges. That set of drawings became the source and inspiration for all the rest of my work at art school, it changed my paintings and my approach to painting entirely. I emerged from those angst-ridden interiors (which, when I look back on it, had been so expressive of my states of mind) into a landscape of colour. Whilst I don't want to give the impression that my discovery of Buddhism and meditation was a road-to-Damascus revelation, I did nevertheless experience – more clearly than ever before – real hope, a feeling that at last I knew what my life was about. This new confidence was bound to manifest itself sooner or later in my artwork. At my degree show I called the painting I was most satisfied with 'In Buddha Garden'. It was derived from one of the little coloured sketches I made that morning in the park.

After leaving art school I started making my way in the art world. I sent slides off to galleries, entered paintings for competitions, and tried to organize exhibitions of my work. It was a miserable business on the whole; I'd lug a painting to the other side of London only to collect it a few weeks later with a red 'reject' cross on the back. However, it was on the way back from one of those fruitless excursions that I had my first real experience of love. Alan (now known as Karmabandhu) and I had gone to show some of my work to a gallery in West London. Having been given the usual 'don't ring us, we'll ring you' treatment, we wandered around the trendy shops and coffee bars of Notting Hill, and stopped off for a mozzarella and avocado sandwich before catching the bus home to Bethnal Green.

The two of us had not long been ordained. Since I met Alan on my first weekend retreat a friendship had gradually developed between us. Not that we hit it off straightaway. He was into politics, psychedelic music, and women. I found the music he listened to positively painful, and even though we both had political leanings, we tended to lean in different directions. As for women, he had started going out with Maria, the same Maria I'd been living with in Brixton, the friend who'd encouraged me to go along to the Buddhist Centre in the first place. So we had Maria in common at least, though not always very happily. I'll have quite a lot to say about Maria later on.

When I moved in above the Centre, Alan was already living there. We happened to share the same bathroom, our rooms being opposite each other, off one of the long corridors that were a feature of the converted fire station that housed the Buddhist Centre and community we lived in. As we brushed our teeth and got ready for bed, we would talk, make jokes and, more often than not, argue. In those days we tended to disagree about most things – ideas, politics, art, sex, Buddhism – you name it, we could disagree about it – and we usually did, at night, brushing our teeth. Despite locking horns over the toothpaste, we would usually come to some sort of resolution, a deeper understanding of each other, before saying a fond goodnight. What we didn't disagree on (ever, really) was that we wanted to dedicate our lives to Buddhism. We railed against things, criticized the Order members for not living up to our unrealistic expectations, and resisted changing ourselves, but deep down we wanted to practise the spiritual life.

We requested ordination at about the same time, went through the process of figuring out in dialogue with Order members whether we were ready to be ordained, and we were finally invited on the same four-month ordination retreat in Spain. We shared the same hut, talked during the long periods of silence, and brushed our teeth together at night. We were friends, and our bright new Buddhist names expressed that. We were both called 'bandhu'. I was Maitreyabandhu, or 'kindly friend'; Alan was Karmabandhu or 'friend of action'. We disagreed about that too. I liked his new name and he didn't – at least not at first.

It was some while after we were ordained that, returning one evening to the community, I had my experience of overwhelming love, sitting at the front of the top deck of a number 8 bus. As with so many important experiences, I remember some very specific details with crystal clarity. I remember during a lull in the conversation, while we waited for the bus, being tempted to criticize a mutual acquaintance. Both of us found this person rather difficult so I knew he would agree with the criticism, indeed I was tempted to voice it for that very reason. Only too often we try to ingratiate ourselves with one person by disparaging another. However, I clearly remember checking the impulse and, in the absence of collusive gossip, finding myself without much to say. Then came the ride home – the rocking and swaying of the bus, the headlights of approaching cars, the sensation of sitting together, of chatting idly for a while, then falling silent. It was during that silence that I felt it, an upwelling of love such as I cannot remember ever feeling before, not erotic or romantic love but a deeper love for my friend pouring through me. While the bus made its way through the darkened streets of London, lurching to a halt now and then as people rang the bell to get off, I felt wave upon wave of love. They came upon me quite by surprise and I felt confused and even alarmed by the strength of them. I had never realized before the potential depths of emotion involved in friendship and the sheer force of my feelings startled and unsettled me. There is something about the experience of unselfish love that makes all other feelings seem insignificant, a poor copy of a pure original.

In a way, friendship isn't a very good word for friendship. It might be more accurate to call real friendship, based on an attraction to the good, *love*. A different kind of love, perhaps, different from the love of lovers or mothers, and rarer than both. Of course, we might have trouble believing that such love exists. Many, when I describe my feelings for Karmabandhu that night on the bus, will assume that what I am *really* talking about is sex, or at least romantic attraction. After all, I am gay, I suppose – not that I think of myself in those terms, and you might assume that that is what all this love and friendship stuff is really about. Even Maria had her doubts about my feelings for Karmabandhu. She couldn't quite believe it was friendship and not something a trifle steamier. Perhaps for her there was an element of feeling threatened. If love and strong feeling could exist between men friends, where did that leave her? Women, it seems, often feel they detect an element of homosexuality in men's friendships. Perhaps they get suspicious of those late nights with the lads in the pub, the woozy backslapping camaraderie they result in. On the other hand, men often assume that friendship between women is merely a substitute for erotic love, a prelude to the main attraction, which is, of course, them. Nowadays we see sex in everything. We are used to attributing dark Freudian motives to our attraction to others, used to the idea that somewhere in our psychic cellar lurk all kinds of monsters, homosexual urges, and strange desires. The assumption so often is that strong feelings *must* be sexual. My feelings for Karmabandhu that night were of an entirely different order. It wasn't the usual love.

Our conception of friendship has degenerated. No longer is it a lofty human ideal expressive of strongly felt love, as it was for the ancient Greeks, but rather a trivial thing, a fill-in between sexual relationships, a way to pass the time, even a way to avoid facing ourselves. Often what we call friendship is merely the prelude to the main attraction and sometimes it really *is* sex dressed up to look respectable. But 'friendly feelings' do not describe the strength of emotion I felt towards Karmabandhu on the bus that night. Friendship, to our modern ears, sounds rather too cool, too casual, too much like mates or chums. Love, on the other hand, sounds too inevitably romantic, erotic, and overblown. Yet love is what real friendship is based on. It is a kind of love that we have no precise word for in English. In ancient Greek the word would be *agape*, a feeling of brotherly or sisterly love as distinct from *eros*, or sexual love. Buddhism has its own word for this kind of love – *mettā*. In fact, not only does Buddhism have a word for it, but – nothing if not practical – it gives you a way to actually develop it.

The *mettā bhāvanā* meditation is one of the many Buddhist meditation practices passed down to us through the ages. The word *bhāvanā* means something like 'making to become', developing, or bringing into being. *Mettā* means love, in this case the same non-sexual, unselfish love I felt on that bus ride to Bethnal Green, except that *mettā* at its most profound is felt for all beings, everywhere. When John Lennon sang 'All You Need is Love' everyone felt he was right. All we needed, all this beleaguered old planet of ours needed, was love. The trouble is he didn't make it especially clear exactly what he meant by love, or how you go about developing it. Love in Buddhism is no soppy sentiment, no romantic crush or 'love the world' cliché, it is a vigorous sympathetic identification with all beings, especially all human beings. Gradually, with patient and regular practice, the *mettā bhāvanā* cultivates within us an ever-deepening feeling of loving-kindness for all that lives. Instead of relating to others in terms of what we can get, we relate in terms of what we can give. Instead of treating planet Earth like adolescents treat their bedrooms, leaving it a mess for mother to clear up after them, we treat it with care and concern, leaving it habitable and beautiful for those who come after us.

Many Westerners come to Buddhism and meditation with what amounts to a chronically underdeveloped emotional life. They may be intellectually sophisticated, hold down a decent job, have an exciting social life, and be practically capable, but when it comes to their emotional life it is – well – not very alive. If this is true of the emotions in general, it is all the more true of positive emotions in particular. In the West so many have got so much – from power showers to personal computers – yet so many are anxious, unhappy and isolated, in conflict with themselves and others, stressed out and wound up. We complain about being short of money or short of time, but actually what most people are most short of is positive emotion. There is an international shortage of positive emotion: kindness, generosity, patience, inspiration, joy, friendship – you name it, most of us are short of it. The *mettā bhāvanā* is a direct way of remedying this.

And friendship is *mettā*'s first fruit. To develop *mettā* is not to dream of a perfect world like that in Coca-Cola advertisements where everyone is young and smiling and bathed in flattering sunlight. It is first of all expressed in a desire to make friends with actual human beings. The *mettā bhāvanā* is divided into stages. First we develop feelings of loving-kindness towards ourselves. Then we develop those same feelings towards a friend. From there we go on to develop *mettā* for someone we don't know very well and don't have much feeling for one way or another, and then on to someone we dislike or instinctively avoid. Finally we try to develop feelings of loving-kindness towards all beings. Friendship is what happens when the practice starts to work. Sitting down and doing the *mettā bhāvanā* is the cultivation of friendship from the inside outwards.

To be a friend is to love and to express that love, that *mettā*, in thought, word, and deed. 'It should be a part of our private ritual to devote a quarter of an hour every day to the enumeration of the good qualities of our friends. When we are not *active* we fall back idly upon defects, even of those whom we most love.' So writes Mark Rutherford in his *Last Pages from a Journal*. He would have understood what *mettā bhāvanā* was about. He would have appreciated the need to cultivate positive thoughts and feelings towards a friend.

A year or so after I had moved in above the Buddhist Centre, I went on a two-week meditation retreat in North Wales. I had gone on the retreat with some trepidation. The only other time I had done an intensive meditation retreat had been something of a nightmare. Not used to hours of sitting, I had suffered from an aching back, aching neck, aching knees, in fact aching everything. So it was with a few qualms (and much foam rubber to sit on) that I set off for North Wales. The theme of the retreat was the *mettā bhāvanā* practice, and as we arrived the retreat leader suggested we put the same persons in each stage of the practice all the way through. I chose Alan (as he was then) for the friend stage. Day after day I would sit on my cushions (buoyed up by copious amounts of foam rubber) and try to develop *mettā* for him. Sometimes I felt *mettā*, sometimes I didn't, but each day I brought him to mind and tried in my imagination to be a friend. Of course I'd quite often find myself not developing *mettā* at all but thinking, 'It really *annoys* me when he does such-and-such. When I get back I am going to have to bring that up with him.' Then I would realize what was happening and would in my imagination try to understand him more deeply and let go of my annoyance.

Sure enough, the night I got back we were in the bathroom

again, among the towels and the toothpaste, and sure enough, as we brushed our teeth and talked, the friendship between us blossomed. He'd had a hard time while I was away, I can't now remember why, girlfriend problems perhaps, or difficulties at work. As we talked about it I became aware that I was not 'catching up with him', not picking up the friendship where I had left off before the retreat, but that for me the friendship had continued while I had been away. It had moved on during those many hours on my cushions in North Wales. I didn't bring up my irritations after all, but told him simply and straightforwardly why I liked him, what qualities I perceived in him, and how much I valued his friendship. He went to bed that night considerably happier. I went to bed feeling that all this spiritual practice stuff, this meditating for hours and hours, was well worth it after all.

We need to let our friend know how we feel about them; we need to express our friendship in words. True friendship is mutually reciprocated *mettā*. The more *mettā* is mutually felt and mutually acknowledged the stronger and more vigorous the friendship becomes. There came a point in my friendship with Karmabandhu when I felt I had to declare my intentions – to say in so many words, 'Will you be my friend?' Saying such a thing in the school playground when I was a boy seemed quite straightforward. I would just go up to someone and say, 'Will you be my friend?' and that would be it. I remember, for instance, on one of my first days at junior school, asking a boy about my age to let me play with his toy fire engine. It was a big red fire engine with the special feature of a small black hose that squirted water when you pressed a concealed trigger. We became friends on the spot, and confirmed the new alliance by racing around the playground squirting water at the girls and generally creating havoc. Saying 'Will you be my friend?' to Karmabandhu was a rather different matter. Having grown out of fire engines and playgrounds, we had almost grown out of acknowledging friendship too. Reluctant to name it, and embarrassed to feel it, both of us felt self-conscious and awkward and keen to change the subject. Of course, as we grow older and more sophisticated, we find the simplicity of asking to be someone's friend uncool in the extreme. No more 'Can Christopher come out to play?' Rather, we protect ourselves with a posture of independent autonomy and a façade of being thoroughly grown up. Part of friendship is the willingness to strip ourselves of this pseudo-sophistication and to admit once again that we want someone to be our friend. Friendship, to be worthy of the name, must be named.

A fundamental rule of friendship is that if you want a friend you must *be* a friend. It's no good just waiting around for someone to befriend you or bemoaning the fact that nobody loves you. You yourself must go out and make a friend. (If this sounds like the sort of thing your mother told you on the way to your first day at school, she was right, and many of us have yet to learn the lesson.) One of the reasons we don't go out and make friends is that we lack a positive sense of self-regard. We secretly feel that no one would want to be our friend in the first place and, if they were foolish enough to do so, they would soon regret it once they got to know us better. This, unfortunately, easily becomes a self-fulfilling prophecy; either we avoid people in the first place or, when we do try to develop friendships, we do so with so much mistrust and suspicion that we take offence only too easily. Taking offence is a great destroyer of friendship. Cicero was well aware of this. 'Some people,' he said, 'make friendship very unpleasant because they are so ready to believe they have been slighted. However, the characters who adopt this attitude are usually those who have a strong suspicion that they deserved the slight.' There are all sorts of permutations of lack of self-esteem. I have met many people who, underneath a jolly and seemingly confident exterior, harbour half-acknowledged feelings that they are in some strange way bad and unlovable, and that if they allow anyone to get too close that person will see that and reject them.

To make friends is to take a risk. To make friends is to risk rejection, to risk *feelings* and the expression of feelings. Friendship means admitting openly that you matter to each other, that you care for each other, and that you want to spend time together. Sitting in my room with Karmabandhu one evening we told each other how much we liked each other, how much our friendship had come to mean to us. It felt risky and strangely exhilarating, as if we were breaking some kind of taboo. Somewhere at the back of our mind was that old Freudian bogey man, sex. Fear of homosexuality is one of the many blocks to friendship between members of the same sex, especially men. Basically, you're frightened that feelings of warmth and attraction for a friend will inevitably lead you up the garden path and into bed. This usually unspoken fear means that you back off from friendship. So Karmabandhu and I had to tackle this at some point. I had been too frightened to express the feelings of love I felt for Karmabandhu on the bus that night coming back from West London. I was nervous that he might think I fancied him, so I kept quiet. It was all rather unsettling; perhaps I did fancy him *really*, but I wasn't conscious of it. Karmabandhu had felt similarly nervous about his feelings for me – but could they have included an element of that? We talked it all through somewhat awkwardly and were able to admit our fears while still committing ourselves to the friendship. But what if there is an erotic tinge in the friendship? Does it really matter? You can just acknowledge it and get on with the much more important task of developing deep friendship; it shouldn't get in the way of that. Anyway, you don't have to act on it, and usually – in my experience – if you devote yourself to the friendship the erotic tinge, if there is one, soon dies away.

When we start to speak our friendship we enter a new emotional reality, a vividness of emotion at once challenging and invigorating. Often enough we leave the positive unspoken; we leave it implied and are embarrassed if it becomes apparent in any way. If we do express our positive feelings we often do it indirectly, like when you go back to your parents for a visit and, after a cordial handshake with your father, your mother says fondly, 'The dog has missed you.' It's strange that we can live in a world where the dog seems more capable of expressing its canine feelings of being pleased to see us than the humans. Some dogs strike one as being bowed low with the weight of misplaced affection, the mute receivers of showers of affection – 'You're a good dog, such a *good* dog!' – while our nearest and dearest, our closest friends, get a curt hello and, if we are lucky, the offer of a cup of tea. We might have strong feelings of love for our friend, but we don't often get around to saying so. It may never occur to us to give expression to our appreciation and delight for our friend; it may never occur to us to express our friendship in words of affection, encouragement, and praise. Perhaps our friend would get suspicious if we did, assuming we were after something or trying to butter them up. If you want a friend you need to express friendship. If you love a friend, let them know – often.

We need to express the *mettā* we feel for our friend (having developed it in the *mettā bhāvanā* practice) in thoughts, words, and deeds. Perhaps, though, it's the deeds that count most. It's the deeds that really show us where our heart lies. In the most essential sense, what we do *is* what we feel. I don't very often feel the strength of love I felt for Karmabandhu on the bus that night. It was a peak experience such as we all have from time to time. I often felt irritated by him, critical and mistrustful, and he often felt the same about me. But the love was there as a reference point, a guiding star to plot my course back towards the heart of friendship. The deep feeling of love I have for Karmabandhu arises most often in crisis situations, for example, when his mother died tragically and unexpectedly. I went up to Manchester to be with him. We sat in his parents' kitchen all day – the place alive with sudden loss, each ordinary household object a potential landmine of painful remembrance – eating the soup she'd made before that terrible headache had begun so suddenly. What can you say to the suddenly bereaved? The years of friendship between us, of fighting it out and making it up, were what mattered, not the words especially.

What's important is not so much the feelings as the action in which the feelings result. If I profess a love for opera but never go to see one, I clearly don't really love opera. If I profess a love for Karmabandhu but don't spend time with him, help him when he needs it, put myself out for him, and visit him when he's sick, then it's not love – not really – it's sentimentality. Love needs a lot of sorting out. It needs sorting out from erotic attraction, romance, and parental love. It needs sorting out from that low-level flirting that is so common between men and women, and it needs sorting out from sentimentality. Sentimentality is feeling on the cheap; it's all the drama of feeling, the local colour, the special effects of tears and sighs and heartfelt protestations but without the expense of feeling, the action that true feeling leads to. It is mock feeling, not really feeling at all. Really it's a kind of showing off. We want to be credited with a big heart and powerful emotions but don't want to pay the price of *action* those emotions demand. There is no such thing as sentimental depression or sentimental envy because, unlike sentimental love or sentimental grief, no one will admire us for it.

Unfortunately, I've not been entirely free of sentimentality myself; probably very few of us have been. Sometimes my friendship with Karmabandhu has been characterized by self-dramatizing emotional volatility, at least on my side. Luckily for me, Karmabandhu's aggressive honesty has meant he's been quite happy to tell me, in so many words, 'You're acting like a fool!' I remember him saying it as I stormed out of an argument over something or other, full of high umbrage and sentimental indignation. It shamed me into going back a few minutes later, spiritual cap in hand, and saying, 'You're right, I'm sorry.' Sentimental friendship is not friendship. As Roger Scruton, the British philosopher, puts it, 'The sentimental friend is not a friend: indeed, he is a danger to others. … He enters human relations by seduction, and leaves them by betrayal.' If love is the basis of true friendship it expresses itself not in lots of feeling but in lots of action, from sending them a postcard from your beach holiday to helping them sort out their bank balance.

In the earlier days of my friendship with Karmabandhu I put too much stress on emotions and their expression. I was always talking over some new emotional nuance, some fresh psychological glitch I'd turned up in our nightly tooth-brushing sessions. Also my love for Karmabandhu did at times shade over into a need *to be loved*, rather than a genuine feeling of *mettā*. And sometimes Maria was right; my feelings for Karmabandhu became something more unhealthy, a quasi-romantic fixation. But, for all of that, for all my imperfections and foibles and for all his, the underlying love of the good in each other has always been there as something to call upon, a witness to the spiritual in our friendship, solid ground to build upon, again and again.

There is something almost indescribably lovely about real friendship, a distinctive and pervading atmosphere that can best be described as an atmosphere of love. It is by no means always as dramatically felt as my experience on the bus; more usually it is far more subtle, like walking through mist which, without your really noticing it, gradually saturates you. Sometimes Karmabandhu and I felt it in laughter – the two of us bent double over a joke in the corridor outside the bathroom – sometimes sitting having a coffee and a pastry, sometimes talking on the phone after he moved to Rome. Samuel Johnson called this rarest kind of love 'a peculiar boon of heav'n'. It can feel like that sometimes, like a blessing descending from a higher and more beautiful realm. I've felt it unexpectedly and in unusual places: in the middle of a disagreement, packed sardine-like into the Underground at rush hour, walking around Sainsbury's, sitting at a kitchen table eating matzos after a funeral …

Then there was the time we got stuck in traffic on our way to the dentist. I was in one of my bad moods, crunching the gears and getting wound up. But as we made our way through Highbury and Islington, crawling from one traffic light to the next, my mood, thanks to him, gradually changed. By the time we arrived for our check-up, it was as if three of us got out of the car, Karmabandhu, myself, and between us the much neglected, softly beautiful angel of love – called friendship.

5

BURIED TREASURE

I do not wish to treat friendships daintily, but with roughest courage. When they are real, they are not glass threads or frostwork, but the solidest thing we know.
  Ralph Waldo Emerson, 'Friendship'

My friendship with Karmabandhu has always been a rather stormy one. In contrast, my friendship with Paramabandhu has always been pretty much plain sailing. In fact the waters of our friendship have run so smooth, the tide of feeling so calm and level, that it took me about three years to realize that we had a friendship at all. I met him when he was still called Ian (actually I met him when we were *both* still called Ian). He sat next to me at lunch one day at the Buddhist Centre and introduced himself. He was a junior doctor, he told me, planning to train as a psychiatrist. This was an immediate black mark as far as I was concerned. I had inherited a dislike of doctors from my nursing days and, after only a cursory glance at the books of R.D. Laing, I had decided I was anti-psychiatry. I immediately grilled him about electric shock therapy: Would he do it? Should he do it? How could he do it? It wasn't long before I let him know my feelings on the subject of doctors in general and of psychiatrists in particular. For some odd reason he liked me.

After that, nothing very much happened; we had one or two arguments, perhaps, but nothing much really – not like the weekly set-tos that Karmabandhu and I habitually engaged in. I remember, even after I had known Paramabandhu for a few years, still being rather chary about calling him a friend. 'Friend' was a very serious word as far as I was concerned and I had to be really sure before I used it to describe my relationship with someone; anyway, Paramabandhu was so odd! At the time (before we were ordained) I thought of friendship in terms of emotion – the thing to do, it seemed to me, was to have lots of it. A sure sign that you were friends with someone was to have emotion swilling about all over the place. Strong feelings about this, that, and the other – traumas from the past to be unravelled, interpersonal conflicts to be resolved, difficulties to be surmounted. I tried to do all that with Paramabandhu, but he didn't seem to have any strong feelings or, come to that, any childhood traumas. I spent a year or two poking around trying to find his secret 'wound' but I couldn't really come up with anything. He liked gardening, was always in bed by eleven, and tended to be happy. I just couldn't see how friendship could be possible with such a person!

We had been ordained a few years when it became obvious that a new community was needed. There were some men around the Centre at the time who wanted to practise Buddhism more intensely and were interested in the idea of living together. So Paramabandhu and I decided to invite them to come and live with us. We moved across the courtyard of the Buddhist Centre into a large flat above a Buddhist-run restaurant, shared a small room (which I painted bright yellow), and got on with the business of creating a new community.

I remember performing a ritual to symbolically dedicate the community to spiritual practice and friendship. After reciting some verses we ritually walked around the somewhat cramped rooms, wafting incense and chanting mantras. If anyone had seen us from the houses opposite they would have thought we were quite mad, and perhaps we did feel a bit self-conscious as we all crowded into the bathroom waving incense and intoning ancient Buddhist chants. But the little ceremony did express our aspirations. We wanted to live *together*, to share our life with each other, especially our spiritual life, and as the seven of us squeezed in each other's little bedrooms, smiling awkwardly and waving incense, I felt that we were embarking on something deeply significant and worthwhile.

Our little ceremony that night was a ritual confirmation of the reasons we had decided to live together. This was not going to be another case of flat sharing, with the fridge full of items of food with people's initials on them, or those curt little notes left around the place saying, 'Could the person who last used the shower please clean up after them!' We were living together to develop friendship, by which we meant we were living together to strive towards a common ideal. If mutually acknowledged and expressed *mettā* is the earth from which friendship springs, a transcendent ideal is the sun towards which it grows.

To have an ideal is to have a definite vision of potential, for yourself, for the world, and for each other. It may not be fully formed, but somewhere in the back of your mind is an ideal towards which you feel yourself to be moving. In my experience of friendship I have a sense of what an ideal friendship would be like and I try to orientate my *actual* friendships in that direction. It is analogous to my experience of painting. When I paint I have a powerful if diffuse feeling for what the painting is aiming at. There is an image in my mind, though still unclear, that I am trying to actualize. In painting I grope towards that image, try to realize it on the canvas. Of course I make many false starts and go down many a dead end, but my sense when I'm painting is that I am struggling towards something. At times the painting seems to make progress towards that something and at other times it seems to be moving away. Friendship is like that. Within friendship is an ideal, a felt sense of possibility and potential, towards which, at best, you feel the friendship is making tangible progress.

Perhaps another reason for the current decay of friendship is the general decline of idealism. Nowadays we are suspicious of idealism. If someone starts talking about his or her ideals we fold our arms only too quickly and, with an air of smug complacency, wait for their ideals to crash down around their ears. To some extent our suspicion is justified, either because, looking back in history, we see some of the terrible misery caused by apparently well-meaning 'idealism', or because we remember our own naïve and short-lived flushes of it in our youth. Ideals can, it is true, be naïve, ill-informed, and even dangerous; however, a lack of them can be a catastrophe. Our little ritual, despite the out-of-tune chanting, was an expression of our common idealism. We wanted to change ourselves and the world, make both better, and, grand and impossible as it may sound, that was why we were living together.

Of course, all this is very out of kilter with the current climate of 'been there, seen that' self-satisfaction. Perhaps two of the most striking features of modern cultural life are trivialization and a kind of cool, cynical posturing. Buddhist monks now appear in flashy adverts for cars and razors, images of revolution and religion are turned into designer chic, and what once communicated profound meaning is now trivialized, dumbed down, or mocked. Television, as far as I can tell, is more trivial than ever, and even the so-called quality newspapers aren't above a bit of know-it-all cynicism.

This baleful atmosphere is antithetical to any authentic idealism, indeed it is antithetical to any genuinely positive emotion or quest for meaning.

Setting up that community has been one of the best things I have ever done. I have grown as a person by doing so and, if only in a small way, helped others to grow too. What I didn't anticipate was the effect this shared project was to have on my friendship with Paramabandhu. Creating something that went beyond our friendship had the effect of enhancing our friendship; no amount of meeting up for cappuccinos could have done that.

Soon after forming the community we started to meet up regularly to talk about our practice of meditation. In many ways Paramabandhu and I don't have much in common – for instance, we are temperamentally very different. He is altogether 'neater' than I am, more organized and disciplined and with a steadier and more emotionally level disposition. I have, for want of a better term, an altogether messier psyche. I tend to be more emotionally intense and turbulent and my thinking is hotter and more passionate. This difference in temperament must partly stem from our very different histories and backgrounds. Take our respective mothers. His mother is *extremely* indulgent. If the young Paramabandhu was even slightly ill he would be whisked off to bed and given all sorts of treats and favours until it could be proven beyond a shadow of a doubt that he had fully recovered. In contrast, I would almost have had to be certified dead before my mother would have consented to my missing school. Paramabandhu was the golden boy of the family, going to study at Cambridge and then training to be a doctor. I was, if not quite the black sheep of the family, at least a somewhat strange creature, and a source of worry and mystification to my parents. I went to Henley-in-Arden High School where I excelled in talking but not much else. In terms of personal history two of the things we have in common are we are both congenitally bad at sport and neither of us thinks of himself as a meditator. It was to try to improve our meditation practice that we set aside half an hour last thing at night on a twice-weekly basis to talk about how our meditation was progressing.

Whilst meeting up and talking about meditation has improved the overall quality of our meditation practice, what is perhaps more striking is that it has improved the quality of our friendship too. When we were ordained we each took up the meditation practice of visualizing a bodhisattva figure. These figures are extremely beautiful; they have gently smiling faces and their bodies, adorned with fabulous silks and jewelled ornaments, are aglow with soft and luminous colour. You could think of them as being the closest image you could get to what the experience of Enlightenment *feels* like. Imagine meeting the Buddha in the street one day. An old Indian man, perhaps a little bent with age, walking with a collected and dignified bearing up the high street towards the bank. You might be struck by his calm composure but in most respects he'd look like anyone else. Now, say you had a magic camera that could photograph not external appearances but internal ones, a camera that could photograph states of mind. The figures that Paramabandhu and I meditate upon are what the Buddha would look like, as it were, on the inside. Meditating on an image that is a symbol for Enlightened consciousness is not simply a matter of holding a picture in your mind, but of trying to get some sort of feel for the reality that image is pointing towards. At 7 o'clock every morning the two of us would sit down and try to connect with our life's goal imaginatively – try, as it were, to *see* the Buddha. So, when Paramabandhu and I talk about our meditation practice, we are talking about how we are progressing in our attempt to apprehend, even to get a glimmer of a feeling for, the state of Buddhahood. Trying to 'see' the ideal and to move towards it in our day-to-day life is what Paramabandhu and I have committed our lives to.

I had assumed that the way forward in our friendship was to be found in delving ever deeper into the murky depths of each other's psychology, whereas actually what ignited our friendship was our increasing capacity to strive towards a common ideal. It is the ideal of Buddhahood, and our attempts to move towards it, that guides our friendship. Not that Paramabandhu and I wake up every morning thinking, 'Today I'm going to *really try* to become Enlightened.' Practising the spiritual life isn't like taking part in an everlasting workout video; Buddhist practice is to do with a gradual reorientation of one's entire being towards one's highest aspirations.

We all have our moments, our peak experiences, our time of miracles. I remember walking home from school in my scruffy uniform one day, tie done up so the knot was as fat as possible, swinging my satchel, and suddenly feeling unaccountably happy. Everything – as I rounded the corner past the cattle market – was suddenly *just right*, as if the world and I had finally clicked and everything had resolved itself into harmony in a moment. But it was only a moment – it didn't even last as far as the paper shop. We have probably all had them, these moments out of life, moments that give us a clue to what life could be like. In these moments we instinctively feel that life should always be like this, that this, more than anything else, is what life is really about. Some people experience such moments in the midst of terrible trauma, some in heightened aesthetic experience, others in the midst of the utterly humdrum. For one friend it was just the sight of a plane hanging heavily in the sky, preparing to land, viewed for a few timeless moments through a window. We can never fully explain or describe these experiences even to ourselves; they elude us, and remain in some mysterious way beyond the world of thought and knowledge. But it's moments like this that turn people to God or to philosophy or to art. It's moments like this that prompt us to ask bigger questions. Practising the spiritual life, being a Buddhist, means dedicating your life so that all of your life lives up to the best moments in your life. Of course, what we make of these moments makes all the difference. If you think you have been touched by the hand of God, that will take you in one direction; if you think that it's just to do with getting out of school early or having a decent lunch, that will take you in another. I didn't make anything of my 'moment' at the time but, years later, it came back – and with far greater force.

I was on retreat. After one morning meditation I walked out into the garden en route to the lavatory. For some reason I decided to imagine that every time I took a step a lotus blossom would appear under my foot. According to the story, when the Buddha was born he immediately walked, and as he did so magical flowers blossomed under his tender baby feet. I took the story as a symbol that says, 'When you are really deeply aware and concentrated, it feels *as if* lotus flowers bloom under your feet' – an ancient Indian version of 'walking on air'. As soon as I thought it, everything was perfect, had always been, and always would be. Thought fell into the deep recesses of my mind and my whole being was suffused with radiant happiness. All I could think was, 'I hope I never get to the toilet.' All I knew was that I wished this moment would go on forever.

But it didn't. What I made of it, though, is still with me. I took it as a prefiguration, a sneak preview, a special private showing of what it would be like to be a Buddha. All I had to do was dedicate my life to that experience. And there was a time when my determination to do that became effective, a time when it stopped being a dream sincerely wished for and became an ideal I could effectively live out. That was when I got ordained.

We were ordained together, Paramabandhu and I. Marooned in a valley in Spain for four months, with Karmabandhu and I sharing one little hut and Paramabandhu and Lokabandhu sharing another. After an intense few weeks of preparation – long bright days of silence and meditation among the olive trees and gorse bushes of our secluded valley – finally came the day of the ordination ceremony. There were fifteen men waiting to be ordained that day. We all gathered beforehand, our heads newly shaven, excited, and slightly nervous and apprehensive about the step we were about to take – a step we knew would change our lives for ever. The moment of full ordination within the Western Buddhist Order is marked when a kesa is finally and ceremonially hung around your neck. The kesa is actually a belt – or rather it derives from a belt. Traditionally, when you were ordained as a Buddhist monk, the person who ordained you – your 'preceptor' – gave you your robes and hung the belt for them around your neck as a symbol that you were now ordained. Not that we were being ordained as monks – our ordination showed that we were dedicating our lives to the ideal of human Enlightenment.

Wearing our shining new white kesas, the four of us had our photos taken, as you do after any special ceremony. We stood under the endlessly blue Spanish sky, the cliffs at the edge of the valley towering behind us and catching the late afternoon sunshine. The photos say it all, really. A group of four close friends smiling into the camera and, emblazoned on the new whiteness of our kesas, the three precious jewels in a halo of fire.

The first jewel embroidered on our new kesas is a golden yellow jewel. This represents the potential to become a Buddha which we all share, the realization of the highest goal of life. It is yellow because it symbolizes the light of the Buddha's wisdom. The second jewel is the deep blue jewel of the Dharma. This represents the Truth, the way things really are, as well as all those teachings and practices that lead us towards that Truth. It is blue, like the fathomless depths of the ocean, because the Truth of the Dharma is deep and very profound. The third jewel, a glowing ruby red in colour, is the Sangha, all those men and women who have realized the Truth for themselves. It is red because the Sangha is characterized by that rare kind of love, *mettā*. The Sangha jewel represents the ideal community, a community of Enlightened individuals relating to each other on the basis of mutual *mettā* and highest wisdom. But 'sangha' can also be used more loosely to mean all those who are trying to realize the Truth, all those we could justifiably call Buddhists. In this sense the Sangha includes the four of us standing with arms round each other's shoulders, smiling and making jokes into the camera.

Since that four-month retreat, and especially in the context of setting up a community and meeting regularly to talk about our meditation, what I have experienced in my friendship with Paramabandhu is a shared and increasing desire to seek out these three precious jewels and to commit ourselves to them. This commitment is usually expressed in Buddhism in terms of 'going for refuge to the Three Jewels'. Both of us see the ideals of Buddhism, symbolized by the Three Jewels, as constituting the real meaning and purpose of life, and both of us want to realize and embody those ideals more and more. So what Aristotle would call friendship based on 'the good' I would call friendship based on commitment to the Three Jewels. When I say I am attracted to the good in Paramabandhu, what I am saying, in more Buddhist language, is that I am attracted to his commitment to the Three Jewels. In other words, I am attracted to that urge within him to aspire to become more than he presently is, to become wiser, kinder, more aware, and more alive. My own commitment to the Three Jewels resonates with that self-same desire in him. Perhaps the most remarkable thing about my friendship with Paramabandhu is that, underlying all our differences – differences in temperament, personal history, and background – is a fundamental sameness of aspiration, a deep underlying harmony, the beauty of which transcends us both.

One of the lessons I've learned from Paramabandhu is just how important it is to look for idealism in friendship. Previously I'd always been attracted to someone's personality, their witty repartee, seemingly glamorous lifestyle, or high-voltage emotionality. Paramabandhu was distinctly unflashy. It was only as I got to know him that I saw how radical he was willing to be, how committed to spiritual life and friendship he was. As our friendship deepened, I got a taste for his quieter qualities, his steadfastness and lack of pretension. For friendship to survive and thrive, you need an ideal that goes beyond you, that transcends your separate individualities. After all, personalities clash soon enough, disagreements arise, and arguments ensue. Or friends drift apart. The evening course you did together comes to an end and – despite your good intentions – so does the friendship. To keep a hold on friendship in the face of obstacles or separation you need to have an *ideal* of friendship, something above and beyond you that helps sustain it when it is in trouble or when it would otherwise fade. If you want friendship you would be best advised to seek it out with someone who holds friendship as an ideal, an ideal for which they have a definite feeling, or even a passion.

You also need to speak the same language. When the four of us were ordained, this showed we were united by a common ideal and by a common language expressive of that ideal. That common language is the language of the Three Jewels. It is the language of Buddhism, of treading the path of the Dharma, the path that, 2,500 years ago, the Buddha opened up to all beings. It is the language of the Sangha, the spiritual community, and friendship as an ideal and as a path towards that ideal. So when

I talk to Paramabandhu about friendship, we both understand what we mean by it. We both understand that it means time and effort and commitment, that we're talking about not just run-of-the-mill knockabout mates but real friendship, a commitment to help each other tread the path together.

The experience of a shared idealism is more important than whether or not you initially like each other or whether or not you have interests in common. Differences of race, gender, class, and temperament can all be overcome and transcended if there is, at the centre of our understanding of friendship, an overarching ideal that transcends our perception of ourselves as a fixed and separate *me*. The more that ideal is mutually felt the more friendship, like a rare and lovely flower, will flourish. Of course it is very pleasant to like someone and to be liked by them. Of course it is very pleasant to have all manner of interests in common. These things may help the friendship get started but they are not what sustain it, not what make it true friendship.

One of the things I do have in common with Paramabandhu is that we both happen to be gay. Actually, even our response to that has been characteristically different. His was one of open-minded exploration, mine of angst-ridden secrecy. It never seemed to occur to the adolescent Paramabandhu that being gay was a problem, whereas it never occurred to me that it was anything but! Of course, when we first met, the fact that we were both gay did mean we had something in common superficially, something we could talk about and agree upon – but that didn't last long. We soon ran out of things to say about it and our shared stories of coming out soon became a bit boring. Friendship based on mutual interests or common life experiences can easily become rather dull. I've known people whose conversation revolves almost exclusively around their history of drug-taking – the biggest spliff they've ever had, the dope cakes they've eaten, the bad trips they've been through. Apart from the very early days, my friendship with Paramabandhu has never really been based on the fact that we were both gay. If anything, I am nowadays rather wary of forming friendships on the shared basis of being gay. Not only can it be rather dull, but in my experience it can also be extremely fragile. Friendship based on common personal history, especially if it's a history of feeling oppressed in some way, is really friendship based on use. Certainly there was a phase in my life when I needed other gay friends to help me feel at ease with myself and with my sexual orientation, but common history and usefulness go only so far, and basing friendship on that can go only so far too. I experience, as I've said, a deep underlying sameness with Paramabandhu, but it is a sameness of aspiration: it is to do with what we hope to become, not with what we have been. Our friendship is based on something that transcends not only our differences but also our similarities.

I remember one evening, when Paramabandhu and I lived above the Centre, before we were ordained, the whole community going out to see a play. What an odd bunch we seemed as we hung around waiting for everyone to get ready, collecting our hats and coats and checking that we had our money and tickets. There was Paramabandhu, training to be a psychiatrist; Lokabandhu, who had grown up with maids and whose father had been governor of the Cayman Islands; David, from a poor council estate outside Manchester; Dhammarati, from working-class Glasgow; Karmabandhu, who came from a Jewish family background and who'd learned Hebrew at school. Some were heterosexual, some were homosexual, and some were somewhere in between. Some dressed trendily, others eccentrically. Some looked smart and some looked scruffy. Some were tall and some were small and some were tending to tubby.

Once everyone had been rounded up, and the inevitable pro-crastinators finally prised out of the house, off we set, a ragtag bunch of men of different shapes and sizes, making our way in a disorderly fashion to the tube station. What, I wondered, would people make of us as we effectively commandeered the pavement, blocking the way for all but the most determined? At the church fêtes of my childhood there was always someone asking you to guess the weight of a cake in order to raise money for the church steeple or something. What if something similar were applied here? Instead of guess the weight of the cake, guess what all these men have in common. An unsuccessful pop group? An old boys' reunion? A men's therapy group? I remember that evening because what struck me at the time was both how different we all were and how united. I would never have chosen to live with many of them, and quite a few I found either strange, irritating, or perplexing. And yet we were, in a palpable way, united; there was something between us that went beyond class loyalties, ethnic grouping, social status, or temperament. There was something in the air that evening, as we waited for the Tube or made our way across Waterloo Bridge, that struck a deep chord within me: an ideal of friendship, of real human fellowship beyond all adventitious differences. That night has, in my imagination, become an image of the potentialities of the future made manifest in the simple realities of the present. It symbolizes what for me is a powerfully motivating ideal – friendship cutting through and going beyond all differences without at the same time negating them.

Friendship as I have described it is a source of hope for the world. Walking down to the tube station today – past the off-licence and the bottle bank – I see women dressed in burkas, handsome young men wearing those funny-looking shoulder bags with one strap, and old ladies with shopping trolleys. I pass an elderly Afro-Caribbean guy leaning in a doorway waiting for the bus, looking a bit forlorn and clutching a small loaf in a brown paper bag. I see middle-aged East End women in unbecomingly tight skirts, children in football shirts and baseball caps, Bangladeshi schoolgirls dressed in colourful *shalwar-kameez*, eating Magnum ices and talking about boys, men in sharp city suits and slicked-back hair, and black guys in cars with darkened windows and thudding music. By the time I get on the Tube the whole world's on it with me. Oversized American men in loose-fitting surfy gear, Turkish Cypriots, an old Japanese lady clutching her shopping, and a wrecked-looking builder falling asleep on his way home from a tough job. This is one of the great things about living in London, the diversity, the richness of one culture cheek by jowl with another. But with it comes the potential for endless misunderstandings, antagonisms, mutual incomprehensions, tensions, prejudice, and violence. Even among the little group of practising and sincere Buddhists involved with the London Buddhist Centre, conflicts and mistrust easily arise between members of different social, ethnic, or racial groups. Differences of race, gender, and outlook go very deep indeed. The potential for ghettoization, for fear, mistrust, and hostility is ever present. What the world needs is friendship. True friendship goes deeper than difference, deeper than black and white, young and old, gay and straight.

Friendship is a wholly human affair. At its most developed it strikes deep into the very heart of what is most human about us – the urge to grow. After all, humanity itself is something of an ideal, often more of an aspiration than a reality. Friendship is the meeting of two persons relating with mutual *mettā* on the basis of a shared ideal. There is something, some treasure deep in the heart of humanity, which we all share and which can be discovered by anyone with the good sense and integrity to look. Buddhism is saying, 'It's as if at the bottom of our hearts, hidden from ourselves and each other, there are Three Jewels.' These jewels are our potential, the potential we all share and which

I glimpsed for a few precious moments as a young teenager on my way back from school. Friendship is looking for that treasure together, finding it out in each other, digging beyond superficial likes and dislikes, differences and similarities, down to that common urge to evolve, to grow from less to more and from more to most.

Perhaps that all sounds rather grand, and perhaps in a way it is. Thinking of my thirteen-year friendship with Paramabandhu, I remember that the steps on the way to true friendship are very small. We have gradually clarified our ideal, lived it out more fully, and related to each other more and more on the basis of it. From the time he first sat next to me in the Buddhist Centre and told me he was a doctor to our setting up a new community together, we have worked on our friendship and on the ideal that inspires it. In the two hundred times two million ways, in the accumulation of the smallest acts of kindness and honesty, we have grown towards our ideal and, as a consequence, grown towards each other.

As I write this in my little shared room in our little community, I can hear Paramabandhu come in from the garden to make a cup of tea before he goes off to work. Later, the community will meet for the evening to talk about how we are getting on, and after that Paramabandhu and I will get together once again to see how our meditation is going. It seems to me that what I thirsted after in childhood is here with me again – friendship and wonder. Here again I am with a group of close friends, friends who will leave me cards and little gifts when I come back from retreat or who later on (as we take it in turns to cook) will call me in for supper, like the family of brothers who called to me over the hedge to come and play: we, the trying to be grown up, have our own pursuit, the highest of all, Enlightened humanity – mysterious Buddhahood.

6

THE EDUCATION OF THE HEART

(The flame of romantic love) is more active, hotter, and fiercer, but it is a reckless and fickle flame, wavering and changeable, a feverish fire prone to flare up and die down, which only catches us in one corner. In friendship there is a general and universal warmth.

Michel de Montaigne, 'On Friendship'

I am never quite sure what to call Gary; given the fact that I am nearly forty, the term 'boyfriend' seems positively ironic. 'Lover' is far too mawkish and I've never liked 'partner'. Concubine has a certain ring to it but it is rather out of date, and 'sweetheart' is, well, rather too sweet.

I got to know him on a picket line designed to stop men going into a women-only night at a local gay pub. I was at the height of my political right-on-ness at the time, and every week, along with a few others, I would turn up, swathed in coat, gloves, and scarf, to keep watch for unsuspecting men trying to get into the pub. Should such an eventuality occur, one of us would rush over and try to dissuade them. As it happened, very few men attempted it, and those who did were only too happy to be put off. They were gay men after all, and, all things considered, not especially interested in gate-crashing a pub full of women. As a consequence, we didn't have very much to do. Most of the time we sat on a wall on the other side of the road and whiled away the time with talk and jokes. Occasionally one of the women would take pity on us and bring us out a pint or two and perhaps a packet of crisps. I was twenty-four at the time and passionately idealistic. Gary was the same age and, while he had a much milder temperament than mine, he nevertheless had his own brand of idealism. He had joined a left-wing political group in his native New Zealand and for him the picket was part of a whole political agenda, one that has lasted up to the present. For me, those winter evenings sitting on that wall with Gary were to be the very pinnacle of my political correctness; since then it has all been rather downhill.

Actually I am no less idealistic now than I was in my twenties; if anything I am probably more so. What has changed is not so much my idealism, my desire to change the world, as my views about how exactly that might be achieved. In my nursing days I had come to the conclusion – under Sam's anarchic influence – that I was a Marxist. Actually I'd never read Marx. I'd been on one or two CND marches and I had a few vague notions about class struggle, but really that was about it. Later, at art school, I became influenced by feminism and gay politics. I volunteered to help run a crèche for the children of lesbians (which is where I met Gary). I read books about how to be an anti-sexist man, and took part in the afore-mentioned picket.

With hindsight, it seems to me that I was trying to find the answer to a question that had tormented me since childhood. The question was 'What causes suffering?' In many ways I was an unhappy child. Without quite knowing why, I found life difficult and painful. As I grew into adolescence and adulthood, and as I slowly became aware of the pain and suffering that surrounded me, my question 'What causes suffering?' became all the more urgent. At first I thought that the cause of suffering was to do with class, with the oppression of the majority by the minority. Then I decided it was patriarchy, the oppression of women by men. When I became a Buddhist I decided that the cause of suffering was to be found in the human heart. This new conviction changed my life.

I suppose, from Gary's point of view, I changed from politico to weirdo. Only a few months after those romantic winter's evenings outside the Fallen Angel, I made my decisive bike ride to the London Buddhist Centre. From that day on he watched me become more and more involved with Buddhism. He watched as I set up a little shrine at the end of my bed, complete with candles, incense, and miniature stone Buddha figure. He witnessed my first attempts to get up early to meditate, chant mantras, go on retreats, and regularly attend classes. It cannot have been easy for him when I decided to move into the community above the Centre, and when I stopped painting to become the cleaner at the Buddhist Centre he thought I had either lost my sanity, or been finally sucked into some weird cult.

Along with changes in my lifestyle came changes in my views. One of the areas in which my views changed was to do with romance and sexual relationships. When I first met Gary I had been 'searching, looking for love' (as a gay anthem at the time proclaimed it) for some considerable time. Emotionally volatile and hopelessly romantic, I had high expectations of my new-found relationship; so much so, in fact, that it wasn't long before I was writing him tortured 'do you really love me?' letters and complaining of his lack of undying devotion. However, as I started to meditate, and especially as I started to understand Buddhism and the Dharma more deeply, my views about all that changed, and changed irrevocably.

One of the most urgent demands on our time as we get older is finding a mate, building a nest, and populating it. Certainly for me, as a young adolescent, finding that much lauded 'significant other' was not so much an occupation as a career. Learning to drive was part of it, as were buying trendy clothes, going to discos, agonizing over whether she did or did not love me, and buying all manner of anti-acne creams which I applied in secret shame locked in the family bathroom. And all that was *before* I actually started going out with someone! As I gradually came to terms with being gay I set my sights on getting a boyfriend. This meant the gay scene and much angst on my part. Trying to pick someone up is a nerve-racking business, no matter what your sexual preference. I well remember the terror of asking a girl to dance at the local disco, or the subsequent trepidation I felt approaching a dark and relatively handsome stranger. Most of us – one way or another – have put a lot of time and energy into finding and then keeping a partner, whether it means spending a bit longer than absolutely necessary looking at the young lady sitting across from you on the Tube, or the demands, financial and otherwise, of starting a family. If we look at our lives, we will probably find that more of our life is taken up with the sexual–romantic impulse than we care to admit; after all, 'the world must be peopled.'

One of the consequences of the time and attention we lavish on sexual relationships is the phenomenon of the disappearing friend. We have all done it or experienced our friends doing it. It starts when you are ten or so. You have a friend, spend lots of time with them, and if you are a boy you spend a lot of that time talking about girls and how you want nothing to do with them, not like Chris or Dave who's just got himself hitched to Cindy or Carol, how soppy! No, 'we're friends,' you think, 'we'll always be friends.' Then one day – puff! – they disappear. You see them a week later sheepishly holding hands with Meryl from the newsagent's. Of course, as often as not a month or two later, when the lovers have fallen out over something, the friend reappears again, heartbroken or bitter or 'I've learned my lesson this time,' and you are friends again – until next time.

As you move from your teens to your twenties, friends disappear more often and for longer. After hardly hearing from them for months they're on the phone again, suggesting you meet up. It turns out that the love of their life has left them for someone at the badminton club and before you know it they are crying on your shoulder and having one too many in the local boozer. Not only do your friends tend to disappear, sometimes without trace, but just about everything you read, every television show you look at, every pop song you hear, says more or less overtly that you'll never be happy until you find Mr or Ms Right. The experience of disappearing friends can be a very painful one. In the world of the couple, being single can be a very lonely affair.

How many times has romantic association gradually diminished our little circle of friends? It reminds me of those old-fashioned films I used to watch on rainy Saturday afternoons. A band of intrepid explorers set off into a wild uncharted jungle. A snaking line of men in white pith helmets cut their way through dense green scrub. Then comes the inevitable sound of distant drumming. The dense foliage suddenly parts and the last man in the line gets jumped on, their body dragged noiselessly off into the undergrowth. 'Good God, sir, something's happened to Johnson!' One by one, the friends we shared our life with suddenly disappear. They're not always dragged off; most go willingly enough into private worlds of coupledom. And it's not just that we hardly see them; on the rare occasions that we do, something seems to have come between you, as if they carry in front of them some fine-meshed muslin screen that faintly obscures them from you. Something of them is no longer available: a part of them is closed to you, locked into the world of lovers.

By the time you are thinking of getting married or your friends are thinking of getting married, friendship becomes more and more of an adjunct to the couple: a kind of optional extra, an accessory. Like Noah's ark, people meet two by two. Couples meet other couples in the pub, on skiing holidays, or at the local garden centre. If you are single you either feel something of a gooseberry, and stay at home, or you get yourself hitched as soon as possible. One thing I have noticed is how partial friends can be when relationships break up or marriages disintegrate. With hardly so much as tuppence worth of real understanding, the so-called friends decide who's guilty and who's innocent, then take sides with one against the other. Many people can lose their partner and just about all their friends in one fell swoop; that is, of course, if they have retained any friends. We can so overcommit ourselves to lover and spouse that, when the relationship breaks down (as it so often does), we find we have ignored our friends for so long that we no longer have any. Our world, once lit with intimacy and warmth, is suddenly rent with pain and loneliness. When my brother got divorced he found he had hardly any friends to speak of, never mind to speak to.

If we look dispassionately at the history of our sexual relationships we find that, over the years, they have afforded us much in the way of pleasure, satisfaction, enjoyment, and affection. We might also find we are tempted to dwell on that alone, to remember only the thrill of the first kiss, the passionate embrace, the time he or she turned up unexpectedly to meet us at the bus station. But if we look closer we will find a bitter to match the sweet. We find that along the way we have caused ourselves, as well as inflicted on others, much pain and suffering – the 'love' relationships that suddenly break up in mutual recriminations, the torturing petty jealousies and insecurities, the betrayals and the cover-up jobs, 'working late at the office' – all that is there too. But it's not that sexual relationships are bad or dirty or bound to end in disaster, or any of those things. It is just that sexual relationships are both limited and, dare I say it, limiting.

Unfortunately it's difficult to really get the correct tenor of these limitations. To start with, Judaeo-Christianity has rather queered the pitch when it comes to sex, making it either sanctified and blessed within marriage, or dirty and sinful outside of it. Whilst we may no longer believe in God or have even so much as a passing interest in Christianity, we have nevertheless imbibed from it an incoherent background noise of contradictory views about sex. The modern Western world (and more and more of the world is becoming 'modern' and 'Western') is, broadly speaking, excessively preoccupied with sex. I notice this very clearly when I come back from a retreat. I've just spent a week or two in the countryside meditating, developing friendships, trying to cultivate positive emotions, trying to cultivate peacefulness and calm, and I come back to the city and the first thing I notice is *sex*. Sex on the advertising hoardings, sex in the newspapers, sex on television, sex in the bookshops and over the radio – it's everywhere. The young man sitting next to me on the train home is reading one of those new 'men's magazines', which at first glance seems to consist primarily of photographs of one lightly bronzed cleavage after another. The newspaper read by the woman opposite promises sixty ways to improve your sex life.

But this is only half of the story. The other is a shrill new sexual puritanism. Sex has become so important, so overburdened with expectation, that if anything goes wrong with it, or someone has it with the wrong person or in the wrong way, those self-same magazines and newspapers are full of sex scandal stories – 'the vicar does it with his surplice on' sort of thing. We're very confused about sex.

We're so used to reacting to the idea that sex is horrid and sinful that many seem determined to believe that sex is wonderful and that everyone should have lots of it all the time. Actually, sex is just sex. It can be pleasurable and fun but it's hardly worth basing your life on, one way or another. In many ways we're hypnotized by pleasure, even addicted to it. We often fail to notice the other side of sex, the side that's not so nice. The times when we want a cuddle and the other person wants something more, the times when we feel it's all been a bit of a waste of time and energy. Then there are the compromises we make, the painful preoccupations, the gnawing pangs of unsatisfied lust, the seedier side of it all. The main problem areas with sex, though, are not so much the sex itself (though clearly some people do get compulsively hooked on it) but rather the emotional dependence and exclusivity that usually accompany it.

A year or so after I was ordained, a friend called Devamitra asked me if I would like to accompany him on one of his visits to the Antipodes. He regularly went out to visit the Buddhist centres in Australia and New Zealand and suggested I go along with him. I didn't know him very well at the time, but I was keen to travel, and he was an Order member of many years' standing, so I thought I might benefit from spending time with him.

In the course of the trip he and I naturally spent a lot of time together. We shared a room everywhere we went, sat together on the seemingly interminable long-haul flights, and spent many hours together standing around in airport terminals. As a consequence we got to know each other very well. Every night as we prepared for bed we would talk about how we were getting on, about our perceptions of the situations we were visiting, about what we had been reading and thinking. My appreciation and respect for him grew quickly, and I soon found myself trusting him and confiding in him. Sometimes, in the midst of one of our conversations, or as we sat silently reading, I would feel that self-same feeling of *mettā* for him as I had felt for Karmabandhu that night on the number 8 bus. It came upon me with the same unexpected strength and, like the time with Karmabandhu, it mostly left me feeling tongue-tied and embarrassed. Perhaps it is this particular feeling of love that Montaigne is getting at when he talks of friendship as 'a general and universal warmth'. For myself, the experience of *mettā* seems to partake of something I can only describe as purity, a sort of innocent purity. I mean pure in the sense of undiluted, unmixed with anything less elevated, especially unmixed with romantic attraction or sentimental attachment. It in no way compromised me as an individual or diluted my sense of myself; rather it augmented both.

It so happened that Gary was visiting his sister in Sydney at the time. She and I went to the airport to meet him. I'd missed him while I'd been away and I was pleased to see him finally appear amid the holidaymakers and businessmen wearily pushing baggage-laden trolleys. He looked a bit bedraggled himself, his blond hair ruffled, his eyes red from lack of sleep. We spent much of the following week together, hanging out on the beach with his sister and her boyfriend, going swimming, and taking in the sights. I loved him too, but the love, whilst perhaps being of the same in kind, was wholly different in quality. Mixed in it were heavy doses of neediness, sexual lust, emotional dependence, and projection. I don't think this applies only to me; it is, to one degree or another, the nature of romantic sexual relationships across the board.

Romantic love approximates to love in friendship as instant coffee approximates to freshly ground Colombian full roast: they are both called coffee but the experience of each is qualitatively different. Instant coffee has all sorts of additives in it: romantic love is much the same. The most significant additive as far as the spiritual life is concerned is emotional dependence. Emotional dependence has to do with a feeling of being incomplete, an uncomfortable sense that, deep inside, something is missing. What we tend to do is seek to make up for that feeling of incompleteness from outside ourselves. We seek to appropriate from without that which we hope will make us feel complete within. We do this in all sorts of ways. For instance, there's the late-night toast crisis. Let's say you've had a really good weekend. It's Sunday night and there is nothing good on telly. You really ought to get to bed, but somehow you can't quite persuade yourself to go. Perhaps you vacantly open the fridge door and stare into it for a while, or you leaf through last week's copy of *Time Out*. You are wanting something but you don't quite know what it is; there is just this background feeling of vacancy, of something-missingness. Then you hit upon it: toast! That's what's missing! So on goes the grill and out come the jam and butter. When you finally get into bed that night, somewhere in the far suburbs of your mind you know that the toast hasn't really done the trick. All that's happened is you've gone over your calorie count and tried (in vain) to cover over a deep existential sense of incompleteness with a slice of wholemeal bread and a spoonful of strawberry jam.

If we're honest with ourselves we'll notice a gap, a 'something missing'. The Buddha taught that our mundane life is shot through with *dukkha*, 'unsatisfactoriness', with what we might call incompleteness. No amount of covering that over with money, expensive clothes, or beautiful lovers will make up for that. Like a stubborn greasy stain on a wall, which no amount of overpainting can hide, *dukkha* is always there. The only thing we can do is face up to the reality of the situation and find another way, a real way to deal with it. If the goal of the spiritual life is Enlightenment, the beginning of it is some awareness of our incompleteness, for it is only in the experience of Enlightenment that our deep yearnings for wholeness are ever truly satisfied.

The Buddha said there are two ways of responding to *dukkha*. Either we set off on a never-ending search for pleasure to try to fill the gap, or we set out on a quest for meaning, for something that finally makes sense of our deepest aspirations. Usually, our natural response to the feeling of incompleteness is to crave something to fill the gap. That's really what the late-night toast crisis is all about. If only toast and jam were all we had to work on! Unfortunately, the 'business end' of craving, the main area in life in which we endeavour to feel whole and complete again, is that of sexual relations and romantic love.

Emotionally dependent sexual relationships are those in which both partners have decided it is the other that will make them feel complete. This is when we look to our boyfriend, girlfriend, spouse, or lover as the source of all happiness, security, and love. Sexual relationships *can* be a source of pleasure, security, and fulfilment, but they can never offer us the pleasure, security, and fulfilment that we expect and hope. They can never take away from us that gap, that something-missingness. The attempt in sexual relationships to get the other person to fill that gap for us, to save us from our incompleteness, is futile, and causes us and them pain. I am friends with a couple who tell me they love each other. What this 'love' seems to mean in practice is that they give themselves carte blanche to punish each other with unrealistic demands, complain of each other's lack of love, bore their friends with constant agonizing over their latest tiff, and torture themselves with petty jealousies, suspicions, and insecurities. 'I love you' can mean many things. Often enough it means something like: 'I'm insecure. I feel empty in myself. I do not love myself. I need someone who will make me feel whole, who will take the pain of life away and love me for ever.' It can also mean 'I want to have your children,' or simply 'Please remove your clothes.'

Sex is the glue that attempts to bind two incomplete people together. In sex we try to get to that 'you inside me, me inside you' experience which is at root our deepest urge for wholeness. However, that experience of wholeness and interpenetration can never be achieved on the physical plane; it can only be experienced in deep experience of oneself and within the highest reaches of human communication and friendship. Sexual relationships always have some degree of emotional dependence. At best they are warm and enjoyable, with both parties living a life independent of each other, realistic as to what they can expect from each other, and with genuine and committed friendships outside the relationship. At worst, they take the form of an anxious and insecure alliance of two people obsessed with each other and at the same time each tortured by the fear of losing the other.

Of course, whilst love 'works', in those halcyon days of young romance, it's hard to see what the problem is. You bathe in each other's eyes, reassure each other of your continued love, and it really does feel that you've found a way of making life that rich and wholly satisfying experience you always hoped it would be. And then something happens. You start to notice that it's not quite working, that in one way or another your hopes for each other and for the partnership are unrealistic and illusory – or you notice that sense of incompleteness still nagging at you, following you around like a stray dog which has taken a liking to you and will not be brushed off. Travelling to work one morning after that magical romantic evening, you notice, among the afterglow of memory, the feeling of incompleteness resurface, undealt with and unresolved. Either you go back again and again to a love which will never finally do the trick, or you decide (or begin to decide) to face up to that feeling within yourself, to find some way to resolve it within the depths of your own heart. To the degree that we choose the latter, we choose even if unbeknown to ourselves to begin the practice of the Dharma.

I suppose many would argue that their lover, partner, wife, or husband was in fact their friend. I suspect that this is very rare, so rare in fact that such relationships, where they do exist, should be put on the endangered species list! I've done it myself, of course, not very convincingly, but I did go through a period where I decided that Gary was just a friend I occasionally had sex with. The real test is when you break up. It is then that you *really* see to what degree you are friends. I have known people split up after ten or twenty years, who – once they have got a new partner – quickly forget the last, despite all the talk of friendship. In a way that's not so bad an outcome; when sexual relationships break down, the speed with which 'love' and 'friendship' turn to resentment and bitterness often prove that the 'friendship' was an illusion in the first place.

The way you find out how emotionally bound up you are with your partner is to leave them or let them leave you. It's so easy to have an inflated idea of your own independence in sexual relationships. I remember being horribly disabused of this when, a few years ago, I ended my relationship with Gary. I had thought I was pretty much independent of him; I was a practising Buddhist after all, and was cognisant of the reality of the situation. I knew all about craving and how craving led to pain and how dependent sexual relationships limited spiritual growth; I knew all that and agreed with it, saw it to be true. However, not long after I finished with him I felt, to my surprise and distress, that a great portion of my life had gone with him, that somewhere along the line I had given part of my life away to him and that now I grieved for that missing part of me. I had in some quiet way located the source of love and affection and comfort within him and I was bereft without them. A sense of loss and grief overwhelmed me.

I remember meeting him a few weeks after we had finished in the very pub we'd picketed all those years before. I remember the pang of seeing him again, the feeling of familiarity and strangeness as we talked about our relationship and how it had gone wrong. I ended up in paroxysms of tears. In the middle of a crowded pub, full of men and women trying to have a night out, drinking and making merry, I started to feel the depths of attachment and neediness within me; I started to learn how far I still had to go.

I must admit, I wish that romance worked. I wish that yearning for completeness *was* met in romantic love. I wish life was like those romantic films where everyone lives and loves happily ever after. Or like those photographs of families on the back of the cornflakes packet: pretty young wife in a sweatshirt, hubby with an attractive square jaw, a selection of healthy pink children, all gathered round a glowing bowl of cereal. I wish life was like that, but it's not. Those films, those impossibly happy families are, for all their glamour and apparent wholesomeness, a cause of suffering in the world. How many lovers have agonized over the questions of love: 'Why is it I can't find the right partner?' 'Why did he stop loving me?' 'Why do I always mess it up?' How often in the tender moonlight have we asked ourselves 'What's wrong with me?' How many parents have lain awake wondering whatever happened to their marriage, asking themselves over and over, 'Where did I go wrong?' The films and the love songs have all been lying to us, selling us an unobtainable myth. We are easily bought and in the back of our minds we tend to think it's all our fault, that the gorgeous couple on the jeans advert or Mr and Mrs Squeaky Clean on the cornflakes packet really *do* exist – somewhere.

What is needed is a new pattern of relationships that, while perhaps including husband, wife, and lover, also includes – and includes much more fully – a sense of community, friends, teachers, and family. Let us imagine a mandala, a mystic circle. Let's call this circle our life. Within the circle is everything we value. In the centre is what is most important to us, and arranged around it, in order of living priority, everything else. Usually we have put our sexual relationships at the centre: the meaning and purpose of our life. But the centre cannot hold, and the mandala of our life must change (even if it's just to make our sexual relationships more successful and healthier). In a Buddhist life we start to move lovers towards the edge of the mandala, find a place for them perhaps, but one that no longer dominates the pattern. In this mystic circle within which our life moves, spiritual friends – friendships based on the good – move closer and closer to the centre.

No doubt many of us will want to find a place for sex and sexual relationships in our lives. However, if we want to live a *spiritual* life, a life devoted to goodness and truth, we will need to find a place for sexual relationships which does not assume a disproportionate importance. In my experience as a meditation teacher it is romantic love and the domesticating effects of coupledom that are most likely to lead us away from the spiritual path and the search for truth. We need a two-pronged approach. First, we need to practise meditation: the art of developing within that which we are often painfully searching for without. Buddha figures are often seen adorned with jewelled crowns, golden bracelets, and richly embroidered silks. We could see this exquisite finery as symbolic of the inner riches of joy, love, and contentment that we can find deep within in meditation. Secondly, we need to develop friendship. If we want to live a truly satisfying and enriching life, friendship should be as important as – perhaps even more important than – our sexual relationships.

Unfortunately, modern life has turned everything upside down. From advertisements for ice cream and life insurance to pop songs, films, Mills and Boon love stories, and soap operas, the romantic couple is usually characterized as being the one truly significant relationship of life: the final source of meaning and the one true guarantor of pleasure. (The only other contender, the child–parent relationship, often comes in a poor second.) The belief in the ascendancy of sexual love is so deeply held and pervasive that it amounts almost to a religious doctrine, a shared mass belief, dogmatically clung to despite all the rational evidence and experience to the contrary. Pop songs, like hymns of praise, worship it constantly, and the doctrine of true love is every day preached from the pulpit of television. Like most religious doctrine, it is best inculcated at an early age. I can hardly have been six years old before my aunts and uncles started asking me if I had a girlfriend!

The reasons for our current devotion to the romantic couple are manifold and various. In part it is symptomatic of a generalized decay in our experience of ourselves as living within a community. Related to this is the consequence of living in a society no longer bound together by a commonly held spiritual ideal. Once upon a time we lived in an age of gods and spirits. They roared in the thunder and enchanted the woods, sometimes presiding over us and sometimes interacting with our earthly lives. Then the universe was ruled by an omnipresent and all-powerful God ranged about by a host of angels that spoke to us in dreams and ecstatic visions. Now, most of us have, for good or ill, dispensed with the lot. We have 'wiped away the entire horizon', as Nietzsche put it. In this drastically reduced user-friendly universe only the myth of romantic love has survived, our last hope of salvation.

When all is said and done we are driven by our emotions. While we might be inspired by the ideal of friendship, our feeling for it – at least initially – is usually rather weak. On the other hand, while we may assent to the shortcomings and pitfalls of romantic love, our feeling for it – to say the least – is usually rather strong. Whatever the head tells us, it's the heart that makes the decision.

This is why we tend to make the same mistakes over and over again, especially in the area of sex and romance: our heart is famously unwilling to listen to reason. Unfortunately for many of us, a chicken-and-egg situation develops. Because much of our emotional energy is going into our sexual relationships, our friendships can tend to be weak and perfunctory. On the other hand, because our friendships can tend to be weak and perfunctory, our emotions, needing an outlet, tend towards our sexual relationships, or towards trying to find one!

Much of our life is dominated by the search for pleasure. We tend to see sexual relationships as the most reliable source of pleasure and, conveniently forgetting the less pleasurable aspects, we invest very highly in them. For this reason, much of our life is lived in anticipation. We hanker after and look forward to pleasure. The result is that we do not invest much in the present, which means in effect that we are not very alive; after all, life only takes place in the present. My experience of this is that much of my life consists in throwing a large grappling hook into the future. I throw my hook onto a ridge of expected pleasure – sometimes it's a film or the magical promise of time off – often it takes the form of some expected sexual pleasure or romantic interlude. The hook I have thrown into my future is, as it were, connected to a rope, which I am holding in the present. If I'm not careful much of my life will consist of hauling myself up to promises of delight. Meanwhile my life goes by unnoticed, unappreciated, and I only have eyes for the future.

I said at the start of this chapter that the picket I attended with Gary outside the Fallen Angel was part of my attempt to answer the question 'What causes suffering?' The traditional Buddhist answer to that question is *craving*; it is craving that causes suffering. It is our tendency to throw our grappling hook of wanting forever into the future, hoping it will alight on some looked-forward-to pleasure, some soft reward. It is our attempt to find lasting satisfaction, happiness, and security in things that can never provide it. It is because we most often look for lasting satisfaction, happiness, and security in sexual relationships that Buddhism has contented celibacy as one aspect of its goal. When I first started going along to the Centre I thought it would take me about three years to become celibate. I remember talking to an Order member who had, as far as I was concerned, been ordained for ages and still wasn't celibate. 'Why on earth not?' I thought. So I gave myself three years; that seemed perfectly adequate as far as I was concerned. Fourteen years later I am still not celibate. Not only that, I am still in a relationship with Gary, that mild-mannered Kiwi I fell for one winter's evening sitting on a wall outside a gay pub.

I have finished with him at least twice – both times for solid spiritual reasons – but both times I have ended up going back to him, enduring the humiliation of asking him to go out with me again and in the process causing both of us a substantial amount of pain. So the question is: Have I made any progress on the education of my heart these last fourteen years? I certainly have a far more realistic sense of just how strong the forces of craving and emotional dependence are, but have I made progress in renouncing them?

What progress I have made has been of the kind a caterpillar makes as it moves from lettuce leaf to lettuce leaf. Ever so slowly, sucker by little sucker, the caterpillar moves, transferring its weight from one green leaf to another. In the same way, over the years I have put more and more of my weight on friendship and looked less and less on security and love from Gary. Over the years I have put more and more weight on meditation, on retreats, on living out my spiritual ideals, and less on Gary and my relationship with him. I have not allowed our relationship to dominate my time (I see him on average less than once a week), nor have I allowed it to preoccupy my mind and heart. One interesting side effect of this has been an improvement in our relationship. As I put less of my weight on him, make fewer demands of him, he is freer to move, to do what he wants to do. As the relationship is less weighed down with burdensome expectation and overinvestment, so the whole relationship lightens and becomes more enjoyable. Admittedly I have been lucky. Gary hasn't pressurized me to father children or to set up home with him, and on the whole, though he has occasionally complained that he hardly sees me, he has viewed my steadily increasing involvement in Buddhism with patient indulgence, for which I will always be grateful.

I would like one day to be able to become happily celibate, to let Gary (or any future lover) go their way with good grace and well wishing. I would like to be deeply content and alive within myself and not try to get someone else to do it for me. I would like to live life fully as it actually happens, instead of hankering for some future promise of sweetness. I am making progress, after the fashion of a caterpillar. The education of the heart takes time.

7

TIME AND CIRCUMSTANCE

*My friendship it is not in my power to give: this is a gift which
no man can make, it is not in our power: a sound and healthy
friendship is the growth of time and circumstance, it will spring
up and thrive like a wildflower when these favour, and when
they do not, it is in vain to look for it.*
William Wordsworth, letter to Thomas De Quincey

In those long-forgotten days before the advent of the cafetière, the
making of coffee was a much more long-winded process than it is
today. Our family mostly drank tea. My father would make a pot
in the morning and leave it stewing next to the gas ring while he
went out to drive coachloads of noisy children to local schools.
Our kitchen was overpopulated with hungry toast-eating coach
drivers at the best of times, so there was always tea on the go,
over-brewed and orange and thick enough to stand your spoon in.
Even Gren – our benign but irredeemably stupid Alsatian – drank
it, after Mum had taken him over the fields to 'do his business'.
Needless to say, my father eschewed the tea bag, a newfangled
and highly suspect invention as far as he was concerned and one
that went against the whole tradition of tea drinking. Sometimes,

though, at the weekend, my mother would make coffee, *real* coffee, as she called it. It was quite a protracted business. Like an alchemist she would carefully fill the old stainless steel percolator with water, take out the metal sieve at the top, pour in the rich, aromatic ground coffee, close the lid and turn it on. We would all wait and watch as the contraption gurgled and hissed and tiny dark brown coffee whirlpools appeared in the transparent plastic knob at the top. As a boy, the whole process seemed to have the aura of sanctity. Real coffee, I felt, was something special, something out of the ordinary, a cut above my father's tea or our occasional cup of Mellow Birds instant coffee. Friendship is the real coffee of human relationships; like the real coffee of my childhood, it takes time to make.

Nowadays, of course, we tend to want things quick and easy. Had Shakespeare been alive today, one can't help thinking that instead of writing 'All the world's a stage' he would have written 'All the world's a shopping mall'. We live in the age of shopping; we count our worth in the money we earn and the things we own. That nagging sense that deep down something is missing is met not by an urge to plumb the depths, but by an out-of-town shopping centre full to the brim with promised riches and images of satisfaction. In the previous chapter I talked about *dukkha*, our sense of incompleteness, how whatever we get – from lovers to organic fruit juice – won't fill that gap within us. If sex and romantic relationships are our first port of call when it comes to trying to feel whole, our second is shopping; it's our leisure activity of choice. Like a thirsty man crawling through the desert, we yearn to feel rich and truly alive but, unable to experience that within ourselves, we chase mirages. In the desert of Arizona we build a Las Vegas, in the poverty of urban life we set up the lottery, with its godlike sky finger proclaiming, 'It could be you.'

Consumerism doesn't just remain on the level of money-making and object-buying; it filters down into our very being, becoming an all-pervading mentality, an approach to life itself. One of the dangers of books like this is that we might start thinking that friendship can be approached with the same consumer mentality as buying a new CD player or mobile phone. In other words, we start harbouring great expectations of all those *goodies* friendship can bring. Like those user guides you see in newsagents that tell you about the best bargains and the most up-to-date gear, we might imagine ourselves flicking through glossy magazines of friendship thinking, 'Oh yes, I'd like one of those!' One page offers us a friend who will love us unreservedly, another a friend who will lend us money, help us with our housework, and forgive all our little shortcomings. Of course we're not terribly impressed with those rather ordinary human beings around us with their funny ways and irritating habits; we want someone special, an up-to-the-minute, top-of-the-range model, and we want it now.

This consumer mentality undermines friendship, first by encouraging too high an expectation of a friend (and too low an expectation of oneself), and secondly by an unwillingness to put in the time that friendship requires. Friendship is the living out of a common ideal; it's not some shiny designer accessory, something to add on to *me*, but a joint enterprise, a journeying forward towards the best in each other, in yourself, and in the world. It's no good waiting for someone to serve you friendship on a plate. The first rule of friendship is to be a friend, to give friendship, rather than passively waiting around until you get it and then complaining it's not good enough.

Actually you can't even *give* friendship. As Wordsworth says, it is the product of 'time and circumstance,' something that grows between you, not something you can individually give to someone. What you can give is attention – you can give interest and concern;

eventually perhaps you can give commitment, loyalty, and fidelity. Of all gifts, however, the first and foremost is time. In a way, time is all we have.

The essence of friendship is time spent together. Everything else follows from that. All that can be said regarding friendship could be reduced to a simple statement like 'spend as much time together as possible'. Whether you are married with children, are upwardly mobile and single, or, like me, live in a community of aspiring Buddhists, if you want friends you need to put time aside for them, as much time as possible. The question needs to become 'How can I spend more time with my friend?' So if you go swimming once a week, suggest they come too; if they have the kids for the day, join them by the kiddies' playground, if you're planning a walking holiday, a shopping trip or a bit of DIY, do it together. *Share* your life – that's the essence.

This shared life is the *raison d'être* of community living. For four years now I have shared a room with David, an ex-art teacher from Yorkshire. We'd had a bit of a reshuffle in the community. Some had moved out and some had moved in, so, for various reasons, I'd ended up moving out of my room with Paramabandhu into one with David. It's a rather small room dominated by a rather large bunk bed. It might seem strange that, at the age of nearly forty, I sleep in a bunk bed, albeit a home-made adult-sized construction with extra headroom so that David (who sleeps in the bottom bunk) can sit up and read. To me it seems the most natural thing in the world. I must admit, though, that sharing a room has its inconveniences. For instance, David has a tendency to create piles. They start innocently enough at his bedside: a few half-read novels perhaps, a Buddhist book or two, the odd income tax return. Gradually the piles start multiplying and, like geese or swallows, they start to migrate. They invade the desk and the chair, alight on the speakers and generally colonize any available flat surface. With me it's different: I often meet people in the room – effectively barring him from it – or I write, or create a few piles of my own. Despite these inconveniences we have shared not only the bunk beds and a room, but also much of our life. From intense heart-to-hearts to insisting he listen to the new piece of Handel I've just discovered; from talking about the Dharma to messing around chatting before lights out; from 'good morning' to 'good night', we have shared our life and in so doing developed a friendship. Wordsworth was right: friendship *does* grow from time and circumstance. Spend lots of time with someone and, as often as not, friendship will 'spring up and thrive like a wild flower'.

Wild flowers, like friendship, can flourish in the least propitious circumstances. Take the deep friendship that developed between Brian Keenan and John McCarthy, when the two men, half-naked and blindfolded, were shackled to a wall in Beirut. In the dreadful privations of imprisonment, among inhuman brutality, somehow, miraculously, out of the years spent together, the wild flower of friendship thrived. It had, of course, thrived before, anywhere in fact where time and circumstance brought people together. My father used to regale us with stories of the war, of the friendships he'd made in the barrack rooms and dugouts fifty years earlier when he was still a young man. For all the horrors brought on by war, it also brings the kind of time and circumstance out of which friendship grows. The vast overshadowing angel of death – which in a time of war seems to blot out all hope and goodness – leaves in the wake of its destruction a precious gift: a new appreciation of life and a depth of comradeship. Think of the passionate friendships between men in the trenches, or the new-found intimacy between women working in the munitions factories.

Most of us, though, are not thrown together by warfare or imprisonment. We must find the time for friendship within our ordinary lives. At the risk of sounding like a doctor prescribing medicine, I recommend that time to develop friendship be taken at least once or twice a week. It should be taken at regular intervals, if possible for many years. In my own life, nearly all my close friends are people I have either lived with or worked with (or both). Of course I have friends with whom I have done neither of these things but, because of that, I am aware that there is something provisional about them, something untested. Like most people, I can get on famously with someone over the occasional cappuccino, but when it comes to living or working with them, well, that's quite another matter.

Ideally, then, friends would live and work together. They would be committed to a common vision and to working that out in the practical realities of their day-to-day lives. After all, gone are those long, hot, endless summer holidays of our childhood, the freedom and space to spend all our time with our friends. The toys we played with have long been put away and the bell that marked the end of playtime rang long ago. As grown-ups we have to earn our bread and butter; we must pay the rent and feed the cat. The best way to do all that *and* have the kind of comradeship many of us had as children is to live and work together.

I stumbled onto this when I became a cleaner. Not long after I moved into the men's community above the Buddhist Centre, I was working as an artist-in-residence at a boys' secondary school in Barking. Actually the 'residence' that I was artist in was a shed in the grounds, so it wasn't as prestigious a post as it might sound. I had felt for some time that I wasn't making the best use of community life. I was *living* with other Buddhists, yes, but actually I spent most of my time trying to paint abstract pictures in a draughty shed on the edge of what was reputed to be the largest council estate in Europe. At our community meeting one Thursday evening, someone suggested I become the cleaner downstairs in the Buddhist Centre. Why I said yes I don't really know. Talking about it later on, it all sounded vaguely reminiscent of Russia after the revolution. One moment I was an artist trained at a respected London college, and the next, a cleaner. I even had a vision for being a cleaner. I imagined myself like one of those simple devoted monks you see on films about Tibetan monasteries, forever cleaning candlesticks and lighting butter lamps. I suppose somewhere in the back of my mind was the vague intuition that living and working with other Buddhists would strengthen my friendships with them and help me develop spiritually … Looking back on it, I can see I was right.

Not everyone would have done the same. Paramabandhu stuck to his career, moving seamlessly on from junior doctor to psychiatrist to consultant; becoming a cleaner at the Buddhist Centre simply hadn't appealed. Not everyone will want to live and work with other people. Many will have family responsibilities and careers that put it out of the question, at least initially. However, if we are to develop friendship we need to give it regular time. Even if we can only set aside an hour or so a week, it's a start, especially if we occasionally supplement that with longer periods together.

One of the striking features of life around the Centre is how many people develop friendships once they have been on retreat together. I notice this as I lead the newcomers' class every week. At first the atmosphere in the reception room – where we gather before the meditation – is not altogether unlike that of a dentist's waiting room, with people sitting awkwardly round the edges of the room not quite knowing where to look. Gradually, as people start to attend more regularly, they stop pretending to scrutinize the books in the bookshop and start chatting to each other a bit. Then, one day, they all go off on retreat together. The next week the noise in the reception room is almost deafening, and the tea break is buzzing with talk and enthusiasm. There is a marked change of atmosphere: what had been friendly but perhaps a little reserved now becomes much more intimate and animated, as if barriers have dropped away. One of the primary reasons for this is that the people have lived and worked together, if only for a weekend. So we could consider seeing someone regularly and living and working with them occasionally, by going on retreat with them for example.

Friendship takes time to develop – you can't force the pace. You can't insist that someone becomes your friend, you can't force friendship upon them, and you can't become best buddies overnight. You can develop friendship and work on it (as we shall see) but, really, if you want deep friendship, the first thing to do is simply to spend more time together. When you spend a lot of time with someone, gradually, almost without your noticing it, a kind of human osmosis takes place. It's as if our tendency to see ourselves as separate and distinct *from* each other, starts – with shared time and experience – to give way to a new softness and permeability *to* each other. We start to perceive ourselves not as free-floating separate entities but as dynamically related to others, even as being, in some sense, part of one another.

Looking at friendship from above, as it were, taking an aerial view of the terrain so as to get a clearer sense of our direction, we can see more clearly what the overall contours of friendship are. First, there is time spent together. Out of that arises mutual acknowledgement that, yes, a friendship is starting to grow between you. Then comes the crucial stage of commitment, the time when you say, 'I want to be your friend.' This stage of commitment is the beginning of *spiritual* friendship: it marks the place where friendship with a small F finishes and Friendship with a capital F begins. Most people are frightened of commitment. Commitment, after all, implies responsibilities, responsibilities imply duties, duties imply having to do things we don't feel like doing, and having to do things we don't feel like doing implies not always doing as we please. What all this amounts to in most people's minds is the frightening possibility of having their precious freedom curtailed. We are used to thinking that freedom means having no responsibilities, being answerable to no one, that committing ourselves to friendship can feel like volunteering to have our wings clipped.

'We are the hollow men,' said T.S. Eliot. It would be just as accurate to say that we are the bubble men (and women). We float around in a world of mysteries as though in vacuum-sealed bubbles, protected from any larger reality by the rubbery membrane of individualism. We think freedom consists in being able to do just as we please with our bubble selves, to move through life wholly intact and separate from it. Bouncing and wobbling in our precarious inflations, our bubble selves are frightened of anything that pins us down; pins, as we know, cause punctures. When we commit ourselves to friendship we challenge our cherished notions of freedom. Instead of seeing ourselves in terms of ourselves – how *we* feel, what *we* want – we start to see ourselves in terms of others and our responsibilities for them. We start to realize that we are connected to each other and, whether we like it or not, to live implies taking more and more responsibility for that connection. We are not and never can be impermeable, free-floating entities. Real freedom isn't a self-contained transportable bubble; it's the lived experience of *mettā*. After all, things go wrong. People cross us, irritate us, or won't do what we want. We can never really remain safely sealed off in our own private bubble. The only freedom we can hope to attain is a freedom of mind. When we feel *mettā*, we are free from reacting to life and from being dominated by those reactions. We can never control life or other people; the best we can do is learn to love both.

Commitment is the first step beyond bubblehood. This stage of commitment is primarily a commitment to spending time together; that is, spending time together with the express intention of developing and deepening the friendship. Friendship, while based on feeling, is not sustained by it: it is sustained by the simple equation of *action over time*. So when I say 'I want to be your friend,' I need to ask myself what I mean in practice. It's no good my professing friendship for someone and then strangely never getting round to spending time with them, or being unwilling to help them out when they are in trouble or to give them a listening ear when they need one. Friendship is something you *do*; it's not just a nice warm feeling – it's a commitment to action over time. The practice of friendship consists in the mutual willingness to keep repairing and maintaining it. This keeping of friendship 'in constant repair', as Dr Johnson brilliantly summarizes it, is the lifeblood of friendship. It is what friendship *is*.

Even the metaphor of repair has its limitations. In spending time with your friend you are trying to make your friendship *more*, more than it was, more truly friendship and more firmly based in the good. We are foolish indeed if we expect our friendships to be carried along on a tidal wave of mutual *mettā*. Feelings are, as we know, only too prone to change. The love we feel for our friend one day can only too easily become the irritation, boredom, or simple indifference we feel the next. Murray, a friend who'd joined my Buddhist discussion group, told me about his old circle of mates at a local East End pub. Having drunk large quantities of alcohol, they would profess undying friendship for each other. The emotions flowed as fast as the beer and with the same froth and intoxication. Even physical contact, usually highly dubious, became permissible: so that arms would be draped around shoulders for shaky flash photos, and bear hugs and backslapping became the order of the day. 'Where are they now?' he'd say. The undying friendship had all but died with the breath that uttered those words or it had dried up along with the supply of beer.

Good intentions and strong feelings aren't enough. Perhaps, though, my image of friendship being carried along on a tidal wave of mutual *mettā* isn't such a bad one after all. Friendship at its best *is* a kind of effortless surfing on the crest of a wave of mutual *mettā*, but, as anyone who has ever tried that particular sport knows, those moments are rare. To get to those experiences of equipoise when you, surfboard, and wave are in rapturous harmony, you'll have to go through much longer periods of waiting around for waves, falling off them, looking silly, and swallowing lots of salty water. Only ongoing commitment, effort, and persistence will finally win the day. Without ongoing commitment to friendship there is no friendship. Without ongoing commitment you will most likely simply back out when the going gets tough. Or else our seemingly natural tendency towards inertia and passivity brings with it the slow death of friendship. Gradually you find you are seeing each other less and generally taking less initiative until, before you know it, you no longer venture out on the waves at all. Instead you just stay at home and read surfing magazines.

The more explicit you make your friendship the better. The more you are both clear what you are trying to do and how exactly you intend to go about doing it the better. This is one reason why friendships that are most likely to survive the test of time, to thrive and grow *in* time, are those based on a mutually held ideal. So when I say to someone like Karmabandhu, 'I want to be your friend,' both of us know that by friendship I mean commitment: commitment to spending time together, commitment through difficulties, commitment to communication.

Al-Ghazālī, the Islamic mystic scholar, speaks of a 'contract of friendship'. He talks about how in the Sufi tradition two friends freely enter into a contract – a kind of pact of friendship – at a particular stage of their relationship. I've tried it myself. I'd read about the idea in Al-Ghazālī's book *The Duties of Brotherhood in*

Islam, so I suggested that Karmabandhu and I sit down with pen and paper and work out in detail what *our* friendship meant. For instance, what did it mean in terms of time – how much time we were each willing to give to it? What did our friendship mean in terms of 'things'? For example, was I willing to let him borrow my clothes or my books without asking? I'd been inspired by the Sufi story of two friends, one of whom was delighted when his friend came and took money out of his purse while he was away. Karmabandhu and I decided that we *wouldn't* be terribly delighted after all, so we wrote down a 'willing to lend' clause only. Anyway, we went through all these different areas of life: time, objects, money, speech, mental attitude, and so on, and wrote down what we were willing to give in the friendship.

Now whether one actually sits down with one's friends and writes it all out may not be important. What is important is that we realize that friendship involves commitment and, leading on from that, definite duties. It's no use just thinking, 'I'm knocking around a bit with so-and-so. We get on quite well but I don't wanna be too heavy about it so let's wait and see what happens.' If you just wait and see 'what happens' nothing will happen. One of the values of Al-Ghazālī's contract of friendship is in making quite explicit what the friendship means, especially what it means in practice.

Commitment is a serious matter. You are pledging yourself to friendship, to being blood brothers or sisters. You are saying, through thick and thin, good times and bad, 'I commit myself to keeping our friendship in constant repair', not just constant repair but constant improvement and development. When you commit yourself to something you necessarily take on working through all the difficulties and obstacles that will inevitably get in the way of that something. Whether you commit yourself to learning to play the piano or to developing friendship, you are committing yourself to time and practice, effort and perseverance.

What's more, when you commit yourself to friendship, or indeed to anything else, you commit yourself to the unknown. You simply cannot know what you will have to work through as you follow through your commitment. This general principle is strikingly apparent in friendship. All manner of things arise that you could never have foreseen before you expressed your commitment to being a friend. You discover aspects of your friend (and of yourself) that you simply didn't know were there.

Committing ourselves to something positive, like friendship or meditation, is one of the main ways in which we grow and mature. You don't often hear the term 'character building' any more, but that is what commitment does for us – it makes us stronger and more grown-up. Living only on your feelings may be well and good for adolescents but it won't help you develop as a person. Commitment *matures*; only children (of whatever age) have no commitments or responsibilities.

I've likened the time taken to develop friendships to the time and commitment involved in making 'real coffee' in those childhood days when I sat and watched the percolator perform its miraculous transformations. Of course that was before cappuccino hit Henley-in-Arden, before cafetières transformed the whole business, making it quicker and easier but taking away the mystery. However, when I say that friendship is the real coffee of human relationships I mean in terms of purity and richness, not caffeine and buzz. I tend to make a distinction between depth of feeling and intensity of feeling. When my father died and his tea-making days finally came to an end, I was at first rather dismayed by my apparent lack of emotion. I had expected tears and anguish, but when death came – after the weeks in hospital and the humiliations of illness – my response was more in the nature of deep sobriety surrounded in some strange way by an aura of calm. Nowadays, in our hyped-up, fast-track consumer world, we want our emotions big, like advertising billboards. We expect our emotional life to be dramatic and eye-catching, the psychic equivalent of cinematic special effects or wailing pop songs. In fact, intensity of feeling is often more to do with the surface than the depths, with the foam and spray of the waves rather than the fathomless depths of the ocean. Sexual relationships, for instance, are often characterized by a heady *intensity* of feeling, veering now one way, now the other; the relative superficiality of the feelings betrayed by volatile changeability and fickleness. Deep feelings, on the contrary, are often much quieter, more subterranean and subtle. They develop gradually and naturally over time, like the slow development of multicoloured coral. Whether it is in the years that Paramabandhu and I have lived together or in my little shared room – among David's migrating piles – feelings of deep friendship develop slowly, the result of time and circumstance.

8

MAKING FRIENDS

*I must in a particular manner recommend to you a strict
care in the choice of your friendships … Do not lay out your
friendship too lavishly at first, since it will, like all other things,
be so much the sooner spent. Neither let it be of too sudden a
growth, for as the plants which shoot up too fast are not of that
continuance as those which take more time for it, so too swift a
progress in pouring out your kindness is a certain sign that by
the course of nature it will not be long lived.*

George Savile, Marquess of Halifax, *A Lady's New Year's Gift,
or Advice to a Daughter*

Perhaps it's not surprising that people sometimes have insights in
the bath. After the accumulated exertion of thinking or acting, the
warmth and reassurance of the bath can ease the overburdened
mind just enough to allow for a new possibility to arise. As
happened with Archimedes in the old story, a few moments
of relaxation among the soapsuds and *eureka!* – that striven-for
solution, that new synthesis, suddenly flashes before us and we
are running naked through the village. It was a bit like that for
Darren.

He was working in a hospital in Gillingham at the time. Having
been a medic in the army a few years previously, he knew, as
soon as Iraq invaded Kuwait, that it would only be a matter of
time before he was called up. In the army he had worked as an
operating theatre technician, so he was well aware what war
looked like; he had seen it on the operating table: army officers
with gunshot wounds, young squaddies with disfiguring burns,
soldiers maimed by bombs in Northern Ireland. The prospect
of death, insanity, and pain tormented him. Dreadful thoughts
spoiled his pleasures and every otherwise ordinary day seemed
nothing but the painful prologue to an oncoming terror. His
friends carried on their lives as usual: work, the pub in the
evening, a bit of telly perhaps, and sleep; for them death seemed
far off. For Darren, still in his early twenties, it seemed just
around the corner. He took to reading Buddhist books – vaguely,
incoherently searching for answers to the questions that burned
in his mind; but he couldn't make much sense of them, except
that they recommended reflecting on impermanence. He started
taking long hot baths to relieve the tension. There he would lie
for ages, topping up the bath with hot water, using his toe to
regulate the temperature, thinking, 'all things are impermanent,
my body will die, it will return to the earth, nothing will be left
of me …' Then one day it happened. Suddenly, lying in the bath
one evening and still in the grip of nagging dread, he had a flash
of realization. In an instant he saw himself as being perfectly
interconnected with everything and everybody. His tears, when
they came, were tears of immense relief. Paralysing fear and
isolation dissolved away entirely and for a while he was left in a
universe suffused with radiant harmony and peace. For Darren
it was the beginning.

I met him a few years later. He never went to the Gulf; his new-
found conviction that he was a Buddhist and therefore practised

non-violence meant that he'd refused to go. By the time I met him he had gone through a lengthy military tribunal which, though stressful and difficult, resulted in his being granted the status of conscientious objector. He started attending the weekly class I was leading at the Buddhist Centre and, after getting to know each other a bit in that context, we arranged to meet up for coffee in town. I remember the two of us sitting by the window in a trendy café in Covent Garden, Darren in his tattered old jacket, scruffy jeans, and trainers, his long hair tied in a ponytail. He talked about his fears, the tribunal, and his conviction that the only thing that made sense in the entire world was to practise the Dharma. I couldn't help but warm to him. There was something straightforward and good-natured about him, a lack of pretension that I instinctively admired. I don't know whether I sensed then that we would become friends, but it wasn't long before I invited him to join the new community I was thinking of setting up. Soon enough we were living together as well as putting an hour or so aside every week just to spend time with each other, to walk, talk, and drink decaffeinated coffee. Before the year was out I had a new friend in my life.

In many ways Darren was a good contender for friendship. He was close at hand. Living together, we had ample opportunity to be in each other's company, ample opportunity for that osmosis of being I talked about in the previous chapter. It sounds obvious, but if we are looking for friendship, we need to look close at hand. I have met quite a few people who claim that no one in the immediate vicinity is capable of being their friend, or that they just happen not to be attracted to anyone within a five-mile radius! For some, it seems, friendship is always elsewhere. Usually this is an excuse, or another symptom of wanting a *special* friend, someone who sees how special *we* are. After all, friends can look rosy from a distance – we can't see their little blotches and pimples and nor can they see ours. Real friendship needs to be with real people; those ordinary human beings who sometimes don't wash up after themselves or who occasionally get on our nerves at the office. Maybe we can't live with them, but we should choose our friends from people who are close by, from Mr and Ms Average Person whom we bump into at work or sit next to at night school.

Darren and I had the time to be friends. We had time to spend together (our Filofax or Psion organizers were not yet full of pressing engagements), and we were willing to put time aside for each other, just to develop the friendship. We also had the same ideal. Both of us were trying to develop, to make progress along the spiritual path towards Enlightenment, and both of us felt that close friendship was a valuable, indeed a vital, part of that.

But did I *choose* to be Darren's friend? We had the time, the opportunity, and the shared vision to be friends, but is that all that is needed for friendship? In Darren's case, I think our friendship did primarily grow out of time and circumstance. Living together, we naturally spent a lot of time in each other's company, and this meant we could 'hang out' together in the kind of straightforward and unselfconscious way that is the necessary basis of genuine friendship. Nowadays, of course, more and more people live alone. A recent survey suggests that soon a staggering 40 per cent of people will be living on their own. In a famous essay, Virginia Woolf said how important it was to have 'a room of one's own'. Nowadays, it seems, we want a whole flat! This increasing trend towards isolationism means that the kind of easy shared time I had with Darren is getting rarer. Gone are those long Sunday breakfasts like the ones I enjoyed with Maria and the others when we house-shared at art school; gone the late-night beer, listening to vibe music in digs. Nowadays, when most of us want to spend time with someone, we have to make a date, put it in our diary, and try to arrive on time.

So we are faced with the question of whom to give our time to. When it comes to making dates, millions of people will choose the romantic option every time. But some of us will see that friendships – like those golden friendships of childhood – are important, and that to live a healthy and happy life they need to stay important. The main way they stay important is by giving time to them. But to give time to one person is not to give time to another. Darren, when he moved into the community, shared a room with Ian. Ian had, so to speak, all the same qualifications for friendship as Darren, and not only that but I was living with six others. Could I develop friendship with *all* of them? And what about my old friends, the people to whom I had already committed myself? What about Karmabandhu living across the courtyard? What about Paramabandhu and others – was I to pass them over now that a new friend presented himself? Choosing means knowing that to choose one person means – somewhere along the line – not choosing another.

But how do we choose a friend? Despite the supreme value we put on choice in our consumer society, choice can be agonizing. If we are not careful, choosing a friend can be like choosing which checkout queue to join in Tesco. You choose a queue that looks promising only to be frustrated by an old lady in front of you painstakingly counting out her loose change. You decide to hop over to the longer queue a few aisles away which now seems to be moving faster than yours but, once there, you're not sure if it wouldn't have been better to have stayed where you were. The old lady's gone through and the assistant at *your* checkout is waving her arms about and making worrying signs that she going off for a tea break.

We need some sense of what to base our choice on. First, we need to look for those three main ingredients: that they are close at hand, that you both have the time and the willingness to put into it, and that you share the same ideal. However, for most of us, the way we usually choose a friend is to do with whether or not we *like* them. I liked Darren almost as soon as I met him. Over that coffee and chocolate cake, while he talked so openly and frankly about himself, I liked him and I was attracted to him. The question was 'What was it that I was attracted to?' After all, I've been attracted to different people for different reasons: because I found them sexy or hip or entertaining, or because they were willing to indulge me, gossip with me, or grumble with me. Often enough we choose friends simply because they go along with our way of seeing the world.

I have made a few glaring errors in choosing friends. I have chosen to make friends on the basis of the wrong kind of attraction and I've made rash and unrealistic promises of friendship that I wasn't able to fulfil. Sometimes my mistakes have occurred because I was attracted to rather superficial qualities in someone. I didn't know them (or myself) well enough to know if I *could* be a friend. We will return to this. For the moment we have to face the fact that just because we like someone doesn't necessarily mean we can, or will, become friends with them.

The first distinction to make is that friendliness is not friendship, nor is it, in my experience, necessarily a prelude to friendship. I used to assume that the best people to make friends with were those friendly, outgoing, hearty types, those people who'd slap you on the back and say, 'We really *must* meet up!' I thought friendliness and *bonhomie* would quickly mature into committed friendship. I wasn't completely wrong, but I was more wrong than I'd expected. Friendliness is, of course, a very good thing; in fact it is a distinguishing characteristic of people who practise Buddhism. Again and again newcomers to the Buddhist Centre tell me that it wasn't so much the meditation, the incense, the

Buddha statues, or the chanting that attracted them – it was the friendliness of the people. This is how it should be – after all, what would be the value of practising the *mettā bhāvanā* if it didn't result in increased friendliness? But friendliness is not friendship; in fact, over the years, I have come to see friendliness and friendship as quite different things. Both are qualities, but friendship is a more significant quality than friendliness. Friendship is more vigorous and demanding; it goes further into the heart of things, expects more from us. Just because someone is sociable and jovial doesn't mean they'll make a good friend, as I've discovered to my cost. Obviously the fact that someone is *un*sociable and miserable doesn't mean they'll make a good friend either! What we need to realize is that likes and dislikes are often rather superficial matters.

We can like someone for the wrong reasons and dislike them for the wrong reasons too. The latter was forcibly brought home to me with another friend, to whom, when I first met him, I took an instant and marked dislike. I didn't like his accent, his lavish and to my mind pretentious moustache, his mannerisms, his views, and the forceful – indeed voluble – way in which he expressed them. It so happened, not long after we met, that we were both invited to be ordained on the same four-month intensive retreat. This meant we would be spending four months together in an isolated Spanish valley! Apparently he felt the same dislike for me as I did for him (albeit for different reasons) so, as we both realized it would be impossible to avoid each other for four months, we began to have short, civil chats whenever we bumped into each other.

Not long after the retreat began I decided to grasp the nettle and broach what was quite clearly a mutually felt antipathy. That walk in the Spanish hills was the start of a friendship. We talked about what had brought us to this point in our lives, what had been working away in me as a child in Warwickshire, and what dissatisfactions had brought him to a Spanish valley far from his home town in New Zealand. What changed, as we climbed the rocky slopes towards the ridge above the valley, was not so much that we talked about why we didn't like each other (though we acknowledged that), but that I saw that what I'd instinctively disliked about him were only the superficialities, the outward show. Sitting gazing across at the distant mountains as they softened in the early evening light I realized that here was someone just like me – someone who cared deeply about friendship and who was committed to changing himself. That essential similitude, that underlying sameness of aspiration, united us in friendship, dissolving as it did so everything in its path.

Just as I had disliked this friend for the wrong reasons, I have, at times, been liked for the wrong reasons. When I was younger I tended to be liked because I entertained people. I told jokes and stories and generally tried my best to be the life and soul of the party. I was rather popular – until I got involved in Buddhism. As I became aware of the fear and insecurity that my desire to be popular was based upon, I stopped people-pleasing. I just couldn't find the energy for it any more; in a way I no longer believed in it. I lost 'friends' as a result. 'You've changed,' they'd say, darkly, as if change was inevitably a bad thing. 'You're not like you used to be.' Much more recently I fell into the same trap with someone myself. He was such good fun to be with, so witty and sharp and lively, and we had so much in common. Then one evening outside a pub in Hackney, over our orange and lemonade, we disagreed and fell out. The fun abruptly stopped, and in the immediate aftermath of hurt feelings and injured pride we felt we had *nothing* in common. Friendships based on attraction to the superficial glitter of personality are usually fragile and short-lived.

I think in many cases there is a degree of projection at the beginning of friendships. This was in part the reason for my falling out at the pub: I had overhastily judged the friendship, felt we were blood brothers and kin too quickly. In my experience many people enter into friendships in much the same way as they fall in love. Again following the romantic model, there can be a tendency to project unacknowledged parts of yourself on to a new friend. You can think, 'At last, here's someone I can *really* develop a friendship with, someone who really understands and appreciates me.' A few intimate moments over a mug of cocoa and it's friendship at first sight! Like falling in love, friendship at first sight can end in disappointment and bitterness.

It's as if the romantic myth is so pervasive in our culture that we take it as the basic paradigm for relationships. (Even when we talk of 'relationships' we tend to mean sexual ones.) Falling in love – what Freud described as 'the psychosis of normal people' – is largely a matter of projection. You project onto the person those qualities and attributes that you feel are missing in you. We usually experience this most strongly when we think we have met Mr or Ms Right, but it can also happen in friendship, especially in new friendship. Karmabandhu used to criticize me for this. I would find a new friend and, before you knew it, they'd be the flavour of the month. Unlike like old Karmabandhu and his unwillingness to flatter me – or even to agree with me – here, I felt, was someone I really clicked with. In this way we can be lured away from the more tried and trusted (if less attractive) existing friendships by the appeal of newness. Even leaving projection aside, there is the excitement of getting to know someone for the first time and them getting to know you. They laugh at all your old jokes and take you to be penetratingly insightful and interesting. They probably haven't seen you in one of your bad moods yet; nor have they heard your views on such-and-such, which they'd be bound to disagree with. All in all, new friendships can seem just what you've been looking for, and those old friends who aren't so easily impressed by you – who know you in a deeper, more multifaceted way – can seem rather stale and difficult. I know people whose best friend is always their most recent, the light of which casts all others into the shade.

We need to choose our friendships carefully and sensibly because backing out of them once we have committed ourselves to them is painful for both parties and undermines our capacity for friendship. We need to make sure especially that our desire to form a friendship is not motivated by superficial attraction, or if it is that we are willing to get on with the constant repair work of friendship after that initial buzz has died down. Nowadays we are not really sure *how* to get to know people; we are not really sure what is appropriate in a friendship and when. Bereft of the formal niceties of custom and courtesy, we either remain wary and inarticulate or, like pop stars talking about their marital problems on television chat shows, foist a mawkish and inappropriate intimacy on people.

I have occasionally been the reluctant recipient of 'force hugging'. You know the sort of thing: you are innocently en route for your tea break and suddenly someone you have met maybe once or twice draws you into his or her arms. It's a clear case of being given the not-wanted! What *is* wanted is a social space – at once easy-going and yet courteous – where, over time, we can test out our connections with people. We need a new kind of village green where a community of people might sit out the evening together and, among the lengthening shadows, gradually get to know one another. Unfortunately the village green has become a shopping precinct and any genuine community has all but died out in bed-sit land. In the past, the church was once the centre of a living community. One of the things I discovered when I started going to the Buddhist Centre was a community: men and women all living near the Buddhist Centre, going to meditation classes, and shopping in the local Buddhist-run health food shop. Never since those not very happy days in Henley-in-Arden had I bumped into so many people I knew! It was within this community – which a local estate agent called the 'Buddhist village' – that I got to know Darren. During tea breaks at the Centre, or catching sight of one another in the restaurant next door, we gradually got to know each other. There is an almost organic process to friendship. As time goes by, little barriers start to come down one by one: the first time you are physically affectionate, the first time you suggest you meet up regularly, the first time you mention how much you like them, even the first time you criticize them. Together these constitute little staging posts on the way to friendship.

Rather unfortunately, perhaps, the language of courtship comes to mind. Thomas More in his *Utopia* makes what was then the radical suggestion that engaged couples be allowed to see each other naked before they get married. It's similar with friendship; before becoming committed to it we would do well to get to know the other person a bit, to see, as it were, what's under the surface. Friendship at its strongest is a kind of nakedness, where nothing is hidden, covered up, or plastered over. This inevitably takes time, time to see beyond the ephemeral exchanges of like and dislike to the far deeper potentialities for virtue and for friendship based upon it. For want of a better metaphor, there needs to be a period of courtship before you start to voice your commitment to the friendship. However, there does come a time, as I have already said, when you *do* commit yourself. With Darren it felt as if one day we went over the starting line of committed friendship. We acknowledged, if rather awkwardly, that we wanted to be friends and that that meant commitment, responsibilities, and duties. We weren't just hanging out together any more: we were friends.

I have met people who talk of 'keeping in touch' with friends but who, when you dig a bit deeper, mean the odd postcard, the occasional get-together. Spiritual friendship is something much stronger and more committed than that. So, given what I have already said about time and commitment, what becomes clear is that we can probably have only two or three close friends at any one time. Perhaps someone who has a lot of time on their hands and who is especially capable in terms of friendship could have more than that, but generally I would say two or three close friends is what we need to be aiming for. People who think they have ten, fifteen, or more close friends are either fooling themselves or do not have a very elevated concept of friendship. There simply isn't enough time in the day to get to know that number of people in any real depth, let alone commit yourself to the constant repair work that genuine friendship entails. Time and the complexities of human nature impose definite limits on the number of friendships you can have.

Part of the problem is that the English language doesn't contain enough words! The word 'friendship' simply cannot cover what is at one end mere acquaintanceship and at the other deeply committed relationships between two people who are trying to grow. It's a shame we don't have particular words for particular stages or types of friendships: after all, in the romantic sphere we have 'going steady', engaged, and married. To make things clearer, let us imagine a pyramid. At the top of the pyramid are two, three, or four really close friends, people you spend a lot of time with on a regular basis and to whom you are committed in friendship. The next layer down we could call (for want of a better term) 'friendships in potential'. The men and women in this layer of your life are more than acquaintances but not friends in the full-blown sense I have been talking about.

The friendship that began with antipathy, which I mentioned earlier, is a good example. He and I have never, apart from retreats, lived or worked together. He lives in Newcastle, the city in England that is furthest away from London, so we have never been able to spend time together on a regular basis. Nevertheless I do have strong feelings of friendship for him, at least since that walk on our ordination retreat ten years ago. When I go to the various gatherings of the Western Buddhist Order I always seek him out and spend time with him. I occasionally email him and more occasionally visit him. When my father died and I wanted some time to take it in, I went up to stay with him in Newcastle. Visiting him, and my other friends that lived there, seemed the obvious thing to do. So, you see, he is a friend in *potential*. I don't spend enough time with him to really test the friendship out, to put it through the fires of experience. If I did, likely enough we'd become Friends with a capital F, but you never know – the original antipathy might rise up again and need to be dealt with. So 'friends in potential' are those perhaps fourteen to twenty people that you have strong feelings for, drop postcards to, and invite to your birthday party. Given time and circumstance they could thrive.

The next layer down on my pyramid comprises all those we are in good friendly relationship with. In principle this layer could just go on and on: from the dinner ladies at work to your children's teachers. It is composed of those people we say a cheerful good morning to. For Buddhists practising the *mettā* bhāvanā this layer of friendly relationship should always be extending, eventually to everyone you meet or have interaction with.

As you get to know someone and develop friendship, they move up the pyramid. Take the development of my friendship with Darren. First of all he came along to classes; I would say hello to him and occasionally we'd chat in the tea break. I was, I hope, friendly and he was friendly back. So at first he was within that lowest band of, let us call it, 'warm acquaintance'. Then I started to see him around the place a bit more and to spend time with him occasionally. He was then a friend in potential. As I said, when he moved into the community he shared a room with Ian, who for me was also a friend in potential. But Ian moved out and for one reason or another the friendship never developed. With Darren it did. What I began to experience, as I got to know him better, was that he had *spiritual qualities*. It seems strange in a way to call them that. He has always been so completely down-to-earth that saying he has spiritual qualities sounds a bit airy-fairy. If you met him now, selling organic veg over the counter at Friends Foods, you probably wouldn't think, 'Now there's a man with spiritual qualities.' Nevertheless, as I got to know him, it was his spiritual qualities that most attracted me.

Spiritual qualities are human qualities consciously developed. People who are more spiritually developed are people who are more human. I don't mean in the sense of having more human frailties – I don't mean the trendy vicar who has a few pints in the pub like the rest of them – I mean that the truly human qualities like honesty, integrity, kindness, and so on are more developed and consciously cultivated. Darren had spiritual qualities, or at least the beginnings of them. I still liked his sense of humour, the way he chatted at the table, his little eccentricities, but gradually, as we shared our lives with each other, I saw there was much more to him.

First, as I got to know him I found I could talk things over with him. I could speak my mind to him and, even though he wouldn't always like what I had to say, he would often appreciate my saying it. I found that the two of us could work through difficulties and misunderstandings in communication without either of us taking offence or going off in a huff. He was honest, especially about himself, and this made genuine communication, and therefore friendship, possible. Perhaps the main quality, however, that emerged as we got to know each other was Darren's loyalty and fidelity to the friendship.

A year or so after we moved into the community together, he moved out. He had been asked to work in Friends Foods (the

Buddhist-run health food shop I mentioned earlier), and the team who worked there also lived together. I was sad to see him go, but the friendship continued to grow, thanks in large part to Darren's loyalty to it. He would work out with me when I had time and would organize his days off so that we could spend time together. If, as happened on occasion, I was too busy to spend time with him, he would come and help me with my work. Month in and month out he would turn up at the appointed time to spend our weekly hour-and-a-half together. Sometimes we got on well, sometimes it was more difficult; sometimes it was fun, sometimes a bit dull. Whatever it was, Darren was loyal to the friendship and to me. So the friendship grew. It became more and more about getting to the truth, whether the truth was palatable or not – it became, in a word, *spiritual* friendship.

So, when you choose a friend, I suggest you choose one like Darren. First of all, someone who is close at hand, whom you have time to be with, and who shares the same ideals. We need to make sure that the relatively superficial matters of like and dislike do not dictate our choice of friendship too much and we need to enter into friendship gradually, like a courtship. We need especially to choose someone who has spiritual qualities, like Darren, or if we don't like that language, simple virtues. Only these kinds of qualities: honesty, generosity, willingness to communicate and go through difficulties, commitment, and especially loyalty and fidelity, are the real basis for spiritual friendship. The art of friendship is the art of cultivating attraction, not to the bright lights of mundane personality, but to the more subtle colours of virtue and love of the good.

Actually Darren isn't Darren any more. A month or so ago I went to pick him up at Luton Airport. He'd been away for four months. Like me, ten years earlier, he had gone to a remote valley in Spain to be admitted to the Western Buddhist Order. He got ordained because he wanted to dedicate his life to developing spiritual qualities.

A group of us went to meet him at the airport. We all piled into a hired van and as midnight approached we were standing around watching as sunburned holidaymakers, tired businessmen, and young trekkers wheeled their trolleys into the arrivals lounge. He finally appeared, looking, except for a freshly grown beard and layers of fleecy clothing, much the same as he had done four months earlier. He wasn't the same, though, and never would be. Something profound had happened to him; he had dedicated his life to the path of Buddhism; he had committed his life to going for refuge to the Three Jewels. As a sign of that commitment he had a new Buddhist name. The name is a symbol of that person at their best; it says, 'This is who you could be if you really transformed yourself, if you really committed yourself to your spiritual qualities.' Darren's new name was Vajrabandhu, meaning something like 'very real friend'. We crowded around him, hanging paper garlands round his neck, queuing up to hug and congratulate him, and helping him with his rucksack, before setting off in one excitable band into the cold air and the car park. In the van back home we sat next to each other and talked. 'How did it go?' ... 'Any news?' ... 'Are you pleased with your name?' ... 'I rang your Mum while you were away, she seemed fine.' ... 'Do you want a chocolate?' Nothing special, just a friendship – continuing.

9

THE FINE ART OF COMMUNICATION

*What he ought to do … is to exert every effort to increase his
friend's self-confidence and lead him towards a more hopeful
and optimistic opinion of his own capabilities.*
   Cicero, *On the Good Life*

I grew up in a town where no one really talked. We passed
the time of day, made pleasantries, were polite and anxious to
please, but no one, as far as I remember, really talked. It's the
English way.

When I was a little boy, and before my mother started
driving coaches (things were tight and Dad couldn't afford to
hire anyone), she would take me down the high street to do
the week's shopping. We'd only get a few yards from the door
before being ambushed by Miss Denly or Mrs Churchill from
Rose Avenue. That would be it, we'd be stuck there, glued, it
seemed, to the pavement. First it'd be the weather – a topic of
endless description, prediction, and lament – then enquiries
about my father's health. Soon we were on to weightier matters:
the latest death in the town, the family that had just moved in
from Birmingham and 'weren't our type'. As a child such social

niceties on the way to the sweetshop were agonizing, and I was soon swinging on my mother's arm, like a yachtsman hauling the sail to catch the wind. Not that such pleasantries are a bad thing. Of late there has been much mocking of the English manner: the constant apologizing over nothing, the awkward courtesy and 'niceness'. I've come to value it myself, and if I went down the high street now I'd be less impatient with it all, more willing to stop and find an excuse for friendly interaction. Except that I wouldn't know anyone any more. Town and village life is disappearing from England. Local communities exist largely in the mind, in television soap operas, and in Agatha Christie novels. I imagine that nowadays my mother can go all the way to Dillons and back without a single interruption. Admittedly she can get to the post office more quickly – but at what cost?

Despite the custom and the courtesy, no one in my childhood days really seemed to talk; perhaps they didn't know how to. As I grew up, unspoken words seemed to accumulate inside me; unacknowledged even to myself, they churned around in the gloomy depths of my mind, collecting all manner of weird accretions. Fears, dark secrets, unspoken loves, brave hopes, dreams, and black nightmares all mixed together in a confusion of unexpressed words. I think it was partly as a consequence of that that I became attracted to outspoken people, people who said things they shouldn't, in ways they shouldn't, to people they oughtn't.

Toby was like that, as were his whole family, especially his mother. She was something of an idol for me as a schoolboy. Witty and outspoken almost to the point of rudeness, she ruled the household with all the *savoir faire* of a well-bred country lady who had married beneath her. She tended to call a spade a spade and she soon called me one. I liked her. Later on, when I was nursing in Coventry, there was Sam with his persistent tendency to bring leftist politics into the most innocent of conversations, getting everyone thoroughly worked up and hot under the collar. Then there were mad Maureen, Lorraine, and, of course, her mother.

Lorraine's mother, Mrs Despereles, took outspokenness into new and as yet uncharted territory. I was invited to supper one evening. We all crowded around the table: Lorraine, her three teenage brothers, a friend from down the street, and Mr Despereles. The physical slightness of her husband was, as he sat next to her at the table, in marked contrast to Mrs Despereles's massive bulk. She was a very large lady with a booming contralto voice, which – rising in a steady crescendo and subduing all other attempts at conversation – announced half way through the meal: 'Lorraine tells me you're a homosexual.' I sat in dumb horror as – her voice settling into a comfortable *fortissimo* – she declared that this *wasn't a problem* as far as she was concerned. Undaunted by my increasing pallor, she proceeded to procure affidavits of liberal unconcern and solicitous sympathy from the whole table. 'Do *you* find Ian's homosexuality a problem, Darrell?' 'No,' stammered the mortified teenager, eyeing me nervously. 'Do you, Craigie?' 'No, Mrs Despereles' – and so we went on till everyone at the table had assured me that my homosexuality was not a problem as far as they were concerned. Strange as it may seem, this was not a reassuring experience.

Even for my taste, Lorraine's mother took things a bit too far, especially when she threatened to ring my mother and tell her all about my 'tendency' then and there. But I was drawn to outspokenness; it felt like an antidote to the brand of terminal politeness that surrounded me. Perhaps it was honesty that I was attracted to. However bluntly it was stated, by Toby, by his mother, or by Sam, it was at least real. Communication is an art and it's amazing how many of us are unschooled in it – whether it is the inability or unwillingness to go beyond social niceties or the forced confessions in which Mrs Despereles specialized.

Of course we hear a lot about communication these days. Communication has become a burgeoning technological industry, an urgent twenty-first-century need. With faxes, email, and the Internet, a worldwide telephone network, satellite television, and countless talk shows, we have – at least on the face of it – more opportunities for communication than ever before. Nowadays you can hardly get through a train journey without mobile phones jingling and besuited businessmen announcing, 'I'm on the train.' The mad woman talking enthusiastically to herself walking along the street or waiting at the bus stop turns out to be a teenager with one of those telephone headsets announcing that she's on her way to the party, estimated arrival time twenty minutes.

In a society increasingly characterized by a breakdown of any sense of community, a society in which isolation and stress are signs of the times, communication technology is mushrooming. While this proliferation of communication gadgetry has its advantages, it doesn't mean that we are communicating *more* than we used to; my own sense is that we are communicating *less*. It's like the young couple I saw in the local café, sitting opposite each other but each turned slightly away, each talking into their own mobile phone. Communication, like friendship, can always seem elsewhere: at the next table or in the next text message. Despite all the talk about information technology and communication skills, probably more people than ever before are lonely and isolated. Few have real friends whom they can really talk to and many have no clear sense of meaning and value that they can talk *about*. Although more and more people own mobile phones, fewer and fewer have anything to say.

Communication is more than information. In fact, information is the smallest part of communication. I started to realize this on my first weekend retreat. On the first afternoon it was announced that we were now going to do 'communication exercises'. The leader of the retreat asked us to find a partner, sit opposite them, and 'just look' at them in silence. 'Try not to stare each other out or focus on the fact that your partner has one ear bigger than the other. Just simply meet each other's gaze.' Now, as far as I was concerned, I had come on retreat to meditate, to focus within, to get in touch with myself. I hadn't come to look some complete stranger in the eye; I'd come for gongs and incense and mystery. Despite my qualms, I turned to the woman next to me and suggested we pair up. The exercise began by first 'just looking', then in stages adding nonsensical sentences (that is, sentences with minimal conceptual content). The exercise came as something of a revelation to me. What actually happened was that I laughed … and laughed … and laughed. I think I laughed throughout the entire exercise. My partner laughed too. We sat opposite each other and laughed until our sides hurt and tears streamed down our faces. Occasionally we would try to stop – nervously glancing at the retreat leader, catching our breath, clamping our mouths shut – but it was all in vain: our ears went bright red and our stifled giggles burst out again into raucous laughter.

In retrospect, that communication exercise was something of a catharsis, one that was both embarrassing and powerfully liberating. The first thing that became painfully clear to me was that I habitually didn't look at people when I talked to them. I might perhaps catch someone's eye for a moment or two, but often enough I would look over their shoulder or stare awkwardly at their feet. I associated looking someone in the eye with two things: sex and violence. It was either a 'come on' or a square up for a fight. In some ways that communication exercise was the first time I consciously looked at someone and tried to become aware of them as a person, as a living human being with thoughts and feelings just like my own.

When we look at someone we usually don't really see the person. From eyeing up an attractive stranger to figuring out how to persuade them to do the photocopying, we habitually relate to people in terms of what we can get out of them, one way or another. Often enough, we're not even looking; we're distracted, rearranging our papers, eating our lunch, doing something, but missing everything. In the communication exercise we stop all that and become aware of the person, the unique never-to-be-repeated person. I've done countless communication exercises now, and I still find it remarkable, almost miraculous, how just sitting opposite someone, looking at them and saying something like 'the cow is in the field' can communicate so much. It might be difficult to imagine for those who haven't tried it, but it's wonderful just to stop and really look, to really listen – to look and listen not for information or ideas, not for personal profit or imagined threat, but simply to become aware of a person as a person, in all their living mystery.

That kind of communication is what friendship is all about. The communication exercise is really just a 'starter kit', an initial push in the right direction. Eventually you are aiming to communicate like that all the time. Obviously I don't mean sitting on the Tube gazing into each other's eyes and repeating nonsensical sentences; I mean engaging in the spirit of communication itself, the sense of mutual responsiveness and humanity. We learn the art of communication within friendship. When I sat down to do the exercise for the first time, I learned that, although I had done an awful lot of talking in my life, I hadn't done much communicating. I was nervous of revealing myself, shy, frightened of conflict, and wary of intimacy. I wasn't going to work out those issues in meditation, study, or ritual – only in friendship. If we want to learn to communicate, reading self-help books, attending expensive workshops on communication skills or conflict resolution, or even doing communication exercises on Buddhist retreats is not going to do it for us – we learn to communicate by being a friend.

Communication starts simply enough: first look, really look, and then speak. Talking is an art. When we talk we create. What we say can either become more and more beautiful, kind, and authentic or more and more crude, ugly, and superficial. Talking either takes experience and moulds it into a new and more meaningful form, or it poisons and pollutes it. After all, words come so easily – they fly out from the tongue like genies carried on the breath, each one a force for creation or destruction. We can do so much good with the words we speak, with the music and colour of them as well as the form. A few well-chosen words can make all the difference. A few kind words from Karmabandhu in a traffic jam on the M11, a penetrating comment from Paramabandhu – his head slightly tilted to one side, his eyes narrowed – hitting the nail on the head again. Darren's easy company and good humour, the implicit sense of trust between us as we natter on about a film we saw or want to see. Honest or kind, courageous or so simple as to be hardly worth mentioning, words can make everything out of nothing and nothing out of everything that's difficult.

The good we can do with words is matched by the harm we can do. We can hurt people so easily, even inadvertently, with words: the hurtful flippant remark, the quick accusation, the temper tantrum. Often enough the harm we do is caused by gradual erosion as much as by sudden destruction, as much to do with what we don't say as with what we do. Again and again we avoid mentioning something because we are waiting for the right time and place to say it. Strangely, the right time and place never come, and for fear of rocking the boat we let it slowly sink. Perhaps we never get round to telling our friend how much we like them, or we nag and niggle them to a slow death by moaning. Perhaps we go in for dramatic exits, the sudden taking of offence, the argument over nothing. From the unspoken words that, like fossils, lay buried beneath the polite faces and 'how-dos' of my childhood, to Mrs Despereles's well-meant mealtime declarations, every time we speak (or don't speak) we create ourselves and each other. Careless talk costs friends, as does careless *not talking*.

Very few people seem to have friends they can really talk to. They may have turbulent sexual relationships, long-term marriages, or casual colleagues, but very often they have no real friends to reveal themselves to or to make sense of themselves with. Self-revelation is a human need. So important is it that millions of men and women, bereft as they are of genuine friendship, willingly pay therapists substantial sums of money just so they can have someone to talk to. The relief we feel when we finally admit something about ourselves – which perhaps we have never dared acknowledge before – can be tremendous. It is as if our inner life, so often confused and at odds with itself, must come out. In revealing myself to my friends I experience a tangible sense of relief, as if I have been holding my breath, bottling up the words that might have poured out with it.

Friendship starts with the willingness to be honest. To be honest with others we must be honest with ourselves. One of the results of meditation is that we start to face up to ourselves, learn about who we really are, find out, often enough, that we are both worse and better than we thought we were. In friendship we cultivate the willingness to be honest with our friend, to reveal ourselves to them. One of the sparks that first ignited my friendship with Darren was the fact that I was honest about something, something I was embarrassed and ashamed about. We had not long moved into the community together when we started, every Thursday evening, to tell our life story.

I don't know how the telling of life stories evolved, but often enough, when Buddhists join a community or a business, they sit down together and try to communicate what their life has been like. In many ways, it is a practice of honest communication, of trying not to minimize or exaggerate. So when it came to my turn, I tried to speak as honestly and frankly about my life as I could. Some of what I said had a strong effect on Darren, and not long afterwards, on one of our weekly walks, he told me I had said things about myself that he could never have admitted to. Walking around the pond in Victoria Park, making our way through the flock of Canada geese gathered on the tarmac, past people feeding the ducks, past bored-looking men with fishing tackle, he talked about his life, about the things *he* couldn't say, the secrets and the ghosts. I remember that walk very clearly: it marked the beginning of something, the beginning of trust, which in so many ways is the beginning of friendship.

By revealing ourselves to our friends we come to understand ourselves better. Our inner life is often something of a mystery to us, full of shadowy half-knowledge, self-contradictions, and tangles. We often don't really understand ourselves until we talk about ourselves, as if what's blurred and indistinct within us comes into focus only when we try to express it to others. One of the reasons we *don't* reveal ourselves to others – especially those parts we feel ashamed of and embarrassed about – is a lack of trust and a fear of being humiliated. We feel that the other person will have one up on us, or will use our personal revelations to mock and belittle us. We feel that everyone around us is as sorted out and as straightforward as they appear, that it is only we ourselves who are a private mess and have strange sexual peccadilloes, private violent fantasies, and uncomfortable guilty secrets. Clearly you don't start revealing yourself to the first person who happens to sit next to you on the bus, nor do you tell your private secrets to someone incapable of being discreet about them (lest their mother announce them at the dinner table!). Self-revelation and the self-understanding that arises from it can only be part of a committed friendship, a friendship in which both parties are clear that they are trying to cultivate the good in each other.

Self-revelation creates trust, and whatever creates trust creates friendship. If we look honestly at our motivations we often find that what we really want is to be loved. What we often don't realize is that, if our friends are to love us, we need to be more and more transparent to them. We often think that the way to be loved is to make ourselves lovable in some way, whether by trying to be a goody-goody or a crowd-pleaser. But if we want to be loved (and, let's face it, we all do), we must start by having the courage to be open and honest, to reveal ourselves to our friend, to let who we are be seen. If, as T.S. Eliot puts it, 'there will be time / To prepare a face to meet the faces that you meet', there must also be time with friends, friends with whom we can drop the mask of sociability and custom and – like an archaeologist carefully laying out broken shards of fine porcelain and antique statuary – reveal our inner life, often both precious and broken. In friendship we can start to sort out the scattered and jumbled fragments of our inner lives and, with patient care, piece them together into a coherent and harmonious whole.

Many people, it seems to me, don't know themselves very well; they have all sorts of blind spots and funny ideas about themselves. Perhaps they haven't learned how to check out their perceptions with other people or perhaps they are blissfully unaware of the effect they are having on others. Whichever way we look at it, if we are to follow the old injunction 'know thyself', we need to know others and to be known by them. Obviously we can't see our own blind spots; we need someone who knows us well to point them out to us.

Ideally, then, being with a friend is like being with yourself. There is nothing that you can't say, no dark secrets or hidden agendas. You can be completely yourself with them, and they can be completely themselves with you. Looking back on my nursing days, I can see that the strong element of keeping up appearances brought with it a certain ongoing strain and tension. I would often have to get away from people so that I could be myself and relax. A true friend is someone you can be yourself with, someone with whom you can explore what being yourself means.

Friendship is also an energizer and enhancer. As we start to relate to somebody as a person, to lay aside our masks of respectability and fear, we start to communicate more immediately and directly. The result of this sort of communication is an excess of energy.

Communication can either drain you or invigorate you. I can feel drained by my communication either because I am not saying something I need to say or because I am holding the other person at arm's length, so to speak, out of fear. Communication is often draining because one person is not really listening. Listening is as much of an art as speaking, perhaps even more so. Very often what we call communication is really two people performing a monologue: while they say their piece you are simply waiting for your cue to say yours. This sort of phenomenon can be especially irritating within a 'spiritual' context. Someone reads a few Buddhist self-help books and, before you know it, they are dispensing cheery advice, sticking pat solutions onto your genuine problems, or, worst of all, mouthing half-baked spiritual platitudes – all this without really paying you the slightest attention. You come away from such 'communication' feeling slightly dazed and depleted … someone has been practising their communication skills on you!

You can also get energy vampires, or at times become one yourself. Energy vampires are people who buttonhole you on your way to the shops and suck all the energy out of you. They either talk *at* you rather than *to* you, or they moan and grumble and unload all their troubles onto you without any real awareness of you. These people talk in such a way that you feel if you were magically replaced by another person – or indeed by a trained and sympathetic gorilla – they wouldn't really notice any difference. However, communication can energize you. You could even say that communication does energize you and that communication that doesn't isn't really communication at all. Energy is life. It's what we mean by life. So when we talk about communication enhancing our energy we are talking about communication enhancing our life. There is no such thing as a person without energy; what we are, what we mean by a 'person', is energy. For many people that energy is blocked, bottled up, and gradually stagnating from a lack of awareness and of expression, or else it is knotted up within us, tied up in inner conflict or frittered away on trivial distractions. The relief we feel when we are honest and open with someone is a relief because it is a release. Energy by its very nature wants to move.

The real communication that takes place in friendship doesn't end with mutual self-revelation. If it did, that mutual self-revelation would probably decline into mutual self-indulgence: a kind of self-indulgence *à deux*. This unpleasant phenomenon occurs only too often, each person revealing themselves as wounded, fragile, and sensitive souls in constant need of tea and sympathy. For such hothouse creatures, genuine emotion is replaced by wishy-washy sentiment and, instead of encouraging more life in each other, they collude in accepting less. Friendship, as I have already insisted, is based on the good, and its activity consists in the progressive cultivation of the good in each other. To cultivate the good we must, as Cicero puts it, 'exert every effort to increase (our) friend's self-confidence and lead him towards a more hopeful and optimistic opinion of his own capabilities'. The main way in which we do that is through communication. In the previous chapter I said that, when we choose a friend, we need to choose someone like Darren, someone with spiritual qualities. Of course the problem with the idea of spiritual qualities is that it's easy to think we haven't got any, so we need our friends to point them out to us. This is the art of communication, to be able to say to our friend, 'That's right, you've got it, that's honesty all right, and what you said the other day – that was kindness and sympathy. I know there's further to go but you're on the right track – just keep going.'

The art of spiritual friendship is to encourage the good in each other. To encourage the good we must perforce discourage the bad. In friendship we help each other not only to augment each other's good qualities, but also to get to grips with each other's bad ones. Part of the art of communication is facing up to our respective weaknesses and striving together to overcome them. This needs to be done fairly gently, and the mix should include as much, if not more, encouragement and appreciation as it does criticism. However, positive criticism is an essential part of friendship. One of the ways in which my friendship with Paramabandhu has changed over the years is that nowadays he is much more ready to challenge me. In the old days, it has to be said, he tended to be rather too nice. He'd listen sympathetically and try to encourage me, but something was missing. Nowadays – while he is still as tactful and considerate as ever – he won't let me get away with anything. For instance, I have something of a tendency to take offence and to feel hard done by. Like most of us, I can be rather emotionally sensitive, and because of that I can sometimes feel hurt by others. In a way that's fair enough; people, even friends, will at times act insensitively or even harshly, and that is objectively painful. What isn't fair is to react to that by taking offence. Paramabandhu (who knows me well and knows all my little tricks) won't let me get away with it. Far from accepting it and there-thereing me, he tends to challenge me about it. I don't mean that he tells me off; rather, he encourages me to face up to what I am doing and to make an effort to change. That is *Friendship*.

Communication in friendship is, amongst other things, a source of ethical reproach. I don't mean moralistic finger-wagging or holier-than-thou posturing, but a hearty, sympathetic, and vigorous effort to help your friend check his or her negative habits. After all, my tendency to take offence (to use that example) causes me pain. A genuine friend will not want to see us cause ourselves, and often enough others, pain. This point goes further into the heart of friendship. If friendship is based on the good, it is in the interests of both friends not to draw each other into unethical actions. It's very easy for that to happen. Because you like your friend you will naturally want to do what they do; so if you are not careful you will draw each other into behaviour that actually erodes the very basis of the friendship you are trying to develop. An obvious example of this is gossip. Gossip is very tempting, especially if it comes to you on the lips of a friend. They arrive at supper, eyes glinting with a juicy bit of the latest gossip, and before you know it you are huddled together like two conspirators oohing and aahing and feeling very pleased with your penetrating insights into so-and-so's behaviour. By the time pudding arrives you're on to a 'them' conversation: how *they* should change, how naughty *they* are, what *someone* ought to do about it. In the low cheap glitter of scandal and gossip you don't see your own shortcomings; instead you collude with your friend in not seeing theirs.

When friendship is well established, by which I mean that there exists quite a high degree of trust between you, you can be really quite outspoken with each other. I remember on one occasion feeling very much put upon: an Order member I was living with at the time had lost his temper with me. We had been for a walk around Victoria Park. I could sense something was up as soon as we set off, and it wasn't long before I found myself, awkwardly speechless, sitting on the grassy bank of the pond being shouted at for what felt like ages. Now he shouldn't have done this, and I was aware that for a Buddhist, especially one who had been practising for many years, this was simply not on. The incident happened some time before I was ordained myself, so I knew – when I recounted my tale of woe over a digestive biscuit and a Barleycup to Devamitra in his room – that my sense of being hurt and outraged by that Order member's behaviour would be met with sympathetic concern. But when I'd finished relaying my story Devamitra simply said, 'It seems to me that you have been rather weak.' I think my jaw actually dropped with shock! I was speechless. This wasn't the response I'd been looking for; I'd been building myself up for a climax of sympathy and compassion, not criticism! At the same time I couldn't help but be impressed. I thought it was brilliant that he could say such a thing, and my appreciation and respect for him grew. What's interesting, looking back on it now, is that while Devamitra was certainly being critical, not to say blunt, I didn't experience it as being in any way harsh or belittling. It was as if he had an eye to my greater good and was communicating with that in me. The net result was more energy. Instead of going back to my community feeling a poor innocent victim, I left feeling that Devamitra was a friend to be reckoned with and that *I* had a lot of work to do.

Just as some communications drain you, others spark you off and stimulate you. For instance, friendship can stimulate you intellectually. There is nothing quite like a really passionate discussion with a close friend. Karmabandhu and I used to spend every Friday evening together. We'd park up by Waterloo Bridge, walk over to the South Bank, and spend the evening immersed in passionate and full-blooded discussion. Sometimes we would talk about ourselves or argue about some criticism one of us had made of the other. But sometimes, when the mood was on us, we would talk about *something*, often enough the 'meaning of it all' or what the spiritual life was *really* all about. At their best, those conversations were like completely ethical fights between wrestlers who, knowing their own strength and confident in their own skill, were able to fight without hurting each other.

If we're not careful we'll lose the art of conversation: the ability to sit down with a friend or two and really chew something over, really try to discuss a subject, think about it, and together get to the heart of it. Fed on a diet of TV trivia and third-rate journalism, many people never really learn how to think. Sometimes we're so keen to have opinions and so keen to voice them (irrespective of how well informed they are) that we don't actually learn anything. Or perhaps we talk endlessly about the minutiae of our feelings, as if my self and my feelings were all the world and the only thing that anyone could possibly be interested in. Yet discussion about issues that really matter is truly invigorating. I like to imagine that this is what French café society was like when Monet and Zola, Degas and Baudelaire, got together – a bunch of artists, writers, and misfits passionately discussing the new painting, the new thinking, or, like that great conversationalist Coleridge, weaving a spell of fascination, erudition, and wit all around him.

Communication is also a source of inspiration. Not only does friendship stimulate you intellectually and emotionally; it also inspires and uplifts you. Trying to really change yourself, trying to transform the negative into the positive and the positive into the still more positive, is a difficult task (to put it mildly). The Buddha himself said that spiritual growth is *the* most difficult thing you can possibly do. That being the case, we are bound to have periods of despondency, times when we just want to give up and pack it all in. Our desire to change ourselves, to make those tiny steps towards Enlightened humanity, is usually very tentative and unsure and – doubtful of our direction – we easily lose our way. What we need is inspiration, and often enough it is from our friends and our genuine communication with them that we get it. Friends should be like mountaineers roped together for a difficult climb. First, one makes headway, finds a way forward, and then the other follows suit. Whilst at one point you may feel that you have lost your way or grown tired in the difficult ascent, your friend, a little higher up, encourages you, saying, 'Don't give up – see, there is a way up over there, just put your foot on that rock and pull yourself up. It's not as difficult as it looks.' In our bad moods, usually at least one of our friends will be just a bit more in touch with the adventure of the spiritual life than we are and can reinspire and reinvigorate us. We can be inspired in all sorts of ways, from books on the spiritual life to literature, art, and music, but nothing inspires us quite like other people. To see a friend act out of a genuine desire to become more than he is, to see him speak truthfully, with integrity and kindness, is a sight of such beauty that it is almost unparalleled. One honest word, one kind encouragement, and our friend is suddenly higher up the mountain and we cannot help wanting to join him there.

Looking at my own life and my years of practice in the East End of London, one thing becomes clear: the spiritual life is nothing to do with being 'spiritual'. It's not to do with any particular time or place, costume, culture, or practice. It's not to do with gongs and bells and orange robes in the eastern sunrise, not to do with hidden caves on snowy plateaux, not to do with golden pagodas and vast monasteries, chakras, hushed voices, strange paradoxes, or secret teachings. It is not that there's anything wrong with those things; taken in the right spirit, they can help us on our way, but they are not ends in themselves. We can have funny ideas about being 'spiritual'. Some people talk about their 'spiritual side' as if it's a detachable part of their experience like their 'emotional side' or their 'sexual side'. Others find all the 'stuff' tempting – the beads and the bells, the 'spiritual accessories', religious equivalents of designer handbags or sunglasses. It's so easy to be attracted to the outer show of Buddhism, to mistake its trappings, beautiful as they often are, for the life itself. Actually, the spiritual life is a simple matter. If it is to take place at all it must take place here and now and in our most ordinary of lives. All we ever need to do is take a step away from selfishness towards selflessness – there is nothing besides this. What makes something spiritual is that it helps us on our journey away from the constriction and pain of self-centredness towards the freedom and bliss of selflessness. Meditation can do that, communication can do that, and even deciding to make someone a cup of tea can do that! In real communication we gradually feel more and more keenly for our friend; their pleasures and pains become our own, and we – who are so habitually *self*-cherishing – gradually come to cherish *friendship* instead, putting a love of friendship before a love of self.

Friendship is altruism in practice. Altruism begins with taking the trouble to enter into the world of another person. It begins when we start to communicate with someone, to take a genuine interest in them. So often our life resembles a house on a tiny plot of land: a little brightly painted bungalow surrounded by a bit of lawn and a few carefully manicured flower beds. Around our little world there is a white picket fence; it is a fence that marks the boundary between my little world and yours. Your little world is broadly similar to mine, except perhaps you have a pond with a few lethargic-looking goldfish in it and the odd garden gnome. The world is like a never-ending suburbia; row upon row of little plots of carefully tended 'me' all bounded by little white picket fences. What we call communication is very often just a kind of talking over the fence. I stay safely in my little world and you stay safely in yours. Sometimes, of course, we take things a bit further: we put up signs saying 'Do not enter!' 'Say nice things only!' or 'Beware of the bad temper!' Some put up barbed wire, erect lookout posts, and patrol the territory with guard dogs and flashlights; others buy a welcome mat and then lock all the doors. Communication is a two-way process. First we need to be open and honest, inviting our friend into this little world of ours (even though we feel the place is a bit scruffy and in need of attention). Secondly we need to invite ourselves over into the little world of our friend. Instead of being content just to lean on the fence and chatter, we need to jump over it. Of course their little world is a bit strange and alien at first, so jumping over the fence is always a bit of a risk. Even when you're invited you can never be quite sure what you'll find. The little white fence we put around ourselves is made of fear and custom and a desire to remain safely in the known. Friendship is an invasion, a going over the frontiers of self into other; it is jumping over the fence, sometimes even kicking it down.

A real friend will occasionally *insist* on communication, perhaps especially if they feel that what you are doing is hurting yourself or others. Of course, by this point enough trust has been established to do that, and, for all your resistance and complaining, you have in effect agreed to be in communication come what may. I've done a bit of fence-kicking myself, and all my closest friends, from time to time, have done the same for me. Anyway, the keep-out sign that we sometimes put up to protect ourselves often has a postscript printed in small letters at the bottom: 'If you really care about me you'd ignore this sign.'

I hadn't expected the fine art of communication to form such a large part of my spiritual life. I'd assumed that other people would, in a sense, be peripheral, that the real progress would be made sitting cross-legged on cushions. The Buddhist tradition seems to assume the same – that breakthroughs, when they happen, will tend to take place in meditation. So it's easy to think that all this stuff about communication is all well and good but it's not the real thing, not where the action *really* happens. That is until you look, once again, not so much at what the Buddhist tradition *says* happens but at the stories about what *does* happen. According to those ancient sutras, plenty of people make breakthroughs in meditation – no surprises there – but many make their decisive breakthroughs in communication, especially in communication with the Buddha. Sometimes it's the briefest of meetings, just a few words, enough for a realization to take place. Reading the sutras, we can find it difficult to see how. You take them down from the shelf hoping that, by reading what the Buddha said to such-and-such a person, you'll experience that insight into how things really are, which is the goal and direction of Buddhist practice. But you find the language formalized and repetitive, perhaps even a bit dull. And even when the meaning is quite clear to you, it's difficult to see what all the fuss is about. If you have done the communication exercises like I have all these years, or more so if you've devoted much of your life to friendship, you'll know that words are only part of the story. It was the Buddha's *being* that made all the difference – that gave the words, so seemingly simple on the page, their life and force. He was said to have the elephant gaze – if you addressed him, he would, like an elephant, completely turn to face you, give you the whole of his attention. For someone to give you his attention so fully, to be aware of you and your aspirations so deeply, imbues his words with a weight and profundity that no printed page (however accurately reported) could ever do justice to. It was the Buddha's being that gave the words he spoke the effect that they had. The aim of every Buddhist is to communicate like a Buddha: to change their life completely and to communicate that change to others. You start by becoming more aware of yourself *and* your friend and, by communicating together, deepening that awareness.

So the art of communication can take us all the way. For myself, it has taken me from what I experienced as the stultifying lack of genuine communication in the small town in which I grew up, to the communication exercise on that first retreat and the friendships I have made since then. I've learned to be open and honest, at least to some degree (and these things are always a matter of degree). I've developed trust, been energized and stimulated, inspired, admonished, challenged, and encouraged. What progress I have made has been due so much to my friends and my communication with them. And it can go on and on, into realms of ever deeper communication, ever deeper friendship. Eventually it can take us into the heart of the deepest mystery of all, the communication of Enlightenment.

10

FRIENDSHIP IN TROUBLE

*Friendship, as I have just admitted, will inevitably involve
distress, and quite often at that.*
   Cicero, *On the Good Life*

When I was at art college the thing I enjoyed most was *starting*
a painting, especially a big one. I'd go down to the workshop,
buy some two-by-four, cut it to the desired length, and, with the
help of some glue and a few nails, build a stretcher. After that
I would carefully stretch the canvas: pulling it tight with my
thumbs and stapling it to the wood, every now and then checking
the tension by tapping the canvas with my finger until it rang
like a kettledrum. Then I would haul it up to my studio, lay it
on the floor, and, with a six-inch house painter's brush, plaster
on layers of thick white ground. When it was dry I would stand
the freshly prepared canvas against the paint-spattered wall of
my little studio, mix up some paint on top of an old kitchen unit
I'd found in a skip, pour meths and turpentine into jam jars,
and get ready to paint. For a while I would just sit staring at the
vast expanse of pristine white canvas. Amongst the debris of
my studio – the piles of charcoal drawings, half-finished mugs

of tea, paint rags, and old newspapers – it seemed to promise *everything*, so new it was, so white and resplendent. Gazing at it, I felt like a jockey in the starting box, full of high hopes and great expectations. Then I would begin – dabbing, scraping, brushing, and ragging in the paint; walking back and forth, squinting to check the tonal balance and quickly roughing in the basic shapes and forms. In one sudden onslaught the painting would leap into a daze of colour: splashed vermilion against scumbled cobalt and ochre, Naples yellow and viridian dragged over china white; paint spotted, layered on in thick gobs or poured in misty washes of violet-grey. On the newly prepared canvas the paint sparkled and shone, each brush mark clearly etched onto the white ground. It was exhilarating at first. Later on, after that first dash, that first heady rush – my hands full of brushes and my head full of ideas – it would get difficult. The paint, as I applied it layer over layer, would begin to clog and congeal. The colour at first so new and luminous would muddy and mix. Bright verdant greens and blues would get fouled up in a quagmire of lurid reds, and soon great swaths of the canvas would decline into a soupy mix of utterly unpromising dirty browns. Whole areas of the painting would have to be scraped off and started again, and the painting's early promise would be swallowed up in the sheer stubborn difficulty of it all. Just about every painting I've ever started has, at some point or other, reached this kind of impasse, a stalemate in which everything I attempted seemed hopeless. At such a time I would turn the painting to the wall and, feeling dejected and despondent, cycle back to my flat in Brixton, the seeming failure of the painting mocking me all the way.

Friendships often go through the same kind of process; after first embarking on them with great éclat and high hopefulness, they start to get difficult. Cicero knew it – anyone who has really tried to develop friendship knows it – 'friendship … will inevitably involve distress'. Actually it's often a good sign, a sign that you are getting somewhere. After all, much of the time we habitually keep our communication superficial. We meet up with our friend for the occasional cappuccino and pastry and, instead of talking, we chat, often never going further than catching up on the latest news: the film we saw last night, so-and-so's new girlfriend, the latest story about our noisy neighbours – all very pleasant, no doubt, but eminently forgettable. Of course chatting like this is often a good way in. Certainly it's better than portentous seriousness or awkward silence, but if we get stuck at that level we won't develop friendship. Going beyond superficiality will, however, cause problems somewhere along the line.

Looking at my own spiritual life, one thing I can say with confidence is that I have become more substantial, more weighty. This, it seems to me, is the opposite of superficiality. One of the main ways I have put on weight, so to speak, is by deepening my relationships with others, especially with friends, over a period of many years. In making and then staying friends, I have had to reach deeper within myself. I've had to learn how to be honest and kind, loyal and impartial, courageous and intimate; in a word, I've had to grow and become more substantial. At the same time, my friends have helped me to grow: they have pointed out things about me that I have been reluctant to acknowledge; they have reflected me back and helped me see how I am seen by others. It has not always been a pleasant process but, painful though it has sometimes been, I would not change it for all the world.

I think the experience of weight is characteristic of our best readings of great literature. I remember reading *Hyperion* on the train to Colchester. I was on my way to see Toby after many years of estrangement. I'd been memorizing the poem for some time and – reciting it under my breath as I gazed out at the changing landscape – every word was suddenly full of meaning, weight, *gravitas*. There was nothing ponderous about it or heavy (in the pejorative sense), but it seemed full of being, Keats's being. The analogy of reading a poem with true friendship is a good one; as with any decent poem, you need to work at it, give it a bit of time and effort, not give up on it because it doesn't give you immediate gratification. And if you were to try to *write* a poem of substance, you'd need determination, persistent concentrated effort, and, of course, imagination.

When you try to create something, when you *commit* yourself to creating something – a painting, a poem, or a friendship – all sorts of difficulties are bound to arise. Before we commit ourselves, we have hardly started. Perhaps we're lucky enough to have an initial flush of enthusiasm – like when I first slapped the paint onto my new white canvas – but it's only later that the real work begins. When the inevitable difficulties *do* arise, we have a choice: to engage with them and overcome them or to react to them and be dictated to by them. For some, one whiff of a difficulty and they're off to find another friend; others slowly back down, phone you less often, and when you do meet up they try to steer the conversation away from any trouble spots. Some talk a lot so as not to say anything; others smilingly say 'we really must meet up', yet manage to find excuses why they never can. Some of us flare up, others clam up, some take offence, and others lose their rag.

Our minds are like a vast labyrinth of corridors along which many doors present themselves. We usually rush along these corridors driven by the force of a lifetime's habit (perhaps, who knows, even *lifetimes* of habit). As we hurry through the corridors of our mind, we habitually tend to choose particular doors: someone criticizes us and we rush through the door marked 'anger'; a friend doesn't seem especially pleased to see us and we go through the door leading to the descending spiral staircase of 'nobody loves me'. All this can happen so fast that we are not really aware we are doing it, and the more we choose the same door, be it self-pity or mock indifference, the more it becomes natural to us, part of who we are. With the help of meditation and friendship, we can gradually start to notice that we *are* choosing doors and that we tend to choose the same doors over and over again. Perhaps, as we progress, we start to get some sort of insight into why we choose those particular doors. The most important lesson we learn, however, is to stop, so to speak, in the corridor of our mind and consciously start to choose one door rather than another. As the German philosopher Friedrich Nietzsche puts it, 'This is the *first* preliminary schooling in spirituality: *not* to react immediately to a stimulus, but to have the restraining, stock-taking instincts in one's control.' So when our friend criticizes us we stop habitually choosing the door marked 'withdrawal of trust' and start choosing a different one, like 'What is it you are trying to say?'

Actually, our situation is worse than this. Not only do we tend to react habitually, but other people tend to react habitually to us. So very often a kind of negative feedback loop arises between you and me: when I say B, you react by saying A, and when you say A, I react by saying B, and so we go on, getting nowhere. In this way we create each other: we confirm and reinforce in each other the tendency to react in habitual ways, to choose the same old doors to go through again and again.

In essence, the spiritual life is about transforming ourselves from someone who reacts habitually to someone who responds creatively. To respond creatively, we need to stop and see that we are in fact reacting and, by some deeper insight, find a new way of acting, a new way of being. The experience of moving from the reactive to the creative is a very liberating one. In my experience it can be like opening a door onto a new world. Suddenly I find myself in a whole new terrain, as if through some secret door the cramped corridors of my habitual mind have given way to a new open space – a space of exploration and discovery.

Friendship is what happens when two largely reactive minds come together and help each other to become creative. Much of our life is habitual and reactive, not perhaps crudely so but habitual and reactive none the less. Most of us don't fly off the handle at the slightest provocation, but we probably do spend much of our time in a fog of unawareness, of ingrained reactions, habitual responses, and superficial communication. And it's not that we don't have our creative moments, moments when we are genuinely kind, thoughtful, and considerate, but the force of our habitual reactive tendencies is so strong that they easily overwhelm them. What we need is help, help to see when we are reacting habitually, and help to remember that a different response is possible. Where we get that help from is friendship.

I remember one particularly striking example of this with one of the men who lives with me in our new community in Bethnal Green. Though we tried to communicate and be friends, though we tried to live together harmoniously, we often did not get on. One day I went to the café where he works to meet him for lunch. Sure enough, we had hardly managed to sit down and order a decaf before we got into an argument over something or other (albeit in a restrained, half-spoken, under-the-breath, *English* kind of way). Before long it was *A Fistful of Dollars* all over again. Both of us had got to that grim mutual stand-off, like Clint Eastwood and whoever it was standing at opposite ends of the street, cigar between clenched teeth, six-shooter at the ready. I was just considering the merits of walking out in a huff when I reached into myself for something deeper. All my senses had been telling me to go on the offensive or to run but instead I let go of my pride and my fear and, finding new resources within myself, managed to discover a new way forward. The tension that had been building between us dropped away entirely and, having both got to the point of walking out, we found ourselves in a new space of mutual sympathy and understanding. We both learned something that day.

So often in my friendships with Karmabandhu or Paramabandhu (especially with Karmabandhu!) I get to the point where something like this happens, where I have to start facing up to my limitations, my reactions, and my petty preoccupations. I'm in one of my black moods and Paramabandhu insists on turning up in my room and talking to me about it. Those dreaded words, 'What's going on?'… that quizzical face when I say (lie), 'Nothing …' Or Karmabandhu with his knock-you-straight-on-the-nose-with-the-truth approach. How many times (poor bloke) have I reacted to him, defended myself valiantly, or counter-attacked, only to realize that he was right in the first place and have to eat my words. If you think friendship is about nice people saying nice things to each other, think again! Friendship is about two people helping each other transform themselves from reactive to creative. It can be a messy business.

You could say that friendship goes through a series of four successive phases. The first phase for many is the phase of projection. This is when you project onto your friend qualities that are not really there, or at least not to the extent you think they are. It is a phase of friendship tinged with romantic idealization – when, as in a new love affair, you only see the shiny attractive aspects of your friend. In this first phase of friendship you are wearing rose-tinted spectacles.

The second phase of friendship is one of reaction. As you get to know someone, you inevitably discover that they are not who you thought they were. Your projections break down and you are left with a pretty ordinary human being replete with annoying habits, mood changes, inconsistencies, and weird idiosyncrasies. At this point you usually start to react with irritation, aversion, or boredom. It feels churlish to say so, but friendships fairly often go through periods of boredom when you run out of stories to tell or can no longer be bothered to tell them. Perhaps you have run out of common ground – you can't talk about your mutual interest in alternative medicine for ever – or the rose-tinted spectacles have fallen off. It's important to recognize what is happening and just stay with it, talk about it, say the next thing, find a way through, help them put some shelves up. Nowadays with our 'thrills-and-spills' approach to life, we give up too easily. The important thing is not to be put off when you move into phase two, because phase two is a stage of turbulence. You start to disagree with each other, to polarize each other, to get bored by each other – whatever way you tend to do it, you start to react. Actually, I think a lot of people don't ever make it past phase one. I know people who are very friendly but don't seem to have any *friendships*, as if they intuit the turbulence to come and avoid it by filling their diary with a hectic whirl of social engagements.

The phase after the phase of reaction is friendship proper. In this stage reactions still occur, but the capacity to be creative is, more often than not, enough to deal with and to overcome them. The fourth and last phase is that of ideal friendship; this is characterized by ongoing mutual creativity, trust, and unswerving fidelity. Phase four may seem a long time coming. After more than ten years of friendship with Paramabandhu, I am only just now starting to experience it, at least some of the time. The main thing to do is concentrate on moving gradually on to the next phase of friendship; you cannot force the pace.

Of course these four stages of friendship are just a rough map of the terrain, not an exhaustive guide. Every friendship is different. My friendship with Paramabandhu, for instance, never went through the first stage and only briefly touched on the second. Somehow, over the years of living together, he sneaked up into the third without me noticing. In contrast, my friendship with Karmabandhu has been characterized by turbulence pretty much all the way (except for a very brief stage one). Both of us are adherents to Emerson's philosophy, 'Better be a nettle in the side of your friend than his echo', so our friendship has always been a rather fierce one. Other friendships have fallen somewhere between the two.

The transition from phase one to phase two of a friendship can be very gradual or rather sudden. It usually takes place when you spend a block of time together, especially if you start working together or – an absolute classic – when you go on holiday together. There is nothing quite like going on holiday with a friend. When I was young it was, as often as not, a make-or-break experience. Suddenly you can't get away from them! They annoy you at the breakfast table, insist on hogging all the driving, and generally get on your nerves. They discover that you are an anxious traveller, that you insist on arriving hours early for the plane, that you go sullen if you don't get your way, and that you are mean with money. More recently, I remember setting up a Buddhist business with a friend I had been seeing every week for some years. We had got on like a house on fire when we met up for our weekly soul-searching chat; we worked together every day for a few weeks and the house burned down! Phase two of the friendship had been inaugurated.

Aggression is a problem in our lives, one that all of us experience to some degree or another. Unfortunately we very often find it difficult to own up to it. When I first got involved in Buddhism I tended to think I was a good guy: I tried not to interrupt Maria when she was talking; I'd get the milk and papers in the morning if she was tired; I was well mannered and politically correct. I was a touch neurotic, perhaps, and prone to be moody, but in general I felt I was a good guy. Any difficulties I thought I had were socially acceptable ones: vulnerability, sadness, that sort of thing. I hadn't counted on aggression. As I became aware of the depth of it within myself I was shocked, to say the least. My identification as a good guy started to switch to an identification of myself as a bad one. This made it very difficult for me to own up to my aggression, to acknowledge it within myself, and to begin to transform it. Apart from the *mettā bhāvanā* practice, the main way I have learned to take responsibility for my aggressive and critical impulses, as well as how to use them creatively, has been friendship.

Dealing with conflict and polarization is an art. Like any art form, the only way to really learn it is to do it. If you take friendship at all seriously you are bound to get into conflict and disagreement from time to time. Friendship, then, is an important arena, or a sailing ship in which you learn to navigate the choppy waters of disagreement, hostility, and anger. The first rule of any genuine spiritual life is to take full responsibility for our mental states: they are ours and *our* responsibility. Nobody made us angry or made us feel small – we did it to ourselves. Children run up to their mothers crying, 'He made me do it.' Adults, to be worthy of the term, must stop blaming others for the way they feel, be it their parents, their friends, or the state. This is not as easy as it sounds; the temptation to blame goes very deep. Acknowledging and taking responsibility for the darker and less congenial aspects of ourselves is made still more difficult by any tendency to irrational guilt. What guilt does is *complicate* everything. We fear owning up to our hatred or whatever, lest awareness of it confirm our worst fears about ourselves – that we are a *bad* person.

As a young man going along to the Buddhist Centre every week, attending retreats, and meditating every day, I gradually became aware of what I can only call a basement of aggression. In it, hidden away from view (my own as well as others'), I stored all sorts of boxes: boxes full of anger, competitiveness, criticism, and hostility. I tended to invite people only into the respectable front room of my psyche where – perched on a comfy sofa – I hoped to please them, entertain them, and, most of all, be liked by them. Of course, occasionally, as we talked there would be an almighty crash as a pile of boxes locked away in the basement of my psyche fell over, spilling their contents and creating a racket. My friend would look up in alarm: 'What was that?' I'd make excuses ('It's only the neighbours'), change the subject, and try to present myself as an easy-going, laid-back, non-judgemental kind of fellow. As I got to know people better they'd start to ask awkward questions: 'Have you got a basement? I could swear I heard something.' 'Oh no, it wasn't me, it must be you …'

As you get to know someone better you start to relax with them. As you relax with someone you find that you can no longer behave as you used to; your tendency to want to give a good impression becomes unsustainable, simply too tiring. At this point things start to emerge from the basement. It is by dint of willpower that we keep things hidden from other people. As we get to know someone and to spend more time with them, our capacity for censoring ourselves diminishes. We start to get irritated and to find fault. We start to notice aspects of our friend's behaviour that we hadn't noticed before; we see sides of them we just hadn't realized were there. At the same time they start noticing all sorts of things about *us* that they hadn't realized before. This is what happens on holiday, isn't it? You can't cover up the fact that you are grumpy in the mornings or that you find your friend really irritating when they do *that*! So both parties can start to feel rather disillusioned and perhaps even start wishing they had formed a friendship with someone else in the first place. What is actually happening is that the friendship is going deeper. In phase two of a friendship you have to start to talk about the contents of your own particular basement. Come to that, you'll probably have to start talking about the contents of theirs too.

Not that our respective basements are just full of nastiness; we relegate to the basement anything that doesn't fit in with our view of ourselves. I have been struck at times by how much warmth and *mettā* I habitually hide away – finding expressing it particularly embarrassing. And we can feel as threatened by our potential for love and goodness as we can by our capacity for meanness and harm. Anger, though, is especially important to deal with because it is potentially so destructive. At the same time it is important to recognize that there is a lot of energy tied up in anger (which is really just another way of saying there is a lot of ourselves tied up in anger). We need to learn how to curb the destructive tendency of anger, without losing our energy and drive. People tend to think of Buddhism as essentially peaceable, which indeed it is: Buddhism's primary ethic is non-violence. However, Buddhism is not about becoming a 'nice' person, neither is peacefulness a passive or docile state. We need to *transform* our aggression, not stifle it. We learn to do that primarily within friendship, and the first step, as in so many things, is awareness and acknowledgement.

In friendship we learn to speak our mind. This doesn't mean dumping our emotional negativity on to our friend or pretending we haven't got any. Gradually as we practise friendship we make our first faltering steps in self-expression, in saying what we really think and feel. In so doing we are bound to make mistakes. We will sometimes insensitively overdo it and sometimes fearfully underdo it. Working at getting the right balance really is an art and one that is vital to the development of friendship. If we always just blurt out our anger and negativity our friend will instinctively withdraw from us. If we try to keep things nice and polite the friendship will lack any real momentum or substance. Anger *expressed* can destroy a friendship in a single unpleasant row: anger *repressed* can destroy a friendship by slowly poisoning it with resentment. Friendship, as I've said, is the training ground in which we learn the fine art of communication, a forum in which we start to find ways of really speaking instead of just talking, of really listening instead of just hearing.

The golden rule is to discuss, not argue. Arguments are largely a waste of time; you blurt out things you don't mean, take offence over nothing, and create mistrust. You don't learn anything by arguing. Your aim in an argument is to win it, not to learn from it. The first thing to do, then, is *seek clarification*. Instead of jumping to conclusions or taking offence, we need to really try to understand what our friend is trying to say. It's amazing how many arguments come about through simple misunderstandings. We either mistake what people mean by what they say or we mistake their reasons for saying it. What we need to do is to start saying simple things like, 'When you say such-and-such what do you actually mean by that?' or 'I take you to be saying so-and-so – is that true?' Very often when conflict starts to arise in communication the whole interaction starts to speed up, with reaction ricocheting off reaction. What is needed is to *slow things down*. To return to my analogy of mental corridors, we need to stop rushing through the same old reactive doors, take stock of ourselves, and, by seeking clarification, find new ways out of conflict and back into harmony. To do this we need to check out our perceptions and observations of our friend in the spirit of open enquiry, as well as try to understand their perceptions of us. Again and again, in my experience, friendship only survives if it is motivated by an ideal. When we become more interested in the truth and less interested in whether we win or lose the argument, then we are becoming spiritual friends.

Often enough, antagonisms simply dissolve once we have sought clarification. We realize – sometimes rather shamefacedly – that we had jumped the gun, that what we were reacting to was a chimera, a phantom of our own creation. However, sometimes we find that we still have criticisms, or that our friend still has criticisms of us. Often it is an unspoken criticism that stops friendship in its tracks, blocking the free flow of *mettā* like a pebble in a hosepipe. Unexpressed words create blockages. The trouble is, criticism can easily get out of hand, spiralling down to grumbling fault-finding and nagging – and a Buddhist nag is no better than a non-Buddhist nag. In the early days of my involvement with Buddhism I kept hearing the term 'positive critical feedback'. It sounded like something to do with electricity, but I knew that for Sangharakshita it was a jewel, something precious. What he was getting at was that, in order to grow, we need positive (that is, emotionally positive and warm) critical (discerning wise judgement) feedback. Personally I have benefited enormously from this. I have come to see why it is so precious: it helps you to grow. One of my deepest needs is to be taken seriously. When Paramabandhu or Devamitra give me positive critical feedback, I feel they are relating to my highest aspirations, taking them seriously and, in so doing, taking me seriously. Positive criticism (as opposed to habitual fault-finding or cynicism) is about helping your friend to grow. After all, who is above positive criticism? Who cannot learn from it? Who can really do *without* it?

What we are aiming at in friendship is to be able to listen to criticism objectively and non-reactively, sifting out what is and what is not true, and to be able to say to our friend what we think and feel (including what we think and feel about them) kindly and honestly. The more we do these things the more our life will be enhanced, our friendships deepen, and our sympathy for others grow.

Again and again, in my dealings with people I find myself encouraging the person I am speaking with to *talk* to someone, to find a helpful way of telling them what it is they perceive about them. We have so much richness of perception. We are like fabulously sensitive radar systems continually taking the minutest readings of each other. We walk around a veritable treasure trove of perception, intuition, and feeling, much of which, could we but find an effective way of communicating it, would be of real help to those around us. Of course, our readings of those around us are often misreadings, and we find as we start to communicate more fully to our friends that they say more about us than about them. Like so many points in this book, it is difficult to tell the truth about communication to more than one person at a time. Some of you reading this will need to learn to speak more, to say what's on your mind and get it off your chest. Others will need to hold back a bit, to think more carefully before they speak, and to take the other person more into account. There are no fixed rules in the art of talking. However, its aim is clear: an ever-deepening harmony, and therefore an ever-deepening friendship.

Then, of course, there is apology. As I have already stressed, we are bound to make mistakes. Mistakes are part and parcel of what it is to be human. The issue is not whether we make them but whether we learn from them. Friendship therefore involves apology, the willingness to go up to your friend cap in hand, so to speak, and say, 'I'm sorry.' We can be so proud, so unwilling just to say, 'I'm sorry, I've made a mistake.' Saying sorry is a spiritual act. It involves a willingness to go beyond ourselves, to let go a bit of our habitual self-cherishing and pride. When we apologize we re-enter the human race, we reaffirm our connection with others and the impact that we have on them. I remember the day after I had been grumpy at a meeting – sending off vibes of ill will and bad temper – feeling ashamed and, having been gently chastised by a friend, taking someone by the hand and saying, 'I'm really sorry I was such a negative presence yesterday. I was trying to say something but I was in a terrible mood. Please accept my apology.' Simple words, but they brought me back to life again, saved me from the narcotics of self-pity and loathing.

For friendship to thrive, we need to take risks in communication. Apologizing is a risk, asking a friend for their honest opinion is a risk, and pointing out where you think they are being harsh to someone is a risk. We might fail. Just as we make mistakes with our friends, so our friends will make mistakes with us. They are bound to hurt us from time to time, just as we are bound (even with the best will in the world) to hurt them. So we need to learn not only to apologize but also to forgive. To forgive is to let go of our basic instinct to retaliate to a real or perceived hurt. When we forgive we renounce blame, resentment, and bitterness. As Charlotte Brontë puts it, 'Life appears to me too short to be spent in nursing animosity or registering wrongs.' A genuine act of forgiveness is one of the most beautiful, most fully spiritual acts we can ever perform. To be a friend we need to learn how to forgive, for without forgiveness there can be no friendship. Perhaps we should forgive but not forget; after all, we need to know if our friend tends to be quick-tempered or careless with the books we lend them – but if we want friends, we must forgive, again and again and yet again.

Friendship is based on mutual sympathy, literally a feeling *with*. The growth of friendship is a growth in mutual sympathy and imaginative identification. However, we must face facts. None of us feels with our friend all the time. We are too self-centred; if we weren't there would be no need to practise the spiritual life. We may experience sympathy from time to time, but only too often our natural capacity for human sympathy is blocked or distorted by our habitual patterns of reactivity and unawareness. To work on these patterns necessarily means working on them in relationship with others, for it is primarily in relation to others that they occur. As we do this, we start to transcend egocentricity. We start to see beyond the small world of 'me' and start to feel, to resonate, with an 'other'. Our habitual reactive patterns, whatever they may be, are what separate us from others. They are what constrict and limit us. When we seek clarification we go beyond ourselves; when we apologize and forgive we go beyond ourselves; and when we try to imagine how *others* feel we go beyond ourselves. This is what human evolution really consists in, a going beyond ourselves, and each time we do it we grow from less to more. Friendship is the whole of the spiritual life because, at its most elevated, it requires that we change the whole of ourselves.

Friendship may inevitably involve distress, but if we seek to learn from it we will grow as a person and as a friend. Difficulties in friendship are like manure, not pleasant in itself but essential if you want something to grow. As I write, I think about two or three friends I have known for fourteen or so years. I have lived with them, argued and disagreed with them, challenged them, apologized to them, forgiven them, and been forgiven by them. We have grown up together spiritually. I can now go to one of them – Paramabandhu, say, or Karmabandhu – and know I will be understood and loved. Not loved in a soppy, sentimental kind of way, but vigorously met, encouraged, taken seriously, and believed in. I am still challenged by them and we still occasionally argue, but I experience a developing trust and understanding between us, which is one of the greatest pleasures of my life. They are the friendship equivalent of the paintings I used to struggle with at art school.

The best painting I ever did, the one I was most satisfied by, was the one I found the most difficult and testing. I had worked away at it for weeks and it just seemed to get worse. Resolving one problem only created another and at one point I could understand why

Cézanne, in an impotent rage of frustration, sometimes threw his paintings out of the window of his studio – and once had to ask his son to poke one out of a tree with a stick so that he could carry on with it. I had just got to the stage of throwing it out of the window myself when I seemed to find a new depth of determination. I found myself painting with a rigour and sensitivity that I never knew I possessed. I seemed to go beyond my usual habitual self and discover new depths of creativity previously unavailable to me. Fifteen years later the painting hangs above my desk and still gives me a sense of pleasure and satisfaction.

11

MEN AND WOMEN

Some are attracted to Buddhism because they find in it the confirmation of their ideas. It would be better if they were attracted by it because it refutes their ideas.

Sangharakshita, *Peace is a Fire*

I hardly noticed Maria to begin with. In the first year at art school we were all given a bit of wall to work on and told to get on with it. Of course the first year students got the worst walls, so most of us found ourselves in a converted school gym divided up into six little rabbit hutches of white painted chipboard. I was in the bay next door to Maria painting something based on the sinking of the *Belgrano* and the *Sun*'s infamous 'Gotcha!' headline. My urge to change the world had, by the time I got to Goldsmiths, found expression in political art of the rather naïve, preaching-to-the-converted kind. Maria, nervously smoking in the studio next door, was hiding from her fellow students behind a large nondescript canvas of mermaids or some such watery-looking figures. She was eighteen at the time, wore pink National Health Service spectacles, and was always (it seemed to me) rummaging around in her bag for her cigarette lighter. She was just out of school, painfully shy, physically awkward, and rather boyish. Her hair was shorter than mine; in fact, later on, when we visited the same Cypriot barber together we got pretty much the same haircut. She wasn't actually working on the large canvas; it was a kind of screen, a barrier, a security blanket. Behind it she was painting a small picture of her sister sitting at a table with the family's Tibetan spaniel. She never finished it.

 All that could be seen of her as she worked was a plume of whitish grey smoke. One day I rolled an apple behind the screen of her untouched canvas and suggested we go and have a coffee. Gradually a friendship developed. It was an alliance of misfits, really. I was four years her senior, but somewhat ill at ease in my new environment. I felt like a country boy from the sticks, a provincial. I remember someone in my studio telling me they were reading Proust, 'in the original French, of course'. I'd never met anyone who'd read Proust, original French or not. Sam had never mentioned him and no one in Henley-in-Arden would ever have heard of him. I felt out of my depth, unsophisticated, and (worst of all) uncool. For some reason I asked Maria to cut my hair. I hadn't known her long when I asked her, but perhaps I sensed a fellow creature. I was lonely, I suppose. She came over one evening, scissors in hand. 'I've never done this before,' she confided, with that gleam in her eye that I later came to recognize as the reckless confidence and intelligence that lay behind her shyness. Great tufts of hair fell on the carpet while I chatted maniacally. What she gave in silence I made up for with words.

 Soon I was spending all my time with her. In the college canteen, among the polystyrene cups and egg-mayonnaise rolls, in the studio, going to galleries, cooking bacon and potato stews, and smoking dope. It was a period of discovery for both of us. I was reading anti-sexist literature and trying to find a boyfriend; Maria was reading *The Colour Purple* and deciding whether she was a lesbian. It was in the long hot summer of that first year at college that, half in flight from art school, we set up studio together in the short-lease house that she and a few other students rented nearby. It was in that summer that I rediscovered classical music (as a youth I had played the trombone in a local orchestra), so the hot days were spent listening to requiems – Verdi, Britten, Mozart – and painting in the studio, its patio doors opening on to an unkempt back lawn where, at lunch time, we would lie in the sun, drink tea, and talk. Occasionally her mother would come round. She was a small, frail German woman who always encouraged her daughter to paint. She would prop one of Maria's enigmatically beautiful paintings against the sofa and gaze at it in a kind of awe. She was very sweet to me, spoke in a charming cracked German accent, and had a will of iron. Sometimes she'd bring the Tibetan spaniel.

It was Maria who started it. It was she who got me to read Christopher Isherwood's *My Guru and his Disciple* (the book that first introduced me to Buddhism – even though it was about Hinduism). When she was still at school she had visited the Buddhist Society in Eccleston Square with her mother – a broad-minded but committed Catholic – and I think her sister once had a boyfriend who had become a Theravadin monk, so by the time I met her Buddhism was a bit familiar to her. It was Maria who then got me to read *Zen Mind, Beginner's Mind* (which I loved, despite not being able to understand it) and it was Maria who suggested one cold November evening that we go to this Buddhist place in Bethnal Green.

Every week we would cycle from Brixton, through Kennington, across Vauxhall Bridge, past St Paul's, up into Whitechapel, then on to Roman Road, arriving at the Buddhist Centre breathless and usually late. We were as inseparable at the Buddhist Centre as we were at college. I can't remember why she didn't come with me to that frozen converted army barracks in Hemel Hempstead on my first weekend retreat; certainly she came on the next one. I remember us sitting under a blanket together outside the kitchen drinking tea. Soon we graduated from the newcomers' class to the regulars', a switch from Wednesday to Tuesday, from twenty-minute meditations to forty, and from hardly a whiff of religion to incense offerings, chanting, and bowing.

Come the following summer, Maria went on the two-week summer open retreat run by the Buddhist Centre (Battle retreats they used to call them – no symbolism intended – because they took place in a converted prep school in Battle, Sussex). I chose to go to Padmaloka for my first longer retreat. It was a retreat for men. That was the beginning of something, too.

It had come as something of a surprise to discover – as I got more involved with the Friends of the Western Buddhist Order – that quite a lot of emphasis was placed on single-sex activities for men as well as for women. Why I should have been surprised I don't know. After all, most religions tend to keep the sexes apart to some degree, whether in monasteries or convents – and anyway I accepted the value of women-only spaces – so why not men-only ones? By the time I set off for Padmaloka I had met Gary outside the Fallen Angel so I was at the height of my involvement with gay politics and anti-sexism. I was therefore well acquainted with the need for women-only spaces; in fact Gary and I conducted much of our romance trying to secure them. Apart from the afore-mentioned picket, we also helped run a crèche next to the women-only space at the London Lesbian and Gay Centre (the LLGC) – now an upmarket wine bar, I believe.

I was suspicious of men-only spaces; they smacked too much of the gentleman's club or the rugby changing room – all that male bonding which my bible at the time, *For Men against Sexism*, had expressly warned me against as being the very foundations of patriarchy. Of course this was in those bygone days before

Robert Bly came on the scene with his *Iron John*, sweat lodges, and hairy men. Now we talk about the men's movement, male archetypes, the male wound, even the male menopause; you heard none of that in those days, or at least I didn't. Perhaps nowadays we are beginning (once again) to see the value in men spending time together as well as women. I hope so. I hope the men's movement doesn't just regress into the occasional weekend in the country, playing bongos, sitting round a camp-fire talking about vulnerability, and doing group hugs. Whatever happens to the men's movement, back in those days spending ten days just in the company of men was something I had never done before in my life – or had ever thought of doing.

As a child I made no distinction to speak of between girls and boys, that is, apart from a rather worrying physical attraction to the latter. I was if anything more disposed to spend time with girls than boys. My brothers and I never got on: I was extraordinarily sensitive, and they – no doubt sensing that I was different in some way – teased and bullied me. My relationship with my father was distant and strained, and my grandfather (who lived next door) positively disliked me and made no bones about it. I was, I suppose, a mummy's boy. I gravitated towards my sister and to the girls at primary school, with whom I became very popular. Later on, as I moved into the female-dominated profession of nursing, I spent more and more time with women. Looking back, although my best friends have always been men, generally speaking I tended to feel that I had more in common with women. I was a sensitive, rather effete young man, and as a result I tended to feel threatened by other men. Anyway, their primary concern seemed to be standing around in small groups admiring parked motorcycles: 'Look, Bob, it's a Ducati, nice one, eh?' Either that or it was my Dad shouting at the football on the telly: 'What do you think you're doing, Charlton? Kick the blooming thing!' or they were drinking lager, dating girls, or working on the coaches up in the yard. My brothers, my father, the coach drivers who worked for the firm, the doctors on ward round – they all seemed to speak a different language from me, one I thought I would never learn or understand. Women, in contrast, seemed to me to be so much more communicative, emotionally available, and lively, so I tended to gravitate towards them.

Despite all this, for some not very well-formed reason, when someone told me about the forthcoming retreat at Padmaloka and that it would be suitable for someone at my level of involvement, I was keen to go. I arrived feeling a little ill at ease and insecure. Would I fit in? What would they think of the fact that I was gay? Would I find I had nothing in common with them after all?

The retreat was led by a masculine and, to my mind, authoritarian man. He was a tall, handsome, well-built man who, apart from leading the meditations, taught yoga somewhat after the manner of an Outward Bound instructor. He tended to repeat stock phases like 'Beast!' and 'Get those thighs working! They should be pillars of steel, not rice puddings. Pillars of steel!' As the retreat went on, I began to dislike him more and more. I felt that here was just the sort of man I had been oppressed by, a typical 'man', just like my brothers and my Dad: insensitive, bullying, and macho. Despite my sensitivity, I could, on occasion, be curiously outspoken, so, one afternoon after lunch, I asked if I could speak to him. We wandered off and sat on the front lawn in the warm sunshine. I took a deep breath and told him I didn't like him. I don't really know what I expected him to say – perhaps I assumed he'd get angry or something; as it was, he simply looked me in the eye and asked kindly, 'Why not?' In a way it seems unremarkable to me now but the fact that he didn't react to me, didn't take, or indeed give, offence, was at that time a kind of revelation. Significant life experiences are always difficult, if not impossible, to put into words. In the description of them, the vital content, the experience, is always missing. Someone overhearing our conversation that sunny afternoon sitting on a green lawn in a Norfolk village would probably have found little to remark upon. For me it was one of the formative experiences of my spiritual life and something I will always feel grateful for.

For a long time he just sat and gave me his attention, looking steadily at me and leaving me space to talk. I suppose we fell into a sort of impromptu communication exercise. This time, though, there was no stifled laughter or suppressed giggles; instead I experienced a great upsurging of emotion such as I had never felt before. The simple question 'Why not?' had acted on me like the breaking of a spell, as if until that moment he had been merely a screen upon which I projected my complicated feelings about men and about myself as a man. As we looked at each other, a loneliness I never realized I had surged through me in waves of grief and pain; my fear of men, my estranged relationship with my brothers and father, the whole complicated confusion of emotion that was my life seemed to course through me like – as I came to say later – an avalanche in reverse. Talking with Surata, I knew that here was a man I could trust, a man who was a man, who didn't get his masculinity from pushing around the weak or from being macho with his girlfriend. Here was a man – a heterosexual man at that – who valued male friendship. As we sat and talked I felt my view of the world, especially my view of men and women, start to change. On that day, sitting by the oak trees in the garden at Padmaloka, I started to experience the value of friendship between men.

Despite the women's movement and feminism, and despite even the more recent men's movement, one of the most prevalent views in today's society is that men and women are the same. They may have different-shaped bodies with different biochemistry but basically we feel that, in all the most important respects, men and women are the same. This idea is a relatively recent one. Over the last fifty years or so there have been unprecedented changes in the roles ascribed to men and women in society. This change is still going on today, and if anything the pace of change is accelerating. Attitudes to work and the family as well as to sex and career have changed almost beyond recognition, even since my parents' generation. It feels a long time ago now that women were expected just to get married and look after the home as my mother was, or that men like my father were expected to be the sole breadwinner. These changes have been both very fruitful and rather disorienting. What it means to be a man or a woman is very much up for grabs nowadays.

Up for grabs or not, the basic assumption is that men and women are the same. Perhaps of late there has been a bit more talk about the differences between the sexes, but usually they're seen as fairly superficial ones, like the difference between Camembert and Brie. So when, in this book, I talk about friendship, your assumption may be that I make no distinction between the sexes when it comes to discussing with whom to make friends. However, an observant reader will by now have noticed that most of my personal examples of friendship are of those with men, and may start to wonder why that is so. You might suppose that it is simply coincidental and therefore think no more about it. You might think that perhaps I don't like women very much or even that I have something against them. Some might even go so far as to assume that my lack of friendships with women is tantamount to a more or less conscious sexism. Others will come to a rather different conclusion: 'Well, we know he's homosexual, don't we – and, well, you know, he would have friendships with men, wouldn't he?' So perhaps it is time to approach some of these questions head-on.

Actually, when I talk about friendship, especially in the expanded spiritual sense in which I use the term, I am talking principally of friendships within the sexes and not between them. Perhaps it's high time I 'came out' and said why.

I should start by saying what I'm not saying. I am not saying that friendship between men and women is impossible. I have, after all, already emphasized, and perhaps it cannot be emphasized enough, that friendship is a response of the good to the good. In more Buddhist terms, friendship is expressed in mutual *mettā* and based on a common ideal, the ideal of going for refuge to the Three Jewels: the Buddha, his teaching, and all those who have realized it. Although, in many ways, my friendship with Maria was an alliance of misfits – taking refuge in each other from the oh-so-clever art-talk and sophistication that surrounded us – mixed in with it was something deeper, a nascent integrity and a search for truth and value. At art school in those days 'value' was a myth, a patriarchal one, possibly, or one propagated by the bourgeoisie. For Maria and me it was something we yearned for and, in part, our attraction to each other was an attraction (almost without knowing it) to that. It was because of that resonance, that mutual half-conscious yearning, that we cycled to the Buddhist Centre every week. So even in those early days there was between us something of the good, some idealism that we responded to in each other.

The urge to go for refuge to the Buddha, the Dharma, and the Sangha is the urge to discover and live out value. It is the deepest urge of the human heart, so deep in fact that it transcends everything, all differences of age, race, class, and gender. It is the urge within humanity to perfect humanity. Friendship, spiritual friendship, is in essence that urge to perfect the good resonating between two particular people. Any two people can therefore become friends, the old and the young, the black and the white, those with everything in common and those with hardly anything in common. It is a central principle of Buddhism that any human being can become a friend to any other human being.

And yet … my friendship with Maria was a very mixed one. By the time I had my experience talking to Surata on the lawn at Padmaloka, she and I had moved into a council flat in Brixton. I remember coming back from that retreat full of energy and raving to her about it, going so far as to teach her and Gary some of the yoga I'd learned – 'from this really nice bloke who led the retreat' – right there and then in the lounge. But she and I often argued, usually, for some reason, in the kitchen. She would feel that I had turned against her or had withdrawn from her. I would feel that she made too many demands on my time and attention. Sometimes Gary would be upstairs as we argued in the kitchen – he said it was like going out with a married man. In many ways our relationship was like that; we fell out, made up, fell out and made up again just like a married couple, except there was no sex (but then some of my married friends complain about the lack of sex as well). When it comes to arguments there are, broadly speaking, two different kinds. One is productive, where facing up to the problem, talking it through, and resolving it produces more understanding and greater harmony. The other is unproductive and circular and talking merely compounds the problem, taking you both round into tighter and ever tighter circles. Many of our arguments fell into the second category. The rows and resolutions were in part because we were young and, all things considered, immature. Looking back on what was for both of us a painful and confusing time, I think the difficulties had a lot to do with the fact that we were (and indeed still are) a man and a woman. In a way it was not personal. We liked, even respected, each other. She was considerably more talented than I was as a painter and both of us were in one way or another committed to finding truth and value wherever it was – in art, in friendship, or in Buddhism. We tried to be friends but something kept getting in the way.

I didn't realize it then, but men and women are different and difference – after all – makes a difference. I don't know whether men are from Mars and women from Venus, but certainly much of the time in those days Maria and I did seem to be living on different planets (albeit in the same flat). I'd been only too aware how different from other men I felt, but I hadn't realized that the differences between men and women went deeper. My feelings of incomprehension, even aversion, around men were psychological, to do with my own insecurities about being a man in the first place. The difference between Maria and me was something else. But before I say more about the difference between Maria and me – and between men and women in general – it would be as well to remember that, in the most important respect, there isn't one.

Men and women *are* the same in the most fundamental sense. Both wish to be happy (though both often go about it in the wrong way), both want to feel their lives are going somewhere, and both wish to avoid suffering. Both men and women have the potential to become Enlightened and both have a deep, though often buried, urge to grow and develop as human beings. All men and women have the capacity to tread the path of spiritual evolution by practising meditation, developing friendships, studying, engaging in devotional ritual, and any number of other things that help individual human beings transform themselves. However, men and women are also different. They have a different outlook on life, different priorities, different needs, and different issues to work with. Men's and women's journey along the spiritual path will therefore be different. Despite the fact that men and women tread the same path towards Enlightenment, how they tread that path will be broadly different.

Of course, many would argue, 'Yes, men and women are different, but that difference is a productive one. Surely we can use that difference to learn from and help each other.' At art school the 'gender issue' was always in the air as a problem to explore, a stick to beat people with, or a 'concern' to make art about. In Buddhism, when it comes to gender, the goal of the spiritual life is to transcend it. The Buddha was only biologically male. He wouldn't have identified himself as a man as opposed to a woman. The Buddha was just himself, fully awake, psychologically neither male nor female – a new species unto himself. So the goal of spiritual life is to transcend gender. Our aim as we practise the Dharma is to gradually exemplify the best of both masculine and feminine qualities. The Buddha was, so to speak, the very best of both worlds. These 'best' qualities – of masculinity and femininity – are spiritual qualities, and neither is the exclusive domain of men or women. The question then becomes how, in practice, we are to develop these qualities. The feminism I got involved with back at the LLGC assumed that the way forward for men was to be more like women. In the heyday of my anti-sexism, I tried to take this on; I tried my best to be a 'sensitive' and 'caring' male, to listen to and learn from Maria, but this only made matters worse. Really it was just a pretence, another expression of my discomfort with being a man. To attain genuine sensitivity and care I needed to take another path, one that would lead me to spend more and more time with other men.

In my experience, men's well-meant desire to help women often gets in their way and, sadly, all the sexes manage to do after a certain point is inadvertently trip each other up, as Maria and I did in our little flat in Brixton. I couldn't understand why she wanted to talk so much about how we were or were not communicating and Maria couldn't understand why I felt the need to be so separate. It was as if we were speaking subtly different languages, with neither of us really seeing that we had different expectations – of ourselves, our friendship, and our life. Maria must have felt that all I ever wanted to do was get away from the realities of human emotion and intimate relationships. I must have felt that all she ever wanted to do was talk, that in her mind my wanting to do something inevitably meant that I was withdrawing from my friendship with her. I remember feeling an unhealthy mixture of guilt (that I wasn't giving her what she wanted) and resentment (that I wasn't doing what I wanted). Looking back on it now, there was some truth in both our views of each other, but we couldn't learn it from each other – it was all too complicated. So we caused each other quite a lot of confusion and pain. Not that things in our little flat in Brixton were all bad; we often enjoyed each other's company, had a laugh, and even learned from each other, but we kept getting stuck. We both genuinely wanted to help each other in the spiritual life. We both valued honesty and friendship, but we didn't realize that what was helpful to one was a hindrance to the other. We didn't realize that the best way men and women can help each other to progress spiritually is by getting out of each other's way.

What men and women both need is to spend more time with their own gender, and in that context to develop the best of their own qualities, male or female, and the best of the other's. It's not that men need to become more like women or that women need to become more like men; both need to become more like the Buddha. To develop the best of masculine and feminine qualities you need to spend as much time as possible with members of your own sex. When men and women are together they often simply let the opposite sex do the work for them. Obviously I'm more aware how this works with men than with women. In the company of women, men tend either to put on a show of 'masculine' qualities – qualities they don't really have – so as to impress the women, or they are so nervous of being thought macho and sexist that they forget to be men at all. Instead of developing the best of masculine and feminine qualities, men and women can sometimes pick up the worst of them from each other, so that we sometimes end up with cut-throat businesswomen and pathetic floppy men. Men need to develop their drive, refine their aggression, and learn how to care and sympathize. On the whole they won't do that if there are women around to do the feminine side for them. Women, on the other hand, need to strengthen their nurturing qualities, and to develop drive and initiative. They'll find all that difficult if they keep going to men for security.

Men and women tend to misunderstand each other, except perhaps that women think they understand men, which is part of the misunderstanding. Men (in my experience) badly misjudge women, as often as not, seeing them as frail emotional creatures who need them to come and save them, which, in my experience of women, is hardly ever the case. As I've already made clear, human beings tend to misunderstand each other; what is happening between men and women is that the tendency is being exacerbated. Of course relationships between men and women are not always as colourful as mine and Maria's were back in those art school days. As often as not, men and women get along well enough; they may never see that something is missing in their relationships with the opposite sex or that anything could be gained from spending more time with friends within their own gender.

I think that, at their most typical, friendships between men and women tend not to get past what I have called the 'projection' phase of friendship. This is hardly surprising considering how deep those projections go. The first thing someone will want to know about a newborn baby is whether it is male or female, and most mothers will tell you that their boy children and girl children are very different, even though they may take great pains to treat them the same. Even if biology doesn't play a part in gender psychology (and I think it does), the different weight of perception, expectation, and assumption placed on boys and on girls from the word go is immense.

Men and women notoriously project onto each other: whether it's earth goddess, Prince Charming, mother-substitute, he-man, *femme fatale*, tough guy, or virgin queen. These projections go very deep and, because they are not based on real awareness but are the result of a one-sided psyche trying to right itself, they often cause a lot of trouble. Even when they don't seem to cause trouble, when men and women get on well enough, the tendency to project onto the opposite sex limits spiritual growth, tending to keep us subtly, though deeply, over-identified with our particular gender. Obviously the tendency to project certain characteristics onto men and certain characteristics onto women is more marked and polarized where sexual infatuation is involved but, even leaving that aside, projection between the genders is an almost instinctive aspect of their relationship with each other, part of the 'war of the sexes' that we used to hear so much about. Men go to women for mother-comfort, women go to men for protection and security.

What would help would be to have a more realistic view of the differences between men and women. I have come to think that most people are really rather naïve when it comes to their understanding of the opposite sex; they mistake their projections for perceptions and often settle for superficially pleasant relationships based, not on mutual *mettā*, but on mutual fantasy. For myself I tended to be attracted to friendships with women because I felt they understood me and sympathized with my problems and insecurities (it's mother again!). But I also felt that I had to hide a part of myself, the more aggressive and masculine side of myself. I began to hate being seen by women as a 'safe' man – in effect as 'one of the girls'. I think this is part of what caused the problems between Maria and me. I'd be wanting sympathy and attention and so on but I'd also subtly resent the feeling of being somehow diminished as a man because of it. She in turn would pick up that resentment, feel insecure, and want to talk about it. I'd react to her insecurity by feeling hemmed in, and so we would go on. I have met quite a few men who seem to be almost irredeemably silly about women. In the company of women they become like little boys vying for attention from mother. These men are usually somewhat patronizingly sentimental in their attitude to women, tending to go to them for 'succour', for 'there-theres', and for 'communication': the sort of thing that any self-respecting women must surely be sick of! One woman friend of mine tells me she can spot a man on the lookout for a mother-substitute a mile away.

Men and women often gravitate towards each other because they enjoy the more or less overt flirtation and subtle infatuation that so often goes along with it. Even when sex itself is clearly off the agenda, there is often, in the back of the mind, the vague possibility of it. This comes as no surprise. Nature has so arranged things that men and women will be attracted to each other for obvious reasons but, as I've already made clear, this sort of attraction is not the basis for spiritual friendship. Strange to say, you often see a sticky kind of romantic overinvolvement in gay men's relationships with women: my relationship with Maria was a case in point. When (heterosexual) men are around women they often become sexual competitors with other males, as if an archaic biology still courses through the blood, albeit disguised by the thin veneer of civilization. This can be very noticeable when you introduce a woman into a group of men. You'd been getting on fine, then suddenly – almost without your noticing it – you're competing with each other for her attention.

Whether it's out of sentimental projection or Tarzan instincts, men can find it difficult to be themselves around women.

Women, on the other hand, I am reliably informed, can become strangely passive around men, leaving the initiative to them, resenting them for taking it, or in some cases competing with them for it in the first place. When friendships between the sexes do get beyond the projection phase of friendship – and I have stressed that they can – it is almost inevitably because both have well-developed friendships with their own sex. You could say that most friendships between men and women are friendships in potential. This time, though, what is wanting to make them full-blown spiritual friendships is not time and circumstance but established strong friendships within the sexes, and maturity. All the men I look up to have positive and genuinely healthy relationships – sexual or non-sexual – with women, but all of them are conspicuous for their intimate friendships with men; and it is those relationships that are primary.

Not long after the degree show that marked the end of the three-year college course, in the context of which Maria and I had become friends, I made the decision to move into my first men's community – above the London Buddhist Centre. The community was for men only, and women were not allowed on the premises. Maria didn't like this – neither, I imagine, did my somewhat bemused mother. I loved it – eventually. I moved in, primarily, for purely positive reasons. I was a Buddhist; I wanted to become more of a Buddhist and, looking around for how one might do that, I decided that moving into a single-sex community was the way forward.

But why move somewhere where women – including my poor old mother – weren't allowed to visit, even, I discovered, for a cup of tea? In those days I was acquainted, and in broad disagreement, with radical lesbian separatism. I suspected it was an expression of man hatred disguised as a political philosophy. I am still in disagreement with it (assuming that it is still current, which it may not be). I did not believe then and I do not believe now in complete gender separatism, especially if it is an expression of hostility to, or fear of, the opposite sex. What I think is needed for men and for women is a more realistic understanding of the differences between the sexes and a healthy ongoing single-sex dimension to one's life. Anyway, living in a men's community didn't – by a very long chalk – completely separate me from women: I didn't avoid them in the street or hide beneath tables in the restaurant next door, nor did my relationships with women (including Maria) become frosty and cold. I continued seeing Maria, working alongside women at classes, and, yes, visiting my mother. The community had a bell and an intercom, not a portcullis and a moat! Of course, not everyone can or indeed would wish to live or work in a single-sex environment, but, if you want to develop spiritual friendship, some sort of ongoing single-sex environment, be it study groups, retreats, or simply weekends away, are vital, whether you are married or single, hetero or homo. But perhaps I am running ahead of myself.

As the days and months wore on, I started to get my bearings and get to know the men I was living with. Karmabandhu (although he wasn't called that then) was already living there; he moved in eight or nine months before me. I'd already met him on that first retreat, but our friendship was still in the future. Actually, he'd visited the flat quite a bit before I moved out because, not long after that first summer retreat that Maria went on at Battle, she and Karmabandhu started going out with each other. So, for the time being, Karmabandhu was a friendly face, as far as you could see it behind his scraggly mop of long dark hair. Paramabandhu was there too and it was good to have him around, though, because he was fully occupied in training to be a psychiatrist, I didn't see that much of him.

Things were not perfect in this community by any means. Among other things, I gradually became aware of some quite serious breakdowns in communication between some of the men in the community, as well as a tendency for some of them to be rather separate and lacking in intimacy and warmth. This seemed to be reflected in the environment. We sat on broken plastic chairs in a rather austere, not to say uncared-for, environment. The floor was uncarpeted hardboard, we had no curtains, and some of my fellow community members' rooms were not very aesthetically pleasing, to say the least. At first I didn't take much notice of this, assuming it was all part and parcel of the spartan and pared-down life that I took the spiritual life to be. However, I gradually came to realize that, apart from the purely financial considerations, it was in fact an expression of a lack of care for each other; the hit-and-miss nature of the cooking only confirmed me in this.

Just putting a load of blokes together isn't enough, as probably any army barracks or boys' public school will amply testify. Looking back at those days, I see that what had been created, at least in part, was a rather one-sidedly male environment (in the psychological sense of the term). Good conditions, like a single-sex environment, are vital to making spiritual progress, but they are not ends in themselves; they have to be made use of. If you just put a bunch of immature men together you'll easily end up with squabbling boys and messy bedrooms. I'm not sure what happens if you put a lot of immature women together, but certainly what both sexes need is the example of more mature men *and* more mature women. Two sure signs of maturity are a lack of dependence on the opposite sex and the capacity to develop close friendships within one's own sex.

Looking back on it now, I remember one particular turning point. I'd been feeling that the community was not, after all, the spiritual community I'd hoped it would be. Then one night, when we all got together for community night, a disagreement broke out between some of the men. Reaction followed reaction and pretty soon we were getting nowhere. All of a sudden I found myself speaking with a new voice. I found I was able to put things in a way that helped the injured parties understand each other better and helped to re-establish harmony. But it wasn't that I tried to smooth everything over and make it nice again, rather that I was able to challenge people without losing sympathy for them. It was a taste of maturity. That evening I experienced within myself a new potential, a strength that was also a softness, a combination of male and female.

Over time, closer friendships developed in the community, conflicts were overcome, and even the cooking improved! Karmabandhu and I started our daily tooth-brushing sessions, talking into the night, playing the fool, and at one point committing ourselves to friendship. And gradually, between us all, a strong feeling of comradeship arose. I learned a lot in that first community I lived in, from how to speak out in a group and face conflict, to how to develop friendship. I even began to learn – old-fashioned though it might sound – to become a man.

My developing friendships with men, living with them, communicating more deeply and honestly with them than ever before, had all sorts of spin-offs. Having felt so different from my brothers, so antagonistic as a child, I came to see how alike we were, how clear it was that we came from the same pot. My relationship with my father improved. In the years up to his death I put much more effort into getting to know him and communicating with him. I would go and talk to him in the shed when I visited. (He was just about always in the shed; in fact when he died it felt like he was simply spending more time in the shed than usual.) He listened to Radio 3 on a large old- fashioned teak radio he'd bought in a sale and done up. We would talk about the garden, and Mahler, and how he couldn't make head nor tail of contemporary music. Gradually a mutual appreciation developed. He perhaps never came to terms with my sexuality – oddly for him, he had found out by reading a letter from Maria I must have left open on the kitchen table – but the closeness between us was self-evident. Even my relationships with women improved – I became less dependent on them for approval and sympathy, less painfully overinvested.

There is a certain kind of richness – a depth and a closeness – which perhaps can only be experienced in friendships between men or friendships between women. I cannot fully describe it (in a sense this whole book is an attempt to describe it) but I know it and have felt it in my friendships with men. I didn't realize I was missing it when I was young, when Maria and I fought it out in the kitchen. But close friendships with men were missing then just as they are present now. They are my deepest friendships.

And Maria? She found it difficult to understand my decision to move into the community at first. She perhaps felt hurt and rejected for a time, and for a while things between us were a bit strained. After all, both her boyfriend and her best friend were, within a matter of months, living together in what must have felt like an out-of-reach men-only castle, the towering red-brick walls of the converted Victorian fire station perhaps confirming the impression. But gradually our friendship found a new and healthier basis. Our appreciation and respect for each other which, even when things were difficult between us, had always been there, began to grow again. And the mutual affection we'd always felt – from killing ourselves laughing because we'd smoked too much dope together when we first met, to an evening in town reminiscing over a coffee – soon found expression again. But to grow up we each needed to walk a different path, albeit to the same transcendent goal. For myself, I still choose to live just with other men, sharing a room and sharing a life with them. For me spiritual friendship is the rarest thing. It is rare between anyone, between men *and* between women. However, it is most likely to be found within the sexes, not between them. If you're searching for rare jewels, the best place to look is where you're most likely to find them.

Not that moving into a single-sex community is necessarily something you do once and for all. Karmabandhu moved out. He decided to move to Rome to help create a Buddhist centre there. And he decided, after years of community living, to go and live with Maria before his move to a new culture, climate, and language. They shared a flat in Hackney, and I was invited to the flat-warming party. It's strange how things come around. The flat reminded us both of our flat in Brixton, its grand view of the city skyline, the inevitable smell of urine in the lift. But we were different people. As I sat watching the easy affection between Gary and her as they talked, or as Maria came over and chatted to Karmabandhu and me, I felt we had all in our own way grown and changed.

Maria and I are still friends. Recently she came to join the team that runs the introductory meditation class. This meets up for forty minutes before the class to talk about how the class has been going and to check that all the jobs – making the tea, putting out the cushions, taking the money – are covered. This class is the same newcomers' class that Maria and I cycled to fifteen years earlier, so we have, in a sense, come full circle. Listening to Maria introduce herself to the team that evening, I was struck again by how much she has changed. The shyness that once hid her behind a large canvas at art school has completely disappeared; she has become confident, self-assured, and self-possessed. She still has her full-blooded easy laugh, her zest for life, and her almost reckless full-throttle capacity for communication, but she has grown – she has become more. One thing that particularly struck me that evening was what a woman she had become, a real woman. I can't help thinking that this has a lot to do with her spending much more time with women – she hardly ever did back at art school – and developing friendships with women. But perhaps now I am trespassing onto her story, a story that must remain her own.

12

A FRIEND TO LOOK UP TO

I say great men are still admirable; I say there is, at bottom,
nothing else admirable! No nobler feeling than this of
admiration for one higher than himself dwells in the breast
of man. It is to this hour, and at all hours, the vivifying
influence in man's life. Religion I find stands on it; not
Paganism only, but far higher and truer religions, – all
religion hitherto known.

Thomas Carlyle, *On Heroes, Hero-Worship, and the Heroic in History*

'Well,' I thought, standing in front of the slightly shabby front door of his flat, 'here goes.' I rang the doorbell, and waited. This was to be my first meeting with Urgyen Sangharakshita, head and founder of the Western Buddhist Order, 'Bhante', as his followers called him.

I'd not long moved into the afore-mentioned community. Bhante (a term of respect meaning 'teacher') was living next door in a small one-bedroomed flat. I was twenty-five and had been practising meditation for about a year and a half; Bhante, who must have been sixty or so, had been practising it for upwards of forty years. I'd like to say of course I'd read all his books, but I hadn't. I knew about them; they were on sale in the bookshop at the Centre. I'd even dipped into one or two, but I found them rather difficult and, to be frank, somewhat dull and old-fashioned. In those days reading, especially reading books about Buddhism, was still a bit beyond me. I had listened to tapes of talks Bhante had given – albeit ones given way back in those heady 'tune in, turn on, drop out' days of the sixties and seventies. On that first weekend retreat we listened to one entitled 'Breaking through into Buddhahood'. It had a very strong impact on me. Listening to that slow, carefully measured voice was like hearing a close friend tell me who I really was and what I really needed to do to make progress. The experience was startling: 'Who was this man who seemed to know the deepest aspirations of my heart?' I had seen him, of course; he had introduced a talk at some Buddhist festival or other. I noticed his physical movements were as slow and considered as his voice was and, combined with his calm authority, dignified bearing, and sensible jacket and tie, they left me with the distinct impression of a firm but benign junior school headmaster.

Now I was actually going to meet him. I was *extremely* nervous for some reason. As a young teenager I had always wanted to meet Barbra Streisand, or perhaps Jon Pertwee and a few Daleks. Like most adolescents I had my heroes and heroines. When I was a little boy I developed a great admiration for Julie Andrews. I'd seen her in *Mary Poppins* and had started to worship her since then. She seemed so good and clean and gentle, floating around singing cheery songs and doing good works. She was my hero. In fact, when at a children's party I was asked by one of the adults who I would like to be like when I grew up I replied, 'Julie Andrews'. This was a disastrous social *faux pas*, to say the least, but it wasn't that I wanted to be a woman: I just wanted to grow up with her good qualities. At that time, I suppose, Julie Andrews was the nearest thing I could find to a saint.

The desire, even the need, to look up to someone is a natural and healthy one. It is innate in us, part of what it is to be human. Most youngsters tend to worship heroes; not usually *spiritual* heroes, of course, not the great figures of history like Florence Nightingale and Admiral Nelson, or artistic giants like Shakespeare and Michelangelo; mostly it's pop stars like Madonna, Hollywood actors like Brad Pitt, or celebrity footballers like David Beckham. When I mentioned to my young nieces that I'd met the Spice Girls (albeit briefly), they gazed upon me with all the breathless awe and adoration of someone who had seen the face of God.

I suppose as I stood there, waiting for the door to open, I was nervous because I was about to meet a hero of mine, albeit one of a quite different calibre from Barbra Streisand or the latest Doctor Who. Hero though Bhante was, he was hardly the archetypal guru-figure that I had hoped to meet when I first came to the Buddhist Centre. He wore no robes, beads, or sandals; he didn't have a long white beard; and he came from Tooting. Despite his unremarkable appearance there was something about him that I was attracted to. Perhaps I sensed a great man.

The person who answered the door wasn't Bhante. It was, I presume, the person who had been spending time with him just before I arrived. 'Go in,' he said, 'through there.' Then suddenly, in the dark cramped little corridor next to the coat hooks, there was Bhante unresplendent in an open-neck shirt and grey cardigan. 'Hello, Bhante,' I stammered, not completely sure if I should call him that, 'My name is Ian.' I went to shake his hand but thought, 'You don't shake hands with a spiritual teacher, you fool!' And, having raised my hand, I dropped it again – thus causing a bit of confusion. Bhante, seeing my intention, had started raising his hand in response to mine and for a moment we both came to a perplexed standstill there in the hallway. 'You had better come in,' he said in that carefully enunciated way of his, each syllable clear and crisp and etched in the air like black musical notes written on buff-coloured paper.

We were in the lounge. I didn't feel easy enough to notice things much: the desk by the window, the gas fire humming quietly away, the shelves of books, the framed reproduction of Holman Hunt's *Scapegoat* hanging above the mantelpiece. Bhante sat one leg crossed over the other on a wooden chair by the fire looking very much at his ease. I sat on the long, not especially comfortable sofa – that is, I sat on the very *edge* of the long, not especially comfortable sofa. For some reason I had the uncomfortable sensation of being a child again, as if my mother were out in the kitchen preparing Sunday lunch and I'd been left with the awkward and onerous task of entertaining the vicar.

I immediately plunged into a discussion on William Blake, about whom I knew nothing whatsoever. Bhante, I was well aware, had a great admiration for Blake, and for Coleridge, come to that, and for Bach and for … but I couldn't talk about any of them, not really. So my attempts to get Bhante talking about Blake's poetry fell on stony ground. Probably he realized that I didn't know what I was talking about, or was it that he was wondering why I was sitting on the edge of the sofa looking for all the world like a startled rabbit? Things were not going well. I can't remember what else I tried to talk about, but gradually my attempts at conversation ground to a halt and I can only remember thinking, 'When will this ever end!' At one point he took off his glasses to clean them. I took it to be some sort of esoteric teaching like the ones I'd heard that Zen masters went in for. Of course, I intuitively knew what it meant – it was a clear sign that he hated me and no longer wanted to see me. Well, I thought, by now utterly crushed, I hate you too! The bell rang again for his next appointment, and though in literal truth I walked out of the door, metaphorically I crawled out on my hands and knees, groaning.

I suppose I took it for granted that Bhante could see straight through me, that he could see into all those horrible dark crevices of my psyche. The little new-grown shoots of love and devotion I felt towards him were mixed up with nettles and thorns: authority projections, the desire for a father-figure (someone who would tell me all the answers and make everything all right), even perhaps the vestiges of a jealous God who, yes, could see right through me and, no, did *not* like what he found. Also a tendency to self-dislike meant that at first I felt lessened in his company, his size making me aware how small I felt. No wonder the meeting was a disaster, I was looking for a father-figure, a problem solver, a teacher, a perfect friend, and a very nice wise old man all rolled into one!

Of course I had looked up to people before. I remember feeling slightly in awe of Mrs Beasly, my maths teacher at high school. Despite her declaring that I was 'mathematically ineducable' (which was, after all, simply the truth), there was something about her that I respected and looked up to. She seemed to relate to me as a person, not as a schoolchild, and there was something *grown-up* about her, something, alas, that could not be said for many of my teachers. At art school I became devoted to one of my tutors, Elma Thrubron. She would spend the first half of the afternoon going round giving tutorials and the second half going around trying to find her handbag. She would come to my studio, light up, her hand shaking as it habitually did – and sit and look at what I had been doing, which in the early days she obviously didn't like (though she never said so). Once, finding nothing worth commenting on in my work, she gave me an excellent tutorial on the coffee stains left on a plastic tray that happened to be leaning against the wall of my studio – I was mesmerized. She loved painting, and in her husky Lancashire accent would speak in rhapsodies about the wonders of colour. 'I would put a bit of yellow over in one corner and just *let it grow* and then a bit of cerulean, just a dab at first

– then I'd let it grow, let the colours start talking to each other: what were they wanting alongside them, some madder brown, some crimson?' Despite her incomprehension of my early political paintings, she always encouraged me. When finally, at the end of the second year, I discovered what and how I wanted to paint (whilst drawing trees one day, with coloured pastels) it was Elma who was the first to recognize it.

Thinking back on Mrs Beasly and Elma now, I feel a vivid sense of gratitude. Both helped me, not primarily to become a better mathematician or a better painter – though Elma certainly helped me in the latter – but in a more important and far-reaching way. They were *role models*, at least to some extent, and their encouragement helped me to become a better person. In their different ways they helped me find the courage to be myself, to believe in myself. I in turn admired and respected them.

So far, in this book, I have mainly concentrated on friendships with peers, that is, with members of the same sex who are, broadly speaking, on the same level of development as ourselves. I have talked about how Paramabandhu, Karmabandhu, and I grew up together and how we helped each other to grow up: we could call these friendships 'horizontal' in nature.

Now, though, we come to a new species of friendship: friendship with those we look up to and admire. We could call these 'vertical' friendships. In a spiritual context, these are the friendships we have with someone who is more developed than we are, someone who has more experience of the spiritual life and a deeper insight into it. This kind of friendship may be especially rare nowadays. So few people experience themselves as living within a vital spiritual tradition, one that has a genuine transcendental goal, an authentic path towards that goal, and in which at least *some* people have made significant spiritual progress. Christianity has for many years now been in decline, and probably relatively few people go to church expecting to meet wise teachers in the context of a vital spiritual tradition. The ensuing New Age of 'pick and mix' spirituality, from crystal healing to sweat lodges, looks unlikely to fill the gap, so, finding ourselves in a spiritual vacuum, we go shopping. The places of worship have become carpet warehouses or bijou accommodation.

Even our secular teachers aren't afforded much respect nowadays. Having got rid of God (that authority figure in the sky), we have learned to resent anyone telling us what to do or how we should live. Strange, though, given all of that, how so many of us have inklings of devotion and admiration for someone we look up to. Whether it's that strange sense of warmth and gratitude for an old teacher, the adolescent love we had for our big brother, or our devotion to a football hero, we all have a need for a friend we can look up to. But we are no longer in the playground where as a child we would naturally gravitate to the children we admired, be it the gang leader or the especially popular girl. As we grow up our natural urge to be friends with someone we respect and admire becomes more problematic. Disillusioned with our parents, our teachers, even our heroes, we either don't experience admiration any more (sometimes with good reason) or we overlook it or cynically debunk it.

Those tender feelings of hero worship, which many of us experienced as children, are easily crushed. Some people get stuck in adolescent rebellion, thinking they see aggressive authoritarianism everywhere. Some don't grow up in the first place, handing over personal autonomy and common sense to the first person that makes spiritual claims for themselves. Some have inappropriately high expectations of the people they look up to and feel constantly let down by them. Some harbour unacknowledged feelings of envy behind a façade of liberal equality. Some enjoy nothing more than cynically knocking their heroes down to size, whilst others would agree with Tina Turner that 'we don't need another hero'. Actually that is precisely what we *do* need.

We need to learn how to look up to people – to find that vital mixture of respect, receptivity, personal autonomy, and freedom which, as with so many things, we learn in friendship. But it's not as easy as it might sound; like so much in modern life, it's become complicated. I looked up to Bhante, but, in those early days, when I was still a starry-eyed twenty-something, there was no way I could develop a friendship with him. I was too much in awe of him (and awe, after all, is a species of fear). Anyway, he was too far off; the gulf between us – in age, life experience, and, most importantly, spiritual insight – felt unbridgeable. When I sat down for supper with him one evening (the community had invited him round), I sat in awkward silence. He said to me: 'And where have you come from?' I was thrown into a panic. Was it another Zen test? What did he mean 'Where have I come from?' Originally? Metaphorically? Psychologically? What was he getting at? Things were going wrong again. This wasn't the beginning of friendship: it was the beginning of indigestion.

It was in quite another quarter that I discovered a friend to look up to. And, anyway, Bhante has tended to discourage the kind of supercharged guru–disciple relationship that occasionally gets mixed up with Buddhism. He has always encouraged people simply to make friends with those who are just a little more advanced along the spiritual path than we are – that is, people who are near at hand, who can help and guide us along the way. What is needed, if we want to learn *how* to practise the spiritual life, is friendship with men or women who have practised it a bit more intensively than we have. They don't need to be the Buddha incarnate, a saint, or a genius, just someone a little further along the path. 'The spiritual life,' Bhante once said, 'is caught, not taught.' Where you *catch* it is from a friend you look up to.

I caught it from Devamitra. He was living nearby when I moved into my first community, and for one reason or another we started meeting up occasionally. I must admit I didn't particularly look up to him at first; in fact I thought him rather peculiar. We tended to have long and sometimes heated discussions, usually about the value of psychology, a subject of which I was very much enamoured and of which he definitely was not. Off we'd go for one of our evening walks around Victoria Park, arguing passionately about whether or not I had an 'inner child' and, if I did, what I should do with him. He thought I should concentrate on becoming an adult. I tended to think that I should be more in touch with the child within, nurture him, buy him little gifts, possibly. One day, probably after arguing about the merits or demerits of my most recent therapy guru, he said he'd like to be my friend. I felt distinctly uncomfortable. Here was a man considerably older than I was – one of these 'Order member' people, a friend of Bhante's by all accounts – and here he was saying that he wanted to be *my* friend. It seemed really weird! Despite the fact that he was heterosexual, I feared that some sort of sexual shenanigan was in the offing; if not, I reasoned, what was he after? I made a few compliant noises to fob him off, but didn't take him up on his offer.

I don't know what it was that brought sex to mind that afternoon when Devamitra said he'd like us to become friends. Nor did I realize that the seeds of friendship had, in effect, already been planted. In our discussions, whether sitting in his room or walking round the park, I noticed that, even though he expressed his opinions quite strongly and even though some of those opinions seemed to me to be highly controversial, he never once became personally unpleasant. He never pulled ecclesiastical rank ('I've been ordained *fifteen* years, you know'); he never made me feel foolish for disagreeing with him; and he was never discourteous or personally sarcastic. Quite the reverse: he treated my half-baked ideas with real seriousness and the two of us managed to disagree till the proverbial cows came home without the slightest personal animosity. I thoroughly enjoyed it.

But I didn't think that much more about it, that is, until he asked me, not long after I was ordained, if I'd like to accompany him to Australasia. It was on that trip that I started to reciprocate a friendship, which, as I got to know him better, became one of the strongest of my life. Living alongside him for four months, I came to appreciate him more and more. If I was having a hard time (as I was at the time – what with health and boyfriend problems), he would be very kind to me. If I did things that I felt uneasy about or ashamed of, I would confess them to him and he would listen and help me to see if and where I was at fault. If something was on my mind, we'd talk about it. If I came back late to where we were staying, he would leave the light on. If I was tired and a bit ill, he would push the luggage trolley. Basically I came to see him as a spiritual friend, someone who was more than I was: kinder, wiser, more alive, and more radically Buddhist. I came to love those things in him, to aspire to them myself. Unlike so many people I'd look up to as a boy, Devamitra *improved* on knowing. His candour, his kindness, his uncompromising vigour became not only a source of delight but also a source of hope.

Until you meet someone who, you know in your heart of hearts, is more developed than you are, you don't really know if the spiritual life works. Until then, for all you know, Buddhism could be just a collection of nice ideas – colourful, no doubt, but at the end of the day nothing more than a comforting fantasy. You only know that it actually *works* when you start to change yourself and when you meet someone, like Devamitra, who has, by dint of spiritual practice, changed themselves and changed to a greater extent than you have. My friendship with Devamitra increased my confidence that the spiritual life worked, that if I practised it sincerely and intelligently I could become much *more* than I presently was. Having a friend we can look up to, an actual flesh-and-blood friend, not a hero you fantasize about or a distant spiritual teacher you're meekly submissive to, is such a source of inspiration and optimism that I wonder how people can get through life without one.

I've gained so much by my contact with friends like Devamitra. Without such friendships I can barely imagine having a spiritual life at all. After all, one of the principal ways we develop ourselves is by contact with those who are more developed than we are. Even in the simple sense of learning how to speak as a child or learning how to dance the foxtrot, drive a car, or cook a meal, we learn from the more developed, at least the more developed in those particular areas. Education, though, is not just a matter of information-gathering and skill-learning. It has a broader and more profound meaning. Real education is nothing less than the education of our being and consciousness: it is becoming, to use that word again, *more*. You learn to become more from those who are more already.

Ideally, then, at least some of our friendships would be with people we look up to. Of course, that's assuming there is someone around who is worthy of being looked up to. So many, I imagine, live in a world where there is no one at hand that they really admire, to whom they can turn for guidance, inspiration, and support. Some might be richer and more influential, I suppose, and that has a certain superficial attraction. Some will be higher up the career ladder, whilst others merely brag and boast about their disposable income, their sex life, or their connections in high places; but none of this will do if we want to learn to become more, in the way that Devamitra helped me become more. Of course, in a spiritual context some people will *tell* you to look up to them, even go so far as to say they are Enlightened or in direct contact with God: you should take absolutely no notice of that kind of thing!

Part of the problem is that not only are so many people spiritually starved for lack of vertical spiritual friendship, but nowadays we've got it into our heads that no one is more developed than we ourselves are – *differently* developed, perhaps, but certainly not *more* developed. This is understandable, given the disorienting spiritual vacuum in which we live, where life's value, meaning, and purpose are so confused and complicated, but it is a philosophy of mediocrity. This grudging 'no one's better than me' attitude is a sure sign that we won't learn anything; it's a dead end – planet philistine. The trouble is: how do we know if someone is more developed than we are? Certainly not because they tell us so, still less if they insist we treat them with peculiar deference and respect. Devamitra didn't patronize me or tell me how developed he was; he just held out the hand of friendship, even though it took me a few years to take it.

So how do we know? First of all, we need to get to know someone over a relatively long period of time before we can tell if they are more developed than we are. Part of the problem is that we can so easily overdo it and so easily underdo it. We either think that someone is perfect and can do no wrong or that they don't deserve any respect at all; often we start off with the first and end up with the second. For instance, at first I tended naïvely to assume that members of the Western Buddhist Order were, if not quite Buddhas, certainly well on the way. I was rather in awe of them, with their unpronounceable names and their tendency to look you in the eye when they talked to you. I remember listening to one Order member giving a talk and convincing myself that he had a halo around him, or at least a soft golden glow like the one in the Ready Brek advertisement. I must admit that this period didn't last very long. Once I spent more time with them, especially once I'd moved into my first community, I soon became disabused of my naïve and projective hero worship. In fact I tended to swing to the other extreme, the baby of friendship all but thrown out with the soapy water of projection and unrealistic expectation. I became thoroughly disillusioned. I thought I'd found my salvation in these men, I thought I'd found men who were the heroic vanguard of a new society, whereas actually they seemed just like me. So I set to work knocking them off the pedestals I'd put them on. Gradually, though, as I got to know more Order members, I found I was more able to develop friendships with them and out of that I was able to get a more objective sense of how spiritually developed they were.

Having got to know someone a bit, and having gone beyond both that first glowing adoration and the reactive rebellion that so often accompanies it, we need to develop that mixture of respect, receptivity, and freedom that is the hallmark of spiritual (in this case, vertical) friendship. Travelling with Devamitra, I came to respect him, his practice of the Dharma, his ethical integrity, and his judgement. I began to want to hear what he thought about things, and as time went on I increasingly looked to him for advice (though he was wisely reluctant to give it). My respect for him grew quite naturally, and as it did so I found myself wanting to be helpful to him, even to serve him. Of course we don't like the idea of service nowadays; it seems rather demeaning. I aspired to it and still do. As I got to know Devamitra and experienced him as being worthy of my respect, that respect naturally expressed itself in the desire to be of service to him, if only to bring him a cup of tea when he was working.

Respect is what *mettā* or loving-kindness feels like when it is directed towards someone we admire. Of course, respect needs to be present in all friendships, vertical and horizontal. One of the dangers inherent in peer friendship is that you start to lose respect for each other. This used to happen with Karmabandhu and me. We knew each other so well, were so aware of each other's little backslidings and pretensions, that at times we stopped respecting each other. When this happened we forgot to relate to each other on the basis of our common ideal; if anything, we treated each other as if we hadn't got one. This loss of respect can be corrosive. Instead of relating to the best in each other, we expect the worst, peppering our conversations with, 'Oh, you would say that, wouldn't you!' and 'That's just so typical of you!' Unfortunately, you see this kind of thing most commonly in family situations and long-term sexual relationships. But it also rears its ugly head in well-established friendships. When we lose respect for a friend, we lose a friend.

This is also the 'old cronies syndrome'. A bunch of old lads get together for a pint or two and they mock and gibe and poke fun at each other. Sometimes this is affectionate enough but it so easily gets out of hand, degenerating as it does into a veritable stream of little put-downs and gibes. What passes for humour is subtly (or not so subtly) tinged with cynicism and ridicule, thus creating a particularly toxic atmosphere. I remember this kind of thing happening in the first community I moved into, and from time to time it rears its head around the Centre, usually between men, for some reason. However or wherever it occurs, it is antithetical to genuine communication. At root it is basically defensive, a defence against intimacy and emotion. This is not to say that humour has no place in friendship. Humour is an important ingredient in friendship; indeed, it is an important ingredient in life. One should at the very least be able to laugh at oneself, and genuine laughter between friends – laughter that is not at someone else's expense – is a very healthy sign. I enjoy making Paramabandhu laugh; I like the way his face crinkles up in innocent merriment. To respect a friend and to take them seriously doesn't mean always being po-faced and terribly serious.

The word 'respect' has two meanings, what we could call a horizontal one and a vertical one. We respect someone in the sense that we 'respect their humanity', and we respect someone in the sense that we look up to them. As I say, sometimes Karmabandhu and I would lose respect for each other: we would stop taking each other seriously and thereby undermine the friendship and our attempts to practise the spiritual life. So horizontal friendships must at the very least be based on respect in this first sense. Actually Karmabandhu often did things that I respected in the second sense of the term. Sometimes he would act in a way that I really admired and looked up to; perhaps he was especially courageous or kind, or perhaps he listened to my at times rather hostile criticisms with patience and objectivity – vertical friendships are those in which this is true the greater part of the time (even if only by a little). In this kind of friendship, your overall experience of your friend is that they are worthy of your respect and admiration. If you are lucky enough to find such a friend, 'grapple them unto thy soul with hoops of steel', for you have found a treasure.

It took me a while to learn to respect Devamitra. At first I thought some of the things he said were outrageous, almost scandalous, and, to make matters worse, he was so unwilling to indulge me. Once, when I was in one of my 'please feel sorry for me' moods, I complained to him that my spiritual practice felt painfully shallow. His response was simply, 'How very self-indulgent.' It gave me such a shock (though it was said without the slightest trace of unpleasantness) that I was immediately shaken out of my self-pity. Perhaps it sounds perverse, but sometimes 'sympathy' is the last thing you need. I grew to respect his radical and uncompromising nature, his distaste for platitudes and pseudo-spiritual hogwash. I was, I suppose, receptive to him. My respect for him led me to want to learn from him, even to emulate him.

To learn anything, we need to *want* to learn: we need to be receptive. Being receptive doesn't mean passively agreeing with everything someone says, however much we respect and look up to them. It means being open to the possibility that we may have something to learn, that we may not, after all, know *all* the answers, that we may even be wrong. It's amazing how quickly we feel we know it all. Even relative newcomers to Buddhism can start talking as if they already had the greatest of all mysteries under their belt. To learn, we must be receptive. Yes, of course this means questioning, seeking clarification, coming out with our own views on the subject – but without receptivity we don't grow. This is especially true in the context of spiritual life. Without receptivity to those who are, if only to the smallest degree, wiser than we are, we will not make progress. After all, the spiritual life is, axiomatically, a journey into the unknown. You do not know where it will lead you or what challenges you will have to face along the way. By definition, we approach the spiritual life with a less than adequate understanding of ourselves and a less than adequate understanding of what spiritual life actually consists in. You cannot always know what's best for you, spiritually speaking, nor can you always reliably judge whether you are making progress. In fact, in my experience, going forward can sometimes feel like going backwards.

If we all set off on this journey into the unknown together as equals, the most likely outcome is that we will get lost, become anxious, and start bickering. We need people who have gone before us, who know the terrain a bit, and who can say, 'Watch out for that over there!' and 'Ah yes, I remember feeling like that.

Don't worry – in my experience it soon goes.' Certainly our peer friends can help us in this. Together we can help each other find out who we are and where we are going; but we also need someone who can give us *directions*, someone who has actually been there before. Devamitra became that for me. He exemplified what it was to live the spiritual life more wholeheartedly than I did. It's all very well reading about great Zen masters in faraway Japan or Tibetan lamas meditating in snow-bound monasteries, but what *we* need to see is how someone puts the spiritual life into practice in the day-to-day circumstances of life here and now in the West – ordering a pizza, having a conversation, cycling home.

We can learn only if we are receptive. In a way we don't need to worry about whether or not someone is more developed than we are; we simply need to make friends, be receptive, and see what happens. If a vertical dimension is present it will arise quite naturally out of simple human communication and friendship. Anyway, the vertical difference between people is one of degree and by no means fixed. I already have friends who were attracted to me because they looked up to me and whom I can imagine – in the not too distant future – overtaking me.

Any friendship needs to have two ingredients: receptivity and freedom. Interestingly, the word 'friend' is etymologically associated with the word 'free'. To be a friend you must be free, free to be yourself, to think your own thoughts and to run your own life. This means that your friend can have no power over you, cannot coerce you in any way to do things, think things, or say things. If they do, then, at least in that moment, they are not being friends. Friends are not attached as lovers are, nor are they bound to each other by family ties or by allegiance to a group; they are free, free to be themselves and so free to be friends. As Emerson puts it: 'There must be very two, before there can be very one.' So it's not a question of your wise friend, or *kalyāṇa mitra*, ordering you about, emotionally manipulating you or running your life for you, but just of sharing with you their experience of the spiritual life and of your being willing to learn from them.

After my first disastrous meetings with Bhante, I gradually started to become more comfortable around him. I would bump into him on the stairs, or he would come into the kitchen for a bottle of milk, and I would manage a brief chat without becoming too self-conscious. I even started reading his books on Buddhism. And it was through reading them that I really started to experience him as a *kalyāṇa mitra*. In his writings I came to appreciate him more and more deeply: the clarity of his thinking, the radical approach to life he communicated, his humour, his passion for the Dharma. I remember studying one of his books on a retreat at Padmaloka for men who had asked to be ordained. Again I had that experience that everything he said was being said particularly to *me*, to *my* life, to *my* experience. Never have I read a book with so much joy and inspiration. I felt like running around the grounds of Padmaloka with it above my head, just like when someone wins the FA cup and they go round the pitch holding the trophy up to the fans and kissing it. Somewhere in the back of my mind I could hear the theme tune to *Match of the Day*.

It's probably in a similar way that most people experience friendship with the wise. It is often in our experience of the arts – reading a book or watching a play – that we meet a friend who can communicate a higher vision and greater perspective. I remember going to Paris for the weekend with Gary to see an exhibition of Cézanne's paintings. Things had been a bit bumpy between Gary and me. For one reason or another I'd been struggling with feelings of insecurity and jealousy and, as we travelled to Paris, it was those feelings that were uppermost in my mind. It could so easily have been one of these traumatic weekends, those weekends of insecurity, blame, and attachment that are, so often, part and parcel of sexual relationships – it could have been, had it not been for Cézanne. For me, gazing at those magnificent canvases in a room crowded with jostling gallery-goers, Cézanne *spoke*. 'The good conscience of these reds, these blues, their simple truthfulness, it educates you,' said Rilke, looking at Cézanne's paintings eighty years earlier. As I looked at the paintings I experienced communication, a communication not of words or ideas but of meaning.

What struck me about my weekend looking at the Cézannes was that it was like spending the weekend with a friend, a friend who could teach me something. In the company of these paintings I was lifted out of myself, lifted out of my petty insecurities and jealousies, outwards towards the greater significance of the artist's mind. In our most receptive encounters with great works of art we meet the mind of the artist (albeit transfigured into paint or stone or into the music that little black quavers make when played on a musical instrument). In this encounter – which we call the experience of beauty – we are suddenly enveloped in the greater *being* of the artist, and we grow from the experience. This in essence is what friendship with the more developed is all about. After all, one of the translations of *kalyāṇa mitra* is 'friendship with the beautiful'.

But there are many different kinds of beauty. Bhante no longer lives in that flat, so I don't bump into him any more when he comes back from the park or comes in for a bottle of milk. I do still see him every now and then. I no longer feel awestruck and tongue-tied like I used to; in fact he seems so easy to talk to that I can hardly imagine why I was so petrified in the first place. Recently we went for a walk around the park near his new home in Birmingham. It was pouring with rain, so by the time I rang his doorbell he was coated and booted against the elements and we set forth with his large striped golf umbrella, which I held above our heads. We took shelter in a little café in the park and, waiting for the rain to stop, had a pot of Earl Grey and some fruit cake. We talked about this and that, Dante's poetry (which I had actually *read*), how things were going in the Centre, what he had been reading and how his writing was going. Nothing profound in a way, nothing about emptiness or wisdom or the opening of the Dharma eye, just things like 'Is the Centre still running events especially for black people?' and – commenting on Dante's *Paradiso* – 'too much abstract theologizing for my liking'.

Yet, if I have ever met a great man, this is he. As we talked over our tea and cake, or as we ventured out again into the new sunshine (Bhante walking down the small concrete steps with particular care and mindfulness), I experienced such weight of being – if weight can also have a lightness and ease about it. It was not in any particular thing he said, not even in his mindful self-possession which, contained though it was, seemed to take in everything: the mothers pushing prams, the cut-back rhododendrons, the sparkle of sunshine on the lake. There was something about his being that was in all these things – what he said, the quality of his voice and movements – but was not reducible to them. There is something about him, which I can never quite put my finger on, that has the touch of greatness. Not that you would notice; most people as we passed by them wouldn't have given this old gentleman a second look.

13

WHEN FRIENDSHIPS END

The most fatal disease of friendship is gradual decay, or dislike hourly increased by causes too slender for complaint, and too numerous for removal. Those who are angry may be reconciled; those who have been injured may receive a recompense; but when the desire of pleasing and willingness to be pleased is silently diminished, the renovation of friendship is hopeless; as, when the vital powers sink into languor, there is no longer any use of the physician.

Samuel Johnson, *The Idler*, 23 September 1758

I had been friends with Toby for fifteen years when he told me he never wanted to see me again. He and I had become friends at high school. We had been a part of that small band of cronies, Helen, big John, and shy Sharon (whom we rather tormented and who ended up, I believe, marrying a vicar). We played together in the school orchestra, sang together in our school's production of *Iolanthe*, and sat together in the sixth form. Toby often stayed over at my place and he regularly came on our family holidays in Cornwall. At the weekends, or after school, I would go to his parents' house in Earlswood, listen to stories about his mother's latest escapade, be teased by his older sister, or walk Bumble, the dog. When we left school – on that last sunny day when all the exams are over and you sign everyone's shirt 'best of luck for the future, mate' – we managed to keep up the friendship. He went on to music college in Colchester, I to nursing school, then art college. It was one evening – as I was phoning him from the dingy, half-lit corridor outside the bar – that the friendship broke. It was as if over the years we had held onto two ends of a golden thread of friendship which, having gradually frayed (especially in those last months), suddenly gave, and we fell inexorably apart. Despite all the cards I sent, the hopes of reconciliation, the imagined meetings and forgiveness, that phone call – leaning on the wall in my painting clothes, a pint of lager in my hand – marked the abrupt end of what had been at the time the most valuable friendship of my life. It was one of the most traumatic experiences I have ever had.

The causes of the sudden rift between us were a whole confusion of things: injured pride, misunderstanding, unwillingness to back down, unwillingness to explain, stubbornness, taking offence, mistrust, betrayal. I was in my first year at art school, feeling miserable, lost, and out of my depth. I had gotten it into my head that my friendship with Toby was too one-sided, that it was always *me* making the effort, going over and seeing him and his girlfriend in faraway West Norwood, listening to his troubles at work, sympathizing, and so on. I wanted to turn the tables – let *him* make the effort, let *him* be the first to phone. Aside from that, my head was full of art school feminism, gay rights, and deconstruction. I suppose I set about deconstructing my friendship with Toby. The last straw came a week or so before the phone call. I had gone to visit him. He met me at the door smiling, pleased to see me, hoping no doubt that I would explain what was going on. I saw the cue to speak but thought, 'It's always *me* that has to talk and do the explaining and come back round, never him.' I said nothing, pretended – in the pent-up prison of pride – that nothing was wrong. I made small talk. In a thought, in an action (or rather in a non-action), fifteen years of friendship … ended.

Most friendships perhaps don't end so dramatically, though there are quite a few famous examples of those that did: Wordsworth and Coleridge, Nietzsche and Wagner, my great hero Cézanne and Emile Zola. Cézanne and Zola had been friends since childhood. Bunking off school, they had spent days roaming around Aix-en-Provence, days out in the woods sleeping under trees, swimming in streams, and lying in the sun. They were the two 'inseparables'. Then years later, after they had lived in Paris, after Zola had been poverty-stricken and Cézanne refused again and again at the Salon and Zola had finally made it and became a famous author, he wrote a book called *L'Oeuvre*. The main character is a painter, clearly based on Cézanne, but a 'sublime abortion', a heroic failure. Zola, as was his practice, sent Cézanne a copy. Cézanne took offence, it would seem (though there had been rumbles before – Cézanne had never felt comfortable in Zola's new house, often feeling unwelcome and mistrustful in the company of Zola's 'sophisticated' friends). They never saw each other again. Years later, when Cézanne heard of Zola's tragic death (he and his wife died in the night, suffocated by fumes from the bedroom fireplace owing to an inadequately cleaned chimney), Cézanne locked himself in his studio and wept for a day. I sometimes wonder if one of the impulses that lay behind Cézanne's *Bathers*, with the strange figures swimming in sunlit ponds, lying naked on the grass – a theme he came back to again and again – was one of harking back to the freedom and friendship of his youth with Zola.

Before a friendship ends there is a gradual decay, sometimes an almost imperceptible fraying, of 'dislike hourly increased by causes too slender for complaint, and too numerous for removal'. A litany of missed opportunities; flippant, caustic remarks; things said in the heat of the moment; things left unsaid. Probably Johnson was right, the most common end of friendship is the slow death, the gradual drifting apart, the promises to phone, the excuses. People move away to another city, another life, with other friends; the emails stop arriving and the whole thing peters out. If you're lucky you get a card on your birthday saying, 'We really *must* meet up soon!' This will almost certainly be the case when friendship is based on mutual usefulness or pleasure – when use and pleasure come to an end, soon enough the friendship will too. It's not such a big deal. You enjoyed each other's company at the golf club or going out for a curry after the evening class, but now you're moving on again – *c'est la vie*. Some friendships, though, go much deeper than casual friendly affinities in the workplace or at the social club. The end of these friendships, however they come, are much harder to bear. Some, like Toby's and mine, suddenly go up in smoke (though the fire of destruction had been smouldering away for a long time before that). It takes only a few dry days and one spark and the resulting conflagration can destroy years of intimacy.

In friendships that are based on an attraction to the good in each other, to each other's strivings to evolve, one of the most obvious symptoms of decay is the breakdown of trust. In true friendship there is an openness and ease, a mutual unforced transparency and freedom. When such a warm friendship cools, starts to 'sicken and decay / It useth an enforced ceremony'. In other words, if your friend starts to become polite, there is a problem.

All human relationships are built on trust. Without at least some element of trust there can be no personal interaction. Every time we sit in a room with someone we trust them to some degree. For instance, we trust that they are not about to pull a knife on us or go through the contents of our bag while we are in the toilet. Trust is basic to all our meetings with each other. In a noisy café we eat and talk to our friends happily enough, until someone suddenly drops a tray of crockery. For a moment everyone stops talking and looks up – like a gaggle of geese at a perceived threat – then, registering that it is only a few broken dishes, we return to the sentence we were halfway through or the mouthful of food we were eating. Trust is the foundation of society; if we lost *all* trust in people we would never go out – we would go mad. Trust, though, is a matter of degree. While we may trust someone not to rifle through our bag the moment our back is turned, we may not trust them enough to lend them our money or tell them our intimate secrets.

The development of friendship is a development in trust; starting with the rudimentary level of trust that is the implied basis of a civilized society, towards that deep sense of trust and openness that is the mark of genuine friendship. Our capacity to trust is bound up with whether we feel someone will harm us in any way, including whether they will harm us emotionally or psychologically. Though we may trust a friend over a cake and coffee, and though we may enjoy having a laugh with them, we trust them only up to a point. Until friendship is well developed, there are inevitably unspoken and unacknowledged barriers between you. You may not trust them enough to talk about your sex life, your money troubles, or the fact that something they have just said hurt you. Friendship is the *gradual* dissolving of barriers. The protective barriers we put up around us are often not so much to do with any particular person, but with our basic instinct for self-preservation, one that we share with other animals. For some, of course, our natural tendency to be slightly on the lookout for danger is exacerbated by our psychological history – perhaps we have learned to mistrust people, especially those we are closest to.

Even in our more developed relationships we can harbour fears of being emotionally hurt; fears that our friend will try to get one up on us, humiliate us, or take us for granted.

We develop friendship by building trust and by consciously pushing back the boundaries of *dis*trust. We build trust by being open and transparent about ourselves (as I have already said) and by doing what we say we will do. So if I say I will see you next Wednesday at 8 pm that is what I do. All the generosity, kindness, expression of affection, and encouragement that are part of true friendship build up trust. To push back the boundaries of *dis*trust we need to consciously take 'trust risks'. A trust risk is taking the next step in friendship, saying the next thing, the thing in the context of your friendship you know needs to be said. Looked at from the other point of view a trust risk is listening to the next thing. As we take those sometimes tiny trust risks in friendship we gradually dissolve the barriers and boundaries between us. It is rarely a straightforward process. We might go so far and then our friend says something that touches a raw nerve within us and up go the barriers again, like so many steel shutters. We develop and deepen our capacity to trust gradually, with trial and error, apology and confession. In friendship, we need to learn not so much to trust absolutely but to trust more. If we find that our trust has proved to be well founded, then we trust again – and again.

Trust is something that has to be earned. If someone says, 'Trust me,' my advice would be, don't! Trust is something we win, not something we demand, and it develops gradually as friendship develops. We win people's trust by how we relate to them over time. If we keep losing our temper, we create distrust. If we get touchy and defensive every time they make an innocent observation about us, we feed mistrust in ourselves. If we are too proud to apologize we create mistrust. If we talk about our friends behind their back, tell tales on them, or tell others their secrets, we take trust and wring its neck!

When friendship has broken down, trust has broken down. Trust, in my experience, is something that can be badly damaged. It can be misplaced, misused, and misappropriated; it can undergo quite substantial injury, but it can thrive again. One apology, some more genuine communication, a deeper understanding, and it thrives again as fit and as optimistic as ever. When it breaks, however, it can be extraordinarily difficult to put it back together. Once trust has broken, everything is seen through the eyes of mistrust, and the slightest thing sets the mistrust off again. Seen through the eyes of suspicion, a friend's genuine attempts to explain look like just so many excuses, their silence a tacit admission of guilt, their confession proof of your mistrust, their attempts at reconciliation a trick. To the suspicious all things are suspect.

The first rule is to keep coming back into communication, to commit yourself to that and to stick to that commitment. To do that we have to overcome pride. Pride, in some traditions of Buddhism, is seen as *the* basic human flaw: it is our fundamental folly and silliness. Perhaps of all our various sillinesses, pride is the silliest. Looking back on the end of my friendship with Toby, what strikes me most is how almost pitifully silly it was to let vain pride destroy human friendship. And yet pride can be so strong, so deeply embedded in our hearts, so quick to rear up and wreak havoc. One moment you are friends, the next the walls of pride rear up almost insurmountably between you. I have had times in friendships where it seemed a straight contest between my pride – my injured pride – and my friendship. Friends *will* let you down; they will hurt you; they will touch your raw nerves and tread on your toes. Often they will do it inadvertently, sometimes because they are anxious or threatened, sometimes because they are telling you the truth! After all, the truth can hurt. To choose the spiritual life – never mind 'spiritual' – to choose *human* life is to choose friendship again and again over pride, over taking offence, over egotism, and over vanity. Pride (in this negative sense) is a walled-up place of isolation, a fortress perhaps, but also a prison.

True friendship entails the willingness to swallow our pride and get back into communication. At the same time, communication cannot be insisted upon. Friendship, as I said in the previous chapter, can only take place between the 'free'. You cannot force friendship upon someone, just as you cannot force communication on them. You can certainly push and persuade and cajole and exhort, but you cannot force. In the past when my friendships started to flounder I tended to panic a bit and insist on communication. 'Come on, what's wrong? Out with it, spit it out!' Sometimes this worked but sometimes it was counter-productive. For communication to take place both people have to want to do it, even if both of you don't like doing it, would rather not do it, would rather do anything *but* it. Somewhere at the bottom of your heart you know you need to do it, and are willing to do it. To be free to communicate, you have to be free not to.

There are many ways to get back into communication, many ways to mend breaches in trust. The nose-to-nose 'Tell me what's wrong!' approach isn't always the best. Certainly if the breakdown of trust has been very severe and the person is of a sensitive and touchy disposition – as so many of us tend to be – you may need to bide your time, be patient, and build bridges of trust between you and your friend in other ways. The breakdown of my friendship with Toby took place just before I got involved in Buddhism and just before I met Gary, literally a matter of weeks. I sent letters to him trying to urge communication but I just got one short, coldly civil, note back – the basic drift was 'that chapter of my life is over'. I tried via his family but was advised to keep away for a few years. I didn't know what else to do; I felt weighed down by unfinished business. Then, on retreat, someone I looked up to and loved suggested I just send him a card now and then, a little postcard from my holiday or from retreat, just saying what I had been up to, making no demands, no 'when are you going to see sense?' kind of thing. It was good advice and for a long time afterwards that's what I did. Whatever happens with friendship we should always keep it alive, at least keep our side of it alive. Sometimes when communication and trust have broken down all you can do is keep the door of friendship open. Sometimes a tactical withdrawal is called for; you stop pushing at the barriers that have been erected in the friendship and just talk about other things – back off a bit. Sometimes what is needed is to stop doing so much *talking* and just help them in some way, cook a meal with them, help them decorate the flat, look after their cat while they're away on holiday.

Friendship often thrives again if you put it in better conditions for a while. Go on retreat with your friend, go to see a play that you are both inspired by, do something that connects you back to your inspiration and come back together on that higher basis. Talk about your common inspiration rather than your common irritation. I remember once how just asking Karmabandhu how his meditation practice was going was enough. As we sat at opposite ends of the table, our friendship suddenly seemed like the base of an equilateral triangle, with our common ideal the apex above us, holding us together. Whatever way we do it – sending cards, buying them a little gift, changing the subject, helping them move house – the main thing is to keep the channels of communication open. Often, in my experience, you will need at some point to get back to that barrier of injured pride and hurt feeling and – once the initial sting has worn off – try to come to a deeper understanding of each other and to get to the truth of the matter. To do this we need to go beyond personal pride and grudge-bearing.

Once you do come back into communication, and hopefully this should be pretty quickly, the first thing to be avoided is blame and accusation. To push back the barriers of distrust and suspicion we need to be quick to acknowledge our part in the quarrel, or whatever it was that caused the rift, as well as being willing to listen to criticism. It is so tempting to start like children in the playground with accusations of 'He made me, sir', 'He started it', and 'If he hadn't done X, I wouldn't have done Y'. Ideally, both parties in a dispute need to take 100 per cent responsibility for it. Not that disputes and breakdowns in communication are all on one side, either yours or theirs, but we must, if we are to navigate our way out of difficulty, guard against any temptation to apportion blame (usually to the other party). Something else we should avoid is *justification*, especially when it comes disguised as explanation, and more especially when that 'explanation' is a psychological one. With a few morsels of home-baked psychoanalysis we serve up rationalizations like 'Because I had a difficult childhood, I am bound to lose my temper and get resentful; if you were *really* a friend you'd understand and sympathize, not criticize!'

One thing is essential. If a friendship breaks down, for whatever reason, remain true to your friend. Remember their good qualities, keep a perspective on their bad ones, and do not let your injured feelings cast the deadly pall of resentment and bitterness over your friend. So often, when friendship ends we are tempted only to see our now ex-friend's faults. At worst we make their virtues faults in another guise, we bad-mouth them to our acquaintances, gossip about them, recount their intimate stories for cheap amusement, and tell everyone their secrets: 'The bag of secrets untied, they fly about like birds let loose from a cage, and become the entertainment of the town.' Friendship must remain true; even if there are real and justified criticisms and genuine harm done we must never untie the bag of secrets, or use our knowledge of the other person to hurt and injure them, especially in the eyes of other people. This is one of the most painful aspects of divorce, when a married couple, once so tender and so soft-spoken, get stuck in mutual recrimination and vilification (money: who has it, house: who gets it, kids: who sees them). All the secrets are out and nowadays if you happen to be a 'personality' you can sell them to the papers and make a substantial sum out of it into the bargain. Over their breakfast cereal the nation can read about someone's sexual peccadilloes, their lying and cheating, their bank account, and what they did or didn't do with their secretary – all by courtesy of the person they loved.

Perhaps the greatest virtue to aspire to in friendship is fidelity. Fidelity is another of those spiritual qualities that are both the foundation and the aspiration of true friendship. Like honesty, forgiveness, kindness, courage, integrity, idealism, and any number of other qualities to be developed in friendship, fidelity takes us beyond ourselves. What you are aiming for in friendship is to be an absolutely dependable friend: through the vicissitudes of time; through aspects of your friend you were not aware of; through changes in circumstance; through breakdowns in communication; through separation, loss, changes in status and fortune; even through times when your friend takes against you or will no longer speak to you. To practise fidelity is to overcome yourself. To practise fidelity is to overcome your natural tendency to laziness and inertia, to let things drift, to let friendship slip through your fingers. To practise fidelity is to overcome your tendency to find another friend if the going gets tough, or to break off the friendship the moment your friend tells you an uncomfortable truth. To practise fidelity is to overcome your desire to always be liked and agreed with and mollified.

To practise fidelity is to keep trust, to look after them if they are sick, and to stand up for them if they are absent. To practise the spiritual life is to strive to be an absolutely dependable friend. And this will take time. It's a long journey from where we are now to absolutely dependable friendship, but every little step – and this book is an attempt to describe those steps – takes us along the way.

In friendship the circumstances of the life of one of you often change, sometimes radically. Your friend moves to another country (as Karmabandhu has), becomes very rich, or becomes very ill. These are the tests of friendship. Perhaps one of you gets married and has children. Fidelity is keeping the friendship going if that happens to you, and keeping it going if that happens to them.

Something I've not yet touched on is that, when you are someone's friend, you enter into a relationship with their family, whether it be with their parents, brothers and sisters, husband, wife, or children. We take this for granted with couples, but don't often expect it with friends. Because of your feeling for your friend you will quite naturally start to feel for who *they* have feelings for. (For instance, it is quite common that we become friends, at least to a degree, with our friend's friends.) Through the years of my friendship with Toby, I naturally got to know and like his family. In a way, especially when I was at school, they became like another family to me. Being at Toby's house, sitting around the table or watching a film on television, was not *so* different from being in my own – I even became fond of the dog! I was not only a friend of Toby's, but also a friend of the family. I think this is quite common; in more traditional societies it certainly would have been.

So fidelity means fidelity over changed circumstances – for instance, if your friend acquires a family, or when the one they already have requires attention. When Jnanavaca was away being ordained I used to phone his mother every now and then to check if she was all right. In a way I didn't need to. Coming from an Indian family, she had a very extensive family network of support, but my occasional card and phone call helped her, I think, feel in touch with Jnanavaca and his life while he was away. Despite the fact that her spoken English was not that good and my Gujarati was non-existent, I noticed quite quickly that I developed feelings of care and warmth for her, much as I had done, years previously, for Toby's mother.

There are many reasons for the end of friendship. Sometimes the friend was not really a friend at all, rather a sort of pretend friend, the sort of person we meet for dinner and they 'mwah mwah' us on each cheek, tell us how delighted they are to see us, wax lyrical about us, sympathize fulsomely with our difficulties – 'Veronica, that must have been simply *terrible* for you' – but strangely, when we really need them, when we need them to lend a hand, or visit our sickbed, or put themselves out a bit for us, they are not around. Or perhaps our friendship was a rather romantic one, one where we were forever talking about our *feelings* for each other and how the friendship was going. Romantic friendship, like romantic love, often ends up in a bust-up or in a new romance.

Friendship can end with a long fade-out, a quick explosion, or a change of address. It can evaporate or never get going. The main cause of the end of friendship is egocentricity, self-centredness: it is when two egos collide and one or both decide to avoid the other, or stand and fight the other, back off, or run away. Fidelity, once we have committed ourselves to friendship, once we have chosen someone with spiritual qualities, is a journey beyond egotism.

There is another way in which friendships end: death. My friends will die – that I know for sure. I may die before them and some of them may die before me – but we will die. Fidelity means carrying on the friendship when our friend has died. Each of our friends makes an indelible impression on us; they become part of our lives – almost, one could poetically say, part of our soul. There is something about our friend that we can never say or describe – a *themness* which is just and only them, a particularity that eludes description. When I think of Darren or Paramabandhu or any of my other friends, it's their uniqueness that comes to my mind. Yes, there's that hat that Darren has taken to wearing that seems somehow so *like* him, or those little gestures – the way Paramabandhu wrinkles his nose or the way Darren walks into the room when he comes to see me – but there is something about them that defies description; a uniqueness which has become part and parcel of my life, adding so much to it. And when they die that sense of them will remain within me, enriching my life.

None of my close friends, I'm pleased to say, has died, but a boy I was at school with did. We'd been having a clandestine sexual relationship for some time. It was a prepubescent friendship really, with a bit of fumbling on the side. He was knocked off his moped on his way to school. Even now he occasionally comes into my mind, not as a thought really, not as an idea or even an image, but as a *presence*, his unique presence. And perhaps after our friend dies we can keep in contact with that. After our friend dies we can still keep true to them in us, keep them in our hearts and send them *mettā*. After all, who knows what happens when you die? Of course we tend to think that we *do* know – we think, 'Well, that's it, the end, no more, curtain' – but Buddhism tells quite a different story, a story for another book. Certainly, when my father died, my strongest impression was that I really *didn't* know what had happened (including whether he had died in that final nihilistic sense that we usually assume). Life is a journey into the unknown, and death may just be the continuation of that journey, albeit into an 'undiscovered country from whose bourn no traveller returns'. We can be afraid of the unknown, we can try and blot it out and distract ourselves from it, or we can send our *mettā* and love into it – decide to keep the friendship alive even when the friend has died.

It was at my father's grave that I saw Toby again: such things often bring together the estranged. I'd seen him briefly a couple of years or so before. He'd appeared out of the blue with his mother one evening when I happened to be visiting my parents. But we hadn't been able to talk, and anyway nothing came of it. When my father died, my brother went through his old address book and contacted everyone in it. Toby, after all, was a friend of the family, so my brother rang him and told him the news. It was to mix sadness with so much happiness to see him again – and looking much the same as ever, except that his voice had changed and that he'd put on some weight. His mother was there too, as full of beans as ever and just as quick-witted. I went to see him not long after. We spent the afternoon together, walked round the block a few times, pushing the buggy with his little curly-haired boy curled up inside it, waiting for him to fall asleep. We had some supper, a rhubarb and strawberry crumble for afters, and then Toby gave me a lift back to the station. What had I hoped to achieve? I knew that our friendship couldn't begin again; too much had changed between us now and time had taken us both into worlds full of different responsibilities and other engagements. I knew I couldn't turn the clock back. So I shook his hand – something one only does for wedding photographs nowadays – and said 'Goodbye, Toby'. He looked a little taken aback, but that was really all I wanted to say after all these years: 'Goodbye' and 'I'm sorry if I hurt you – I was foolish. Let us shake hands'. For me the friendship had finally come to an end. The unfinished business was finished. As I got on the train back to London I could let it rest.

14

A VISION OF FRIENDSHIP REVISITED

I want to be your friend
For ever and ever without break or decay.
When the hills are all flat
And the rivers are all dry,
When it lightens and thunders in winter,
When it rains and snows in summer,
When Heaven and Earth mingle –
Not till then will I part from you.

'Oaths of Friendship', Chinese, 1st century CE, trans. Arthur Waley

When I am ill Paramabandhu goes down to Friends Foods and buys me a carton or two of orange juice. When I was setting up our Buddhist-run café, Darren came and helped paint the walls and sand the floor. When I come back from retreat Paramabandhu leaves a vase of flowers in my room with a postcard welcoming me home. When Karmabandhu was suffering from chronic back-ache I would press his pressure points before he went to bed so as to ease the pain. If David goes to bed before me, he puts a glass of water by my bedside in case I wake in the night. When Maria was short of cash, I gave her some. Sometimes one of the men in the community folds all my washing and leaves it on my bed. These are the actions of friendship.

When Karmabandhu was sick in bed I cleaned out his vomit bowl and got him some fresh water. When I had to move out of my room Darren came over on his day off to help me. When it is someone's birthday in the community we sit round the table, watch them open their presents, and then each of us says what we appreciate about them. When Jnanavaca went off to get ordained, Paramabandhu and I drove him to the airport. When I was cooking for the community I decided to bake a cake for Bhante, for no reason other than to show my love for him. When I presented Bhante with the cake he smiled at the poor misshapen thing and said, 'Did you make it with your own hands?' Devamitra has a photograph of us both on his bookshelf; we are standing together outside Wellington Airport with our sun hats on, Devamitra has his arm around my shoulder. Sometimes Paramabandhu leaves a little bar of chocolate on my pillow. These are the actions of friendship.

When I am on solitary retreat I think of my friends and chant mantras for their happiness and well-being. Realizing Devamitra needed a new swimming cap I bought him one. When I had a talk to give and not much time to prepare it, David ironed my shirt. When Karmabandhu was running out of funds in Rome I sent a letter to all his friends asking for their help. Bhante phones the two friends he used to live with every week. When I had flu Bhante sent a big colourful book of Tibetan art for me to look at. Paramabandhu bought me a statue of the figure I meditate on, having seen me admire it earlier on in the day. When my father died Devamitra persuaded me not to go off and lead a retreat as I had planned to. Darren gave me a single flower for no reason, except friendship. If Paramabandhu thinks I might like a cup of tea, he makes me one. These are the actions of friendship.

Friendship is a simple thing. In the Zen tradition there is a saying that first of all mountains are mountains, then they are anything but mountains, then the mountains are mountains again. Friendship is like that. At first friendship is just friendship, an ordinary thing, something you hardly notice, something that 'fills up the chinks of one's time'. Then friendship is anything but friendship – it is mutual discovery, love, and *mettā* finding expression. It is learning how to talk, learning how to bring out the best in each other, learning how to resolve conflicts and win trust. It is storm and summer ease, sudden dislike and graceful apology. It is telling the truth and causing a ruckus. It is deciding not to withdraw, being 'equally balked by antagonism and by compliance'. It is staying true to someone even when they take against you or move away. It is a common journey into the unknown. Then friendship is friendship again: something, in a sense, extraordinarily ordinary, marked not so much by storm and fire, showers of love, or vows of eternity, but by the steady heartbeat of friendship.

The heartbeat of friendship is an ongoing undemonstrative generosity, a ceaseless vibration of mutual sympathy, like the deep thrumming beneath the decks of an ocean liner. It is the habit of self-transcendence, of mutually giving yourselves to a common ideal. As it matures, talking and saying ripen into being and doing, and even silence, that neglected restorative, finds her easy resting place between you. When help or work or conversation is needed, friendship responds quickly and straightforwardly. It needs no Sunday best or proud attire, no large statements or grand gestures; when it is true it is as simple as your face in the mirror – unadorned, smiling back at you.

The heartbeat of friendship is the heartbeat of altruism. In Zen they talk about 'mouth Zen', where people talk about Zen, about meditation and voidness and, usually, Big Mind, but it is all hot air: words and no deeds. Friendship, to be friendship, can't be like that. There can be no 'mouth friends' in friendship. To be a friend is to give friendship, to give your time, to give your help, to give *yourself*. As Walt Whitman puts it, 'Behold, I do not give lectures or a little charity, / When I give I give myself.' In this book I have tried to show how friendship is a spiritual practice, how – like meditation – it is something to engage in, improve at, learn from, and grow by. On the path of friendship you gradually leave behind you all that weighs you down: loneliness, isolation, fearful mistrust, and self-absorption. On the path of friendship you learn to understand yourself and to genuinely care for others: you learn how to speak, how not to speak, how to give, forgive, trust, apologize, love, and be loved.

The path of friendship leads to the palace of egolessness. A central metaphor in this book is the metaphor of *more*, that the spiritual life is a movement from less to more. In those terms, egotism is least, altruism is more, and egolessness is most. Egotism (which is really a posh, slightly technical-sounding word for selfishness) is actually less, much less than we are; it is merely the husk of ourselves, a fleeting, inflated, not very enjoyable illusion. For Buddhism, consciousness is infinite, expansive, and luminous, a never-ending play of mysteries. Egotism is trying to force all that wonder into a little cardboard box called 'me'. The irritation, discontent, disquiet, and restlessness we feel is to do with the fact that life cannot be squeezed into our me-shaped box, and our futile attempts to do so hurt us. Perhaps I cannot talk about egolessness from my experience, but I do know that each time I act genuinely positively – when I give instead of take, create instead of react – a new space seems to open up in my life, a new buoyancy, a new freedom. To let go of the ego, to transcend yourself, is to let go of all that separates you from life, all that fixes and restricts you. The Buddha said it is like being released from prison, like finally putting down a heavy load, like getting out of terrible danger, like getting out of debt. To move from selfishness to selflessness is to move from less to more.

To become an absolutely dependable friend we need to overcome egotism, our natural tendency to think always of 'number one'. Egotism is like sand on a beach holiday – it gets everywhere. It gets in your shoes, between your toes, down your knickers, and into your flask. When we get home we keep finding *sand* – in our shirt pockets, in the turn-ups of our jeans, between the pages of our book, and in our pencil case. Egotism is like this; whatever we do (even when we are really trying to think of others), we keep finding little gritty bits of egotism in it. We praise our friend's merits and notice a little aftertaste of wanting them to praise ours. We cook a meal for them and surreptitiously give ourselves the bigger portion. We apologize to our friend while sneakily hoping that they will admit it was their fault. The list goes on and on: egotism gets everywhere.

Egotism and selfishness are natural to us, they are just how the unenlightened mind works. Each of our actions, until we are very developed indeed, will be mixed with egotism. The spiritual life consists in gradually changing the mix of ingredients; reducing the quantity of little gritty bits of egotism and increasing the quantity of altruism.

In friendship all that 'me' – that gets-everywhere self-cherishing egocentricity – gets worn away. The test of *true* friendship is in the everyday person-to-person reality of friendship and all that it entails. It manifests itself not so much in heroic deeds (though it can do, especially in times of hardship, warfare, or danger) but in the tiniest simple actions of friendship. So that when I make myself a cup of tea I ask Paramabandhu if he would like one too, or if I see him out in the garden struggling with a particularly tenacious root growth, I stop what I am doing and help him. That is the practice – it doesn't seem much, perhaps, but if we engage in it, it will change us.

The path of friendship is a path of small things, of generous actions too small to be remembered and words too slight to be recalled. These acts of friendship, so seemingly insignificant, are like snow, each one like the perfectly formed crystal of a snowflake – slowly, almost imperceptibly, gathering. Looked at individually, the actions of friendship seem paltry and unremarkable. Your friend has a sore throat, you give him your Strepsils; she is short on cash, you pay for her Tube ticket. As we practise friendship and as those tiny actions gather, day in and day out, week in and week out, month after month, they become by slow degrees nothing less than a reorientation of our entire being.

Then we can go further. The practice of friendship is the practice of putting yourself out for someone. It is as Samuel Johnson thought of it, the 'readiness to sacrifice one's own pleasure and profit for the pleasure and profit of another ... to go where, and do what, is agreeable to him rather to oneself'. This will take us years to learn, accustomed as we are to think first and foremost of ourselves – but we *can* learn it, gradually. As the caterpillar moves slowly but surely from leaf to leaf, each time we think about our friend's needs rather than our own (or at least just our own), we move beyond ourselves. You iron a shirt for your friend even though you're having a busy day yourself. You give them a lift home even though it takes you out of your way and means you'll be late for bed. When you are thinking of moving away you consider your friends and what they might need. Your friend wants to go to Bath for your day trip together ... you want to go to Brighton ... you go to Bath; when they need you to listen to them just when you're off to see your girlfriend, you stop and listen to them. In other words, you are willing to undergo some inconvenience for them. In this way we learn to treat our friend like we treat ourselves. We think not just of our own needs but of theirs, not just what *I* want but what *they* want.

Friendship teaches us how to go beyond egocentricity in a harder way. We learn to go beyond egocentricity via egocentricity, that is via *their* egocentricity. Friendship is the meeting of two basically selfish people, people who think of themselves as occupying the centre of the universe. If underneath our accomplished social graces we think of ourselves as being at the centre of the universe (as we all do) and if we then start to form a friendship with someone else who also thinks that they are at the centre of the universe, then the result will be friction. This friction is what happens when two egos collide with each other. What is happening is that the being, that is the self-centredness of your friend, *impinges* on you, on your self-centredness, like two great tectonic plates rubbing and colliding and grinding against each other. This impingement of their egotism on yours is experienced as irritation. Friction, after all, causes heat, irritation, and, if extreme enough, sparks. Wants and desires clash. Your friend does things that you don't want them to do, and doesn't do things that you *do* want them to do.

Egotism, as I've said, gets everywhere. It even penetrates into the very stuff of spiritual life. It's amazing how soon you can start to become intoxicated with your spiritual 'attainments'. Perhaps you've had some powerful meditation experiences or perhaps you've just been feeling really good for a while. You start to think that perhaps you are a rather special person, a rather especially spiritual person. When this happens (as it does from time to time), the spiritual life has become something to add on to *me*. This is spiritual materialism. Feeling special is the very antithesis of the spiritual life. If the spiritual life is a journey from selfishness to selflessness, feeling special is like getting on a bus and going in the opposite direction. You cannot 'puff yourself up' and get to feel special with friends. They know you too well; they have seen you do it before. If they are genuine friends they will not pander to that in you – or if you've managed to get yourself very inflated they will make sure they carry a large pin just as a final resort! (Though they will take care to be there when you pop.) Friendship inevitably involves collision and a good few sparks. In that collision you start attenuating the egotism that is the cause of it.

So in this book I have been at pains to show how friendship is a practical path of human evolution. First we practise generosity. We give our friend our time, attention, encouragement, and help. Then, as we start putting ourselves out for our friend (in little ways at first), we come to think more and more of their needs, not just our own. Then, after our ego has bumped and collided against their ego for a few years and all those hard edges of ourselves have been smoothed and polished a bit, after we have lived out in the day-to-day all those tiny actions of friendship – the gifts, the apologies, the communication, the help, the forgiveness, the fidelity – suddenly friendship changes, matures beyond itself. Eventually our feeling for our friend has, by incremental degrees, become so strong that to love them is to love ourselves. To think of our friend, to consider his or her needs, is no different from thinking of ourselves and our needs. You and your friend have ceased to be two. The final flowering of friendship has been attained. Those tiny crystals of snow, each one an act of friendship – silently falling, settling, gathering – in a moment become an avalanche, the force of which propels you on a journey into the infinite. No 'me', no 'mine', no 'self', no 'other'. Life in all its mystery *dawns*.

The main thing to do is to get on and start! Begin it now: make friends. Life admits not of delays; it rushes past us in a torrent – we have no time to lose; we must plunge in. If you think friendship is something you will get around to some day – let that day be *today*. For myself, I still cannot quite believe that I am nearly forty. I have always thought of myself as a young person, much in the same way as I have thought of myself as an arty person or not the type to play football. Being young has become an identity rather than a description. I look up from my page at the winter sunlight catching the shopfront opposite my room and I am nearly forty. 'You, too, are like the sun going down in the western mountains, or like a living corpse whose span of life is nearly over,' says Kukai, the great Japanese master. He whispers it across the centuries to me: 'You, too, are like the sun going down.' Already my bright noon has passed and the light of hopeful brash youth has started to fade. When my sun sets, whenever that will be, what will I have achieved? When I was young I wanted to be Julie Andrews. In my early teens I wanted to be a famous actor or a pop star. When I was in my twenties I wanted to be a great painter like Cézanne. I will probably never be any of these things; I can't be Julie Andrews, anyway. I will probably never produce great art, despite all my art school fantasies about being interviewed by Melvyn Bragg on *The South Bank Show*, or about my latest knockout show at the Waddington Galleries. What I hope is that I will have developed friendships, that I will look back on my life and see a life devoted to friendship – to making friends, developing friendship, and going beyond myself.

Until we die, the nearest we come to death is when things end. When I left my first community they had a little ritual to send Paramabandhu and me off, and to wish us luck in our new community. Sometimes rituals can be surprisingly powerful. Realizing suddenly that my years of living there were coming to an end, what arose strongly in my mind was the wish that I had been a better friend. I looked around the room, and although my relationships were in fairly good repair, I could see in that heightened state that I had never *really* been close to so-and-so, I had reacted to so-and-so, and I could have been kinder to so-and-so. I didn't remember the meals we ate together or the quality of the cooking. I didn't remember much of what any one person said or whether or not they had done their community duties or their fair share of the washing-up. It wasn't even all those petty little grudges and undealt-with niggles that came to my mind, but the simple wish to have been a better friend. At death perhaps we will suddenly come to our senses in this way – see what has been *really* important. Perhaps then we'll see how fame and shopping, sex and nice meals, fitted kitchens and holidays in the sun, digital television and clandestine affairs, morning papers and tea on the veranda, all of it, and a million other things besides, have been a dream – half-forgotten. Perhaps then we'll see that people *are* our life, that it's the depth of our relationships with people that make or mar us, complete us or leave us unfinished. Perhaps then we will *really* see the value of true friendship.

Life rushes on, 'flowing, flowing, flowing into an unfathomable abyss', and no one knows where it will end. Plunge into life and you plunge into friendship. Devote yourself to it now. 'Why,' said the Dodo, 'the best way to explain it is to do it.'

FURTHER READING

BUDDHISM
Chris Pauling, *Introducing Buddhism*, Windhorse, Birmingham 1997
Kulananda, *Western Buddhism*, HarperCollins, London 1991
Sangharakshita, *Human Enlightenment*, Windhorse, Glasgow 1993
Subhuti, Sangharakshita: A New Voice in the Buddhist Tradition,
    Windhorse, Birmingham 1994

MEDITATION
Paramananda, *Change Your Mind*, Windhorse, Birmingham 1999

FRIENDSHIP
Aelred of Rievaulx, *The Way of Friendship*, New City Press, New York
    2001
Aristotle, *Nichomachean Ethics*, trans. H. Rackman, Wordsworth
    Editions, Ware 1996
Cicero, 'On Friendship' in *On the Good Life*, Penguin, London 1971
D.J. Enright and David Rawlingson (eds.), *The Oxford Book of Friendship*,
    Oxford University Press, Oxford 1991
Sangharakshita, *What is the Sangha?* Windhorse, Birmingham 2000
Suvajra and Vidyadevi (eds.) *Reflections on Friendship*, Windhorse,
    Birmingham 2001

INDEX

WINDHORSE PUBLICATIONS

Windhorse Publications is a Buddhist charitable company based in the UK. We place great emphasis on producing books of high quality that are accessible and relevant to those interested in Buddhism at whatever level. We are the main publisher of the works of Sangharakshita, the founder of the Triratna Buddhist Order and Community. Our books draw on the whole range of the Buddhist tradition, including translations of traditional texts, commentaries, books that make links with contemporary culture and ways of life, biographies of Buddhists, and works on meditation.

As a not-for-profit enterprise, we ensure that all surplus income is invested in new books and improved production methods, to better communicate Buddhism in the 21st century. We welcome donations to help us continue our work – to find out more, go to windhorsepublications.com.

The Windhorse is a mythical animal that flies over the earth carrying on its back three precious jewels, bringing these invaluable gifts to all humanity: the Buddha (the 'awakened one'), his teaching, and the community of all his followers.

Windhorse Publications	Perseus Distribution	Windhorse Books
169 Mill Road	210 American Drive	PO Box 574
Cambridge	Jackson TN 38301	Newtown NSW 2042
CB1 3AN	USA	Australia
UK		

info@windhorsepublications.com

THE TRIRATNA BUDDHIST COMMUNITY

Windhorse Publications is a part of the Triratna Buddhist Community, which has more than sixty centres on five continents. Through these centres, members of the Triratna Buddhist Order offer classes in meditation and Buddhism, from an introductory to a deeper level of commitment. Members of the Triratna community run retreat centres around the world, and the Karuna Trust, a UK fundraising charity that supports social welfare projects in the slums and villages of South Asia.

Many Triratna centres have residential spiritual communities and ethical Right Livelihood businesses associated with them. Arts activities and body awareness disciplines are encouraged also, as is the development of strong bonds of friendship between people who share the same ideals. In this way Triratna is developing a unique approach to Buddhism, not simply as a set of techniques, but as a creatively directed way of life for people living in the modern world.

If you would like more information about Triratna please visit thebuddhistcentre.com or write to:

London Buddhist Centre	Aryaloka	Sydney Buddhist Centre
51 Roman Road	14 Heartwood Circle	24 Enmore Road
London E2 0HU	Newmarket NH 03857	Sydney NSW 2042
UK	USA	Australia

ALSO FROM WINDHORSE

Buddhist Meditation
Tranquillity, Imagination & Insight
by Kamalashila

First published in 1991, this book is a comprehensive and practical guide to
Buddhist meditation, providing a complete introduction for beginners, as well
as detailed advice for experienced meditators seeking to deepen their practice.
Kamalashila explores the primary aims of Buddhist meditation: enhanced
awareness, true happiness, and – ultimately – liberating insight into the nature
of reality. This third edition includes new sections on the importance of the
imagination, on Just Sitting, and on reflection on the Buddha. Kamalashila has
been teaching meditation since becoming a member of the Triratna Buddhist
Order in 1974. He has developed approaches to meditation practice that are
accessible to people in the contemporary world, whilst being firmly grounded in
the Buddhist tradition.

*A wonderfully practical and accessible introduction to the important forms of Buddhist
meditation. From his years of meditation practice, Kamalashila has written a book useful
for both beginners and longtime practitioners.* – **Gil Fronsdal**, author of *A Monastery
Within*, founder of the Insight Meditation Center, California, USA

*This enhanced new edition guides readers more clearly into the meditations and
draws out their significance more fully, now explicitly oriented around the 'system
of meditation'. This system provides a fine framework both for understanding where
various practices fit in and for reflecting on the nature of our own spiritual experiences.
Kamalashila has also woven in an appreciation of a view of the nature of mind that
in the Western tradition is known as the imagination, helping make an accessible
link to our own philosophical and cultural traditions.* – **Lama Surya Das**, author
of *Awakening the Buddha Within*, founder of Dzogchen Center and Dzogchen
Meditation Retreats, USA

*His approach is a clear, thorough, honest, and, above all, open-ended exploration of the
practical problems for those new to and even quite experienced in meditation.* – **Lama
Shenpen Hookham**, author of *There's More to Dying Than Death*, founder of the
Awakened Heart Sangha, UK

ISBN 9781 907314 09 4
£14.99 / $27.95 / €19.95
272 pages

Change Your Mind
by Paramananda

An accessible and thorough guide, this best-seller introduces two Buddhist meditations and deals imaginatively with practical difficulties, meeting distraction and doubt with determination and humour.

*Inspiring, calming and friendly ... If you've always thought meditation might be a good idea, but found other step-by-step guides lacking in spirit, this book could finally get you going. – **Here's Health***

ISBN 9781 899579 75 4
£9.99 / $13.95 / €12.95
208 pages

Meditating
by Jinananda

Meditation is a household word, everyone has their idea of what it is, but does this mean that it is more misunderstood than understood? Here Jinananda, an experienced meditation teacher, gives us the Buddhist perspective. He shows us that – far from being a safe, patching-up, therapeutic tool – meditation is a radical, transformative, waking-up practice.

Buddhist meditation is about being true to your experience, and this means getting behind the idea of what is going on, behind the label, to the ungraspable experience of this moment. Jinananda shows you how to start doing this, how to sit comfortably for meditation, and how to do two meditation practices that develop clarity, peace of mind and positive emotions.

ISBN 9781 907314 06 3
£6.99 / $14.95 / €10.95
160 pages

The Art of Reflection
by Ratnaguna

It is all too easy either to think obsessively, or to not think enough. But how do we think usefully? How do we reflect? Like any art, reflection can be learnt and developed, leading to a deeper understanding of life and to the fullness of wisdom. *The Art of Reflection* is a practical guide to reflection as a spiritual practice, about 'what we think and how we think about it'. It is a book about contemplation and insight, and reflection as a way to discover the truth.

No-one who takes seriously the study and practice of the Dharma should fail to read this ground-breaking book. – **Sangharakshita**, founder of the Triratna Buddhist Community

The Art of Reflection *will give teachers insight into Buddhist practice. Even more importantly, it may help to develop the ability to engage in deeper personal and professional reflection.* – **Joyce Miller**, *REtoday*

ISBN 9781 899579 89 1
£9.99 / $16.95 / €12.95
160 pages